Popularizing
RESEARCH

This book is part of the Peter Lang Media and Communication list.
Every volume is peer reviewed and meets
the highest quality standards for content and production.

PETER LANG
New York • Washington, D.C./Baltimore • Bern
Frankfurt • Berlin • Brussels • Vienna • Oxford

Popularizing
RESEARCH

Engaging New Genres,
Media, and Audiences

EDITED BY Phillip Vannini

PETER LANG
New York • Washington, D.C./Baltimore • Bern
Frankfurt • Berlin • Brussels • Vienna • Oxford

Library of Congress Cataloging-in-Publication Data

Popularizing research: engaging new genres, media, and audiences /
edited by Phillip Vannini.
p. cm.
Includes bibliographical references.
1. Social sciences—Research. 2. Research—Social aspects.
3. Research—Methodology. 4. Mass media. 5. Social media.
6. Learning and scholarship. 7. Popular culture. I. Vannini, Phillip.
H62.P643   001.4—dc23   2012006547
ISBN 978-1-4331-1181-5 (paperback)
ISBN: 978-1-4539-0819-8(e-book)

Bibliographic information published by **Die Deutsche Nationalbibliothek**.
Die Deutsche Nationalbibliothek lists this publication in the "Deutsche
Nationalbibliografie"; detailed bibliographic data is available
on the Internet at http://dnb.d-nb.de/.

A website accompanies this book. Both the website and the book are organized into nine parts. Whereas the purpose of this book is to narrate and reflect, the purpose of the website is to show real examples of popularizing research.

To see and learn more about the projects described in this book, go online to www.popularizingresearch.net

Contents

Part 3. Exhibits and Installations

Part 4. Audio

Part 5. Periodicals

Part 9. Publicity

Introduction: Popularizing Research

Phillip Vannini

It was the first year of the new millennium. I was a young sociology PhD student at a research university in the US. Interested in popular culture and popular music in particular, I thought of utilizing a graduate social psychology seminar in which I was enrolled as an opportunity to do some research on personal identity, youth, and Top 40 pop music. I was an eager student—driven to find a secure academic post immediately after graduation. I knew I had to publish research even before my dissertation was defended. So I pitched the idea about my possible paper to my professor—a tenured and well-regarded social psychologist.

"Who cares? It's just pop music, Phillip," was her reaction. Studying popular music and popular culture wasn't quite Sociological, she explained. To be sure, it was sociological in nature, but it wasn't Sociological with a capital "S"—the "S" that rubber-stamps mainstream, institutionalized, respectable American Sociology. She hinted that if I wanted to practice the kind of Sociology that could get me a job, I had to toe the party line.

Digging a little bit deeper the attitude behind her answer—and the broader collective attitude for which it stood—I soon learned my lessons. First, forget the popular and the populace. Surely, as any good Sociologist, I should feel free to speak on behalf of the common (wo)man, but for the most part I should do so only paternalistically and demagogically, without doing anything about it. What they—the members of the populace—like is not what we—respectable academics—like. And what they are like is not what we are like.

Second, and following the first point, I shouldn't bother communicating with laypeople about my research, as it wouldn't get me an academic job. They watch reality TV, listen to bad music, digest dumbed-down knowledge provided by whatever journalists decide to feed them. We, on the other hand, produce intellectual material too precious to be sullied by easily digestible formulas, too complex to be broken down for easier appreciation by their unsophisticated palate.

The story ends years later with my leaving Sociology with a capital "S," slamming the door on my way out, never to return. But that detail is much less interesting than what the story itself reveals: popular research is something that all academics should do at their own risk. So, before I go any further with my writing, I'll need to issue a loud and clear warning: proceed at your own risk. Determine whether your higher-ups will appreciate your messing with the needs and the wants of the populace. Think carefully about it: will your thesis or dissertation committees dig it? Will your tenure mentors value it? Will your grant agencies care? How much time will it take? How much will it cost you? But hey, on the other hand, if you think that life without taking a little risk isn't fun—and if you think that research without imagination is, well, not that much fun either—stick around. This should be a sweet ride.

What This Book Is, and Who It's for

In pitching my proposal to my acquisitions editor at Peter Lang, I loudly exclaimed that this book was meant for people who have had enough of spending months, if not years, to produce research that will be read in less than ten minutes by five distracted readers who will forget what they have read in less than three minutes. That was my raw message. I could have baked it up a bit more. I could have sold it to her by saying that this book was targeted to audiences interested in knowledge mobilization, or knowledge exchange, or knowledge transfer, or research outreach and dissemination best practices, and/or the various flavors of "public" disciplines such as public sociology, public anthropology, etc., but instead I decided to cut to the chase. I promised to deliver a book for the bored and disenfranchised, for those feeling alienated from the drudgery of academic writing and inauthentic about producing more of the same drivel, and for those willing to let their academic imagination play.

She wasn't the only one to really get my idea. Earlier, I had gotten on as many listservs as I could and put out a call for proposals that read:

> I am inviting chapter proposals for an edited book that will show and tell ways that scholars can make research more popular to larger lay, media, and other popular audiences. Much too often research in the social sciences and humanities suffers from an ivory-tower complex, the symptoms of which prevent wide audiences from fully enjoying the processes or appreciating the value and utility of research. As a result, research is often destined for and consumed by a small cadre of readers who have access to both the narrowly accessible media in which research is published, and the difficult lexicon that characterizes academic writing. As new, experimental and blurred genres of research emerge, as well as new distribution media, new academic imperatives, and new ideas and wills, the need to popularize academic research grows. How to popularize research is, however, neither always clear nor easy. Students and scholars often lack a comprehensive vision of the contemporary possibilities available and the procedures involved. The goal of this book is to provide students and scholars with a broad and thorough overview and serve as a companion for any research method course or as a handy reference for career academics. Since the goal is to make research popular, the means themselves should abide by that principle. Therefore, I am not interested in editing a dry, tedious, abstract book. I am seeking witty, fun, funny, enthusiastic, thrilling, suspenseful, dramatic, performative, artistic, documentary, provocative, innovative, sensual, sexy, genre-blurring, multi-modal, multimedia, charismatic, experimental, funky, cool research material. In other words, I am seeking to collect *examples and reflections* of ways in which research in the social sciences and humanities can be more like *popular* culture.

A little less than a month later, I had received over 150 ideas. Two months later, I had twice as many new messages in my inbox, accompanied by at least 50 emails that were not sent to propose anything to me, but simply congratulate me on the idea. I realized that across the disciplines and across the world, many students and scholars had encountered noxious attitudes of people like my social psychology professor. The idea for this book struck a chord with them, and the process of making research more popular—a decade after my encounter with navel-gazing academia in that graduate seminar—was now fully under way for a lot of people.

So what exactly is this book now, after it's all said and done? A tempting sound bite such as "an illustrated guide to making research public" might characterize it in part, but there is more to it than that. The idea behind this project is to *go beyond the book* as medium of academic knowledge dissemination, and to exploit the potential of the web to facilitate access to new media, new research genres, and therefore new audiences that the book alone could not reach. As a result, this book comes with a website, available at http://www.popularizing research.net. The website and the book together deliver a multimodal message about popularizing research, which seems truly innovative to me, for a few reasons.

First, books on *how to* make research more accessible are now legion. And so are books on *why* we should reach out to broader publics. Yet neither of these bodies of useful knowledge are particularly adept or transparent about actually doing it—that is, about showing the outcomes of popularized research.

Second, the web is vastly underused by academic book authors and editors, and academic journals as well. While every peer-reviewed journal these days has a website, and every other introductory textbook does too, the multimodal potential of the web is not thoroughly exploited. Thus, we get websites that mirror text-based content (e.g., peer-reviewed journal websites) and companion websites that mostly mirror some of the most unimaginative material of classroom teaching (e.g., quizzes and text-based PowerPoint lectures, with a few hyperlinks thrown in for good flavor).

Third, despite the potential of the internet to reach more people than the academic book, the organizational state of internet-based popularized research is a sorry mess. Whereas freely accessible broad internet search engines such as Google Scholar and more specialized and restricted academic search engines such as ProQuest provide easy and fast access to overwhelming amounts and types of research, no search engine or directory for non-text-based academic research is available. As a result, searching for examples of popularized research is time-consuming and frustrating, if not downright futile. Try this for yourself on Google, YouTube, or Vimeo.

For all of these reasons and others I don't have the space to enumerate here, combining a book with a web-based directory of popularized research seemed like a good and terribly simple idea. This also seemed appealing to me because this strategy allows me and all the other contributors not only to *tell* the audiences of this book and website how this kind of research is done and why, but also to *show* them what the fuss is all about.

In sum, this book/website package is meant for people like you: students, academics, and professional researchers who are keen on expanding the audiences of their research, and who are tired of producing inaccessible writing distributed through inaccessible media to largely invisible audiences. As I like to tell my communication students, a decade after that miserable exchange with my social psychology professor, it is not sufficient to be familiar with the cultures and the languages of the people we study and to investigate the multiple media through which cultures are reproduced. Rather, what we need to do is find ways to directly employ the cultures and languages of the people we study and communicate with them through the very same multiple media, in order to learn from them and in order to educate and produce new public cultures. If you find this to be a possible, albeit admittedly partial, solution against academic elitism and irrelevance, then this book and website are for you.

Kindred Spirits

The move toward public research is not new, fortunately. Several pioneers in the social sciences and humanities have distinguished themselves throughout the last century for their popularization work. In some disciplines, these pioneers are also recognized as the very founding fathers and mothers of their discipline. For example the ethnographic writings (combined with political activities) of anthropologists Margaret Mead, Ruth Benedict, Claude Levi-Strauss, Bronislav Malinowski, and Franz Boas managed to reach large numbers of citizens throughout the early 20th century, becoming classics not only in their own field, but also of our civilization as a whole. As McClancy (1996) rightly remarks, their success proves that:

> the space between the academic and the popular is not a one-way street but an arena of voices where one may inspire the others. As the example of Ruth Benedict's *Chrysanthemum and the Sword* shows, that space is potentially one of productive dialogue rather than patronizing monologue. Popular anthropology need not be a downmarket derivative of "the real stuff." It is not a cheapened version of a high-quality product which has been allowed to "trickle down" (a patronizing metaphor of treacly hierarchy). It is an integral, contributory part of the discipline, broadly conceived. (p. 4)

Notwithstanding these illustrious kindred spirits, for the better part of the last century, academia as a whole seemed mostly to further cave in on itself. Anthropological writing, for example, became inaccessible because of its technical, theoretical nature (McClancy, 1996). The same happened in sociology (Burawoy, 2005), which had earlier enjoyed a good measure of popularity through writings of authors such as William H. Whyte (1956) and David Riesman (1950). Similar trends unfolded in other disciplines, for a variety of reasons.

Chief among these reasons might be a widely shared affective disposition among many academics: the fear of being popular. Some might view this as the outcome of a bad experience with the media—being misquoted, for example, or seeing one's work dumbed down by a journalist in need of condensing a long and complex argument into a few words. Others might view it as a typical disposition of all those individuals who dedicate years of their life, especially in their young formative years, to the lone pursuit of intellectual matters. After all, who among advanced students has not once looked down in disdain from the high floors of the university library at the masses of raucous students amusing themselves with the moot victories of their sports team or otherwise busying themselves with equally seemingly trivial and crass pleasures typical of the "common man"?

Some might even argue that these dispositions are at the very ideological core of cut-throat academic politics, and that the practices of gate-keeping committees—whether in charge of awarding degrees, tenure, or publication—are in fact nothing but the reproduction of an exclusive and elitist ego-defending attitude disdained with the value of popularity. Whatever the case, what is obvious is that graduation and career prospects in academia have long mostly hinged upon students and aspiring professors preaching to the choir, rather than sullying their hands with the needs and the wants of the populace. What graduate student hasn't been reminded that to make tenure, one must write research and theory monographs instead of textbooks, and peer-reviewed journal articles instead of magazine and newspaper columns? As a result, the scorn and stigma of "pop" psychology, "pop" political science, or "pop" this and that attached to those who dare aim their writings for the shelves of bookstore chains and newspaper kiosks echo through the hallways of the ivory tower, haunting and halting careers, and preventing authentic peer acceptance.

This ideology and shared affect has acted like a vicious cycle across the social sciences and humanities. When being a "generalist" becomes equated with being unsophisticated and superficial, it becomes logical for the social sciences and humanities to splinter. New disciplines such as communication studies and cultural studies and women studies are born from once common social theory. Old disciplines such as anthropology split asunder in cultural anthropology, archaeology, linguistic anthropology, and biological anthropology. Then, geopolitical and organizational divisions compound the effects. Thus we witness splits between social and cultural anthropology, social and cultural geography, the sociology of culture and cultural sociology—and so on. Soon enough then, book and journal publishers realize that their best marketing bet is not to aim for large audiences, but for narrow, specialized niches—an editorial practice that further Balkanizes scholarship and reinforces the idea that 1,000 audiences of 100 are easier to achieve than one of 100,000.

The corollary of all this is that it's rather easy and common for any academic to feel irrelevant. And this is more than just a feeling. In an era of ever-deepening cuts to university budgets and constantly increasing political pressure on universities to contribute to a knowledge-based creative economy, researchers are beginning to deal with shifting political priorities. Whether universities are pushing academics to find commercial applications for their research or to popularize their teaching material and methods to appeal to new student markets, or simply to apply their research to concrete problem-solving and thus more directly benefit communities of stakeholders, the latest trends in academic politics are obvious: researchers must begin to climb down from the ivory tower, and they need to do so swiftly, even though they may not know how.

Such was the realization inherent in various turns toward the publicization and popularization of academic research that marked the beginning of the millennium. In sociology, for example, the turning point was undoubtedly Michael Burawoy's enormously influential (and equally controversial) address to the American Sociological Association in 2004 (Burawoy, 2005). Burawoy had been noticing a growing disconnect between an American political culture swerving toward the right and a sociological culture becoming more and more leftist. Keen on seeing a growth in the impact of sociology on public discourse, Burawoy called upon his colleagues to reach out to American voters and the world. Sociology could achieve this aim by reverting to its traditionally public role and by better appreciating its new organic public function. His incitation is worth quoting at length.

> Public sociology brings sociology into a conversation with publics, understood as people who are themselves involved in a conversation. It entails, therefore, a double conversation. Obvious candidates are W. E. DuBois (1903), *The Souls of Black Folks*, Gunnar Myrdal (1994), *An American Dilemma*, David Riesman (1950), *The Lonely Crowd*, and Robert Bellah et al. (1985), *Habits of the Heart*. What do all these books have in common? They are written by sociologists, they are read beyond the academy, and they become the vehicle of a public discussion about the nature of U.S. society—the nature of its values, the gap between its promise and reality, its malaise, its tendencies. In the same genre of what I call *traditional public sociology* we can locate sociologists who write in the opinion pages of our national newspapers where they comment on matter of public importance....The traditional public sociologist instigates debates within or between publics, although he or she might not actually participate in them. There is however another type of public sociology—*organic public sociology* in which the soci-

ologist works in close connection with a visible, thick, active, local and often counterpublic. The bulk of public sociology is indeed of an organic kind—sociologists working with a labor movement, neighborhood associations, communities of faith, immigrant rights groups, human right organizations. Between the organic public sociologist and public is a dialogue, a process of mutual education....The project of such public sociologies is to make visible the invisible, to make the private public, to validate these organic connections as part of our sociological life. (pp. 7–8)

While inevitably cloaked in the mantra of mainstream American sociology, Burawoy's characterization of a public scholarship attempting to reach out to publics through mediated communication and/or through face-to-face collaboration easily characterizes all of social-scientific research aiming at popularization. In one way or another, all the research discussed in the pages of this book falls into either one or both of his categories.

Public sociology has probably generated more attention and debate than any other version of "public" discipline or field, but it is certainly neither the first kind of popularized research nor the only type. Public anthropology came to life a few years earlier, at first with the publication of McClancy and McDonaugh's (1996) edited book *Popularizing Anthropology*, and then with the formulation of a mission statement for public anthropology by Borofsky (2000; n.d.) and Purcell (2000). As opposed to sociology—where applied work has traditionally meant "social work" and has been almost entirely relegated to a marginal "practitioner" status—anthropology has had a stronger applied tradition. While applied anthropology has clearly not enjoyed the status of its theory-driven, "pure" scholarship cousin, its existence has made the rise of popular anthropology easier, albeit not without controversy (see Gottlieb, 1997; Singer, 2000; Lamphere, 2004; Lassiter, 2005, 2008). In light of this, applied and collaborative fieldwork in international settings have benefited from a broader dialogue on development and education, stimulating and being stimulated by various pedagogies of the oppressed and forms of action research—the kind of work that Burawoy might call "organic."

The importance of the ethnographic tradition of Boas, Malinowski, Benedict, and Mead has also helped anthropology connect with broader publics by way of effective representational aesthetics. According to Gans (2010), ethnography's foci on the personal, the intimate, the particular, and the narrative are key elements for popularization. This opens the way for not only good writing, but also for a sensuous scholarship (Stoller, 1997) capable of appealing to wider publics through visual media such as film (Scheper-Hughes, 2009). This is where public anthropology and another tradition, qualitative inquiry, begin to blend.

Qualitative inquiry is a highly influential movement in qualitative social-science research that rejects the realism and the uncommitted objectivism of positivist scholarship (see Denzin & Lincoln, 1994, 2000, 2005). According to Denzin—the foremost exponent of this movement—qualitative inquiry offers an empirical alternative to the supposedly apolitical stance of positivism and post-positivism. Mixing a transformative drive for social justice, an ethos of aesthetic sensibility, and a commitment to public relevance, qualitative inquiry has expanded the definition of ethnography to encompass more or less all forms of research carried out through scholarly reflexive engagement and in-depth participation of people into the research process.

If qualitative inquiry can be viewed as an offspring of poststructural and postmodern anthropological and ethnographic traditions, one of its manifestations, art-based research, can be viewed as originating from long-standing traditions in the fields of education, arts, and communication. Volumes such as Knowles and Cole's (2008) *Handbook of the Arts in Qualitative Research*, Leavy's (2008) *Method Meets Art*, and Sullivan's (2009) *Art Practice as Research* serve as prominent contemporary examples of the vitality of research strategies that attempt to connect with broader publics. Utilizing old and new media, performative and representational arts, classic, folk, and popular culture genres, these new forms of scholarship manage to popularize research and scholarship writ large by way of constant experimentation, innovation, genre-blurring, collaboration, and application to multiple social problems and issues.

Whether inspired by public sociology, public anthropology, qualitative inquiry, art-based research, or whatever other tradition not covered in this introduction, the popularization of research answers the need to make scholarship relevant to the many, not the few. And whether in communication or education, sociology or anthropology, geography or cultural studies, or whatever other discipline or field, more and more scholars and students are now starting to recognize that a scholarship that wants to be meaningful has to have an audience and has to be consequential to its stakeholders. As a result, outreach activities are now more and more fully recognized by both universities and funding agencies, which now often demand them as as a form of service to the wider community. This has generated an entire new field, which has come to be known by various names such as knowledge mobilization, knowledge transfer, knowledge translation, and knowledge exchange, only to name a few.

Such a growing body of literature recognizes the need for research to be communicated through a variety of media, to be community based, to be consequential and transformative, and truly cumulative in nature. A growing awareness of the importance of knowledge management is changing universities for good (Hardill & Baines, 2009), initiating new partnerships with governmental and nongovernmental organizations (Phipps & Shapson, 2009), and changing the criteria by which good research is consumed by multiple publics (Levin, 2008). It is in light of these trends that the essays in this book and the products on www.popularizingresearch.net must be understood and appreciated, and it is in light of this history that they must be judged.

Plan of the Book and the Website

Following this introduction, the book is divided into nine parts, with three or four chapters each. The parts of the book are organized around a particular medium or genre of research production and distribution. Overlaps between the various parts of the book are inevitable, as these boundaries are merely organizational devices employed to keep things relatively tidy. It should also be kept in mind that the genres and media covered by the book are not intended to be exhaustive—there are undoubtedly more kinds of popularized research that I could have included. As it always goes, however, availability of authors and space were limited.

Without getting into the details of what each chapter covers—since there's a lot to summarize—it might be useful to briefly outline the plan of the book. Part One covers film and video, drawing primarily from the documentary genre. Part Two continues to look at visual media, but switches to still photography and graphic arts, in particular photovoice, cartoons, and poster exhibits. Part Three segues into exhibits by examining art installations and web galleries. Part Four discusses research that uses audio technologies, ranging from radio to music and digital documentaries. Parts Five and Six focus on renovating the potential of the written word. The former examines periodicals and related print media and genres such as op-eds, ethnodramas, and autoethnography. The latter hones in on how books and reports can be produced and distributed to reach broader audiences. Part Seven concentrates on engaging in dialogue with research publics and stakeholders through web cafes, online conversations, and the web

2.0. Contributions to Part Eight examine various kinds of performative renderings of research such as slam poetry, performance ethnography, playback theatre, and performance autoethnography. Finally, Part Nine teaches us how to communicate better with news media gatekeepers—from releasing effective media tips to interacting well with journalists.

Almost all the contributors were asked to deliver a "show" to be uploaded on the website and a "tell" to be featured on the book. The "tell"—authors were told—was meant as a narrative reflection on the experience of producing and distributing popularized research (i.e., "the show"). I asked each contributor to keep their writing accessible; indeed I asked them to avoid terminology entirely, and to write clearly and employ basic language that any student and faculty across the social sciences and humanities could understand. Each chapter discusses unique experiences, but every chapter follows a relatively standard format, touching upon common elements. These elements are intended to tell readers what the research they popularized was about, why the decision to popularize it was made, why certain media and genres were employed, what lessons researchers learned in the process, and how audiences responded.

Each chapter is meant to strike a compromise between two extremes: the practical extreme of teaching technical components of research popularization (e.g., how to use Adobe Creator to edit media material) and the abstract extreme of reflecting on the epistemological value of popularized research. As a result, the information presented in each chapter is meant to stimulate and guide readers to popularize research and to provide them with a rough directory on the possibilities available. On the other hand, advanced readers keen on learning the ins and outs of, say, recording audio documentaries using digital or analog technologies, will find the need to learn these techniques by accessing more in-depth reference material. The same goes with the theorists and the philosophers among our readers, who may find value in accessing edited books such as Denzin and Lincoln (2005) and Knowles and Cole (2008), which provide in-depth reflections on the politics, epistemology, and ontology of qualitative inquiry and post-realist knowledge production.

For easy reference, the website follows the organizational scheme of the book. Most chapters in the book refer to material available on the web, though some chapters did not need additional material and therefore have no web content at all. The website also features this introduction to this book, each chapter's introductory words, and other resources and links. As it often goes with web-based communication, a website is merely a starting point. Thus while some material is immediately available on www.popularizingresearch.net, other material is available on contributors' own websites, and simply hyperlinked from the book's website. Video-based material is available on Vimeo and YouTube, and hyperlinked from the book's website.

One of the most noteworthy characteristics of this book and website, in my mind, is the remarkable diversity of the contributors. From communication to education, and from sociology to anthropology and almost everything in between, both traditional disciplines and new interdisciplinary fields are duly represented by authors' affiliations, training, and subject matter. Further contributing to this diversity is the age of contributors. It was my intent to host a variety of popularization strategies and therefore featuring the work of no one but well-established academics—with greater access to research funds, research assistants, and broad team collaborations—would have been pointless. Thus among the contributors there are academics, but also students and professionals who are not affiliated with universities. Lastly, I am keen on seeing the movement for popularized research cross geopolitical boundaries. Therefore I was happy to receive responses to my call for papers from many areas of the globe. As the author biographical notes attest, at least two dozen countries are represented here by authors' place of birth and institutional affiliation.

While vast areas of the globe remain populated by institutions of higher learning that practice elitist knowledge and thus restrict the freedom of researchers to reach out, and while disciplinary and university politics still limit many students and academics from achieving a greater impact with their research, the prospects for the future are much rosier than they were a decade ago, and infinitely better than they were in the better part of the last millennium. The growth in the opportunities provided by more user-friendly and more democratically accessible media and technologies can only push the possibilities to popularize research in the right direction.

Technology, often touted as the driving energy of change, is only a tool box, however. The true driving force for popularized research can only be a keen determination to do it, a determination unfettered by institutional obstacles, less-than-ideal budgets, and unproven skills. Where there is a will, there is a way—and while this sounds like a cliché, the only real alternative to the will for popularization is to continue to find excuses for remaining irrelevant, unheard, and unimaginative. We all—students, teachers, academics, professional researchers—have a lot to learn from making research-based knowledge more popular, and a whole lot to lose from not doing it.

References

Borofsky, R. (May 2000). Public anthropology. Where to? What next? *Anthropology News*, 9–10.

Borofsky, R. (n.d.). Public anthropology: A personal perspective. Available at http://www.public anthropology.org/Defining/publicanth-07Oct10.htm.

Burawoy, M. (2005). 2004 ASA presidential address: For public sociology. *American Sociological Review, 70*, 4–28.

Denzin, N., & Lincoln, Y. (Eds.). (1994). *The SAGE handbook of qualitative research* (1st ed.). Thousand Oaks, CA: Sage.

Denzin, N., & Lincoln, Y. (Eds.). (2000). *The SAGE handbook of qualitative research* (2nd ed.). Thousand Oaks, CA: Sage.

Denzin, N., & Lincoln, Y. (Eds.). (2005). *The SAGE handbook of qualitative research* (3rd ed.). Thousand Oaks, CA: Sage.

Gans, H. (2010). Public ethnography; ethnography as public sociology. *Qualitative Sociology, 33*, 97–104.

Gottlieb, A. (1997). The perils of popularizing anthropology. *Anthropology Today, 13*, 1–3. Hardill, I., & Baines, S. (2009). Personal reflections on knowledge transfer and changing UK research priorities. *21st Century Society, 4*, 83–96.

Knowles, G., & Cole, A. (Eds.). (2008). *Handbook of the arts in qualitative research.* Thousand Oaks, CA: Sage.

Lamphere, L. (2004). The convergence of applied, practicing, and public anthropology in the 21st century. *Human Organization, 63*, 431–443.

Lassiter, L. E. (2005). Collaborative ethnography and public anthropology. *Current Anthropology, 46*, 83–106.

Lassiter, L. E. (2008). Moving past public anthropology and doing collaborative research. *NAPA Bulletin, 29*, 70–86.

Leavy, P. (2008). *Method meets art: Arts-based research.* New York: Guilford.

Levin, B. (2008). Thinking about knowledge mobilization. Available at http://www.ccl-cca.ca/pdfs/OtherReports/LevinDiscussionPaperEN.pdf.

McClancy, J. (1996). Popularizing anthropology. In J. McClancy and C. McDonaugh (Eds.), *Popularizing anthropology*, (1–57). New York: Routledge.

McClancy, J., & McDonaugh, C. (1996). *Popularizing anthropology.* New York: Routledge.

Phipps, D., & Shapson, S. (2009). Knowledge mobilisation builds local research collaborations for social innovation. *The Policy Press, 5*, 211–227.

Purcell, T. (2000). Public anthropology: An idea for searching for a reality. *Transforming Anthropology, 9*, 30–33.

Riesman, D. (1950). *The lonely crowd.* Hartford, CT: Yale University Press.

Scheper-Hughes, N. (2009). Making anthropology public. *Anthropology News*, 25, 1–4.

Singer, M. (September 2000). Why I am not a public anthropologist. *Anthropology News*, 6–7.

Stoller, P. (1997). *Sensuous scholarship*. Philadelphia: University of Pennsylvania Press.

Sullivan, G. (Ed.). (2009). *Art practice as research*. Thousand Oaks, CA: Sage.

Whyte, W. (1956). *The organization man*. Philadelphia: University of Pennsylvania Press.

Part 1

FILM

CHAPTER ONE

Short Film as Performative Social Science

The Story behind *Princess Margaret*

Kip Jones

Older now, I finally realize that certain moments in my life were pinnacles, not predictors of things to come.

Publish or perish drives much of academic life. It has its origins in hard science where the first to get an experiment, finding, or theory into publication won the prize. Other academic disciplines followed suit by imitating this system. This structure has developed an academic writing style and a vetting process that are both now antiquated and suspect. We are all frequently caught up in this bind, me included.

Qikipedia recently cautioned us on Twitter that "about 200,000 academic journals are published in English. The average number of readers per article is five" (Qikipedia, 2010). Funders are now looking for outcomes from their investments that demonstrate how we will affect change in the wider world; in other words, the world beyond the very few other academics who happen to read a journal article. Fortunately, publishing is evolving, and more and more, supplementary multimedia are requested as part of the publication process. This climate of change presents opportunities to get the products of our alternative methods of dissemination of social-science data to wider audiences—to popularize research.

Writing about *The One about Princess Margaret*

This chapter revisits *The One about Princess Margaret*, one of my earliest cracks at audio/visual script writing, by recalling my initial motivation and enthusiasm for finding innovative ways to express scholarship. My thinking about the use of tools from the arts in social science has evolved since those early days and is reflected upon here. Nonetheless, as I labor to become more sophisticated and skillful in my productions, it is important for me not to forget those initial struggles and uncertainties documented in those early attempts. I don't want this chapter, however, to be simply a rehash of what has been previously published about *Princess*

Margaret. My hope is that interested scholars will follow the citation trail for more information, background, and detail. Rather, my purpose here is to inspire the reader to watch the video more by instigating curiosity than by academic argument.

The story behind *Princess Margaret* recounts an unconventional journey to academic publishing that certainly did not follow the usual route of journal or book publication. At the time of its inception, I was becoming less interested in writing that did not communicate directly with others and more interested in including my "self" in that narrative. Somewhat reluctantly at first, therefore, I began to explore the potential of autoethnography for more personal communication and to investigate the platforms that I might use in order to reach a wider audience. I realized that all I really have to share with anyone is my own experience, though it may be flawed and/or of little value to anyone else. For these reasons, I have since tried to write and produce for various media in a way that will transcend typical academic expectations. By developing skill and craft, I can respond to a wider brief—to popularize research by unifying serious scholarship with popular culture.

When writing autoethnography, I endeavor to remain a minor character and/or a conduit to a time, place, and other people. I become fictionalized through writing. I am the sorcerer who reminds audience of themselves. In terms of visual representation of such stories, I become the keen observer, allowing cultural images to become private and iconic. These remembered images twist and turn and eventually morph in various ways to be included as my own graphic memories. These visual "mash-ups" are truly Ethno-Graphic. Indeed, our visual memories can become imbued with both intense cultural and personal meaning. This is the *visual* autoethnography that I hope to represent in my work (see Jones, 2010).

Over the past ten years or so, along with exploring visualizations of research data, I have also experimented with writing performatively—that is, representing on the page what I am trying to accomplish imaginatively. Examples include the results of an interview with Mary Gergen (Jones, 2004); the script for an audio/visual production about Klaus Riegel and Kenneth Gergen (Jones, 2002a); a very early piece about Akira Kurosawa and gerotranscendence (Jones, 2002b); and, of course, the script for "The One about Princess Margaret" (Jones, 2007a).

Moving our work to arts-based procedures is not a series of isolated acts; it requires an adjustment to how we approach everything in which we engage—including writing for academic publication. For example, this chapter is an illustration of my current writing, which is continual, reminiscent of my blog, and isn't afraid to allow motifs to develop across publications and over time through a body of work. In terms of structure, its composition is influenced more by the arts (frequently music, but also painting), than by academic writing. The allows room for the reader to participate (following Bourriaud's [2002] relational aesthetics). I expect the reader to have questions, even doubts. As a writer, I leave a trail or clues to some of the answers, rather than routinely relying on argument or debate.

How Did the Saga of *Princess Margaret* Begin?

"The One about Princess Margaret" (Jones, 2006a), an audio/visual production on film that recalls my encounter with Her Royal Highness, Princess Margaret, at a New York nightclub in 1965, is a personal story narrated to unrelenting psychedelic screen images. The production ends with a *dénouement* or recapitulation consisting of a whirlwind of photographs depicting the story's places, characters, and time. I conceived it originally as an autoethnographic "visual radio play."

Princess Margaret, like many of my early productions, involved being presented with a particular scholarly puzzle or challenge and then seeking tools from the arts to respond to such questions. My initial query was: How can humor be used to capture time, place, and culture, and how will the results measure up to scrutiny as autoethnography? Thus my personal leap into autoethnography and the development of a fusion of the arts and social science (that is, performative social science, see Gergen & Jones, 2008) began with a research question.

Over time, I have screened the film at four universities in the U.K. to receptive, sometimes quizzical, audiences. The production was never meant to meet "the needs of an audience," however. Its purpose is to provoke and unsettle typical scholastic spectators. In fact, it often makes them forget themselves as academics—a key purpose of my efforts.

Once, however, an audience member bellowed, "What about scholarship? Where's the scholarship?" I immediately replied, "It's in the footnotes!" What I meant was that the scholarship had been backgrounded in order to foreground the more immediate experience of being a member of an audience, sitting in the dark without our usual critical academic hats on, and embracing suspended disbelief. I believe that this approach produces possibilities for the reduction of interpersonal distance by the development of sensibility for the intuitive, emotive, and associative aspects of communication. Those footnotes, nonetheless, contain gems of careful scholarship.

Following the production's initial seminar presentation, it was uploaded to the internet later that year (Jones, 2006a). Since then it has had nearly 10,000 viewings on the web; it is being used both as a teaching tool as well as for popular enjoyment around the world. This was followed in 2007 by an article (Jones, 2007b) written for the online qualitative journal *Forum: Qualitative Social Research (FQS)*. The script (Jones, 2007a) for the audio/visual production was published in tandem with the article. A short piece (Jones, 2008) about the process was created in 2008 for the website *Exploring Online Research Methods* at Leicester University. In 2009, "How Did I Get to Princess Margaret? (And How Did I Get Her to the World Wide Web?)" (Jones, 2009) was published in *Ethnography and the Internet: An Exploration,* and included the original *FQS* article and the complete script and footnotes. These follow-up publications are a representation or record of the original creative act.

Two professional relationships propelled *Princess Margaret* into cyberspace and publication. First, a colleague convinced me early on of the value of uploading it to the internet. Second, because of their familiarity with my work as a copyeditor, the editors of *FQS* were more receptive to my alternative ideas for *Princess Margaret*'s publication.

After viewing "The One about Princess Margaret" on the internet, some viewers ask for permission for their students to download it or to use the film in their teaching. Of course I say yes. This is the nature of the internet, a free and open platform. It is this environment that sidelines the tediousness of usual academic publishing, reviewing, and a hierarchical and closed club of academics too often protecting their own turf.

What Is Performative Social Science?

Is Performative Social Science (PSS) art or social science? It isn't either. It is a fusion of both, creating a new model where tools from the arts and humanities are explored for their utility in enriching the ways in which we research social science subjects and/or disseminate or present our research to our audiences. This does not mean that we simply put on a play (Gergen & Jones, 2008) or make a film. It certainly isn't taking an interview transcription, leaving out a line or two here and there, rearranging them on the page in a stanza format mimicking poetry, and then passing it off as poetic inquiry (and even worse, then calling ourselves poets.) It isn't thinking that our lives are so precious and unique (the "snowflake" phenomenon [Genoways, 2010]) that sure-ly the world wants us to dramatize them—too often through embarrassingly intimate perfor-mances of over-cooked angst. Academics typically present these hysterics to a captured conference audience, the presenter crawling around the floor for half an hour and calling it dance or pro-ducing a monologue that seems to never have a narrative arc or conclusion. As audience mem-bers, we often wish we had instead chosen the parallel book launch with complimentary sherry.

Instead, let us return to what we already know quite well: academic research. I recall the standard suggestion that we routinely make to postgraduate students: "find a research method that best fits the research question(s)." This imperative applies to PSS as well. Within the vast richness of the arts and humanities, which lens, device, technique or tradition might deepen our research process or expand our dissemination plan? Is it a good fit (to the question[s])? Do we automatically put on a play or fashion a film from our research data because we are so many frustrated actors or film directors, without ever asking which art form best fits the research ques-tion or the data that it has produced?

In producing *Princess Margaret*, I did not suddenly transform into an illustrator, scriptwriter, or filmmaker. I remained a social scientist with a particular story to tell or message to get across and explored which media would best help me to accomplish that. I didn't worry about whether I was exceptionally good at the use of a specific medium, but rather I wondered if that means would serve the purpose at hand. I then began the struggle with the specific new methods of communicating. This process itself held many of the joys and frustrations of the project, but also the opportunities to really explore creative problem solving.

I believe that writing up our projects should be ancillary to this new performative work; the text should never be our main output. For me, more interesting as documents are the scripts themselves or the notes or the diagrammatic evidence that our projects leave behind as a kind of trail, trace, or map. When we do publish, these sorts of records certainly hold more relevance as scholarship. I am more and more convinced these days that any academic written texts report-ing our efforts at popularizing research should be supplementary papers supporting our pro-ductions and certainly not the final results of our investigative efforts.

Many who have turned to PSS have shifted to the arts for both inspiration and practical assistance in answer to our own frustrations with more standard research practices. Perhaps typ-ical qualitative academic methods have become shopworn (routinely slotting vast amounts of data into themes and then banging on about "rigor" comes to mind as an example). Possibly the problem lies within our description of data. Do we write too routinely about the "evoca-tive" without knowing what it is that is being evoked and how or, better yet, what our work might provoke instead? Yes, we turn elsewhere, aptly so. The arts encourage us to be at the fore-front of academic change and innovation, challenging the status quo and moving our fields for-ward—the rightful place of scholarship.

What Lessons Have Been Learned from Popularization?

Funders are currently encouraging researchers to find ways to reach wider audiences with their findings ("impact factor") and, because of this, we are beginning to look beyond academic jour-nals or narrow academic subject groups (e.g., presenting to delegates at specialists' conferences—or "preaching to the choir"). Funders now want to know the benefits of our research to society and how it might affect the social order—the potential outcomes of our efforts.

Performative Social Science, when it is at its best and humming along, is a synthesis that provides answers to many of these very requirements. Ideally, our audiences should be almost unaware of the seams where we have cobbled together in-depth, substantial scholarship with artistic endeavor. In my estimation, part of doing PSS is not only breaking down the old boundaries, but also discarding the old expectations and frameworks of what research is supposed to resemble after it is finished.

Nonetheless, we are researchers. We are not actors, directors, filmmakers, dancers, or poets. There are many opportunities and outlets (and frustrations and roadblocks) for those who wish to pursue those professions. We can learn a great deal from these folks who often find it necessary to wait tables and do other menial jobs in order to pursue their dream profession. They may help us look at our own field through new lenses, but let's not insult them by falsely assuming their hard-earned mantles.

In return, a word of caution to artists who might be drawn to working with researchers: the world of academia is not simply a new venue for you to put on a play, dance a dance, or publish a poem. There are both constraints and opportunities in the academic world as well, which we are happy to share with you through our collaborations.

Through interfaces with both practitioners and practices from the arts and humanities, opportunities are presented to work with social-science material and expand its means of production and popularization to novel and creative levels. This requires the fusion mentioned earlier. This necessitates cooperation and collaboration. Communication and common ground are central to successful partnership and union (see Jones, 2006b, p. 71).

The intuitive aspects of shared culture, coupled with a more universal response to life's tribulations and injustices (and, therefore, artistic expressions of these emotive components), compete for resolution with the more rigid academic ethical frameworks and methodological constraints under discussion. By developing a trust in instinct and intuition and the naturally expressive and moral potential of these personal resources, social-science research can become richer and more human, if we only are willing to jettison some of the baggage of the old academic rigor and dry procedural ethics.

A few closing words of caution: some academics would rather incorporate the language of what we are doing into their own publications without ever challenging either their own thinking or production. They subsume the lingo of PSS, but never really re-examine their own routine techniques or dissemination methods. Our developing terminology is, therefore, appropriated within standard academic journal texts rather than representative of any meaningful reinvention of research methods or diffusion.

Most of all, however, let's be careful not to implode PSS through an overblown sense of what we are about. In our enthusiasm, let's not be too quick to anoint ourselves as poets, actors, dancers, or magicians. If we do eventually earn those titles, I am sure that others more qualified to judge will be certain to let us know.

References

Bourriaud, N. (2002; English version). *Relational aesthetics*. Dijon, France: Les Presses du Reel.

Genoways, T. (2010, January/February). The death of fiction? *Mother Jones*. Retrieved from http://mother-jones.com/media/2010/01/death-of-literary-fiction-magazines-journals.

Gergen, M., & Jones, K. (2008). Editorial: A conversation about performative social science. *Forum Qualitative Sozialforschung/Forum: Qualitative Social Research, 9*(2), Art. 43. Retrieved from http://nbn-resolving.de/urn:nbn:de:0114-fqs0802437.

Jones, K. (2002a). The birth of constructionism! Or, on a train from Morgantown, West Virginia, 1976, with Klaus Riegel & Kenneth Gergen (script). Multimedia production presented at the Free University of Berlin, Feb 2002. Retrieved fromhttp://www.angelfire.com/zine/kipworld/Morgantown.pdf.

Jones, K. (2002b). The spiritual dimension: A gerotranscendental take on Akira Kurosawa's film *Ran*. Audio/visual production presented at the *International Association of Gerontology 34th EBSSRS Symposium on Ageing and Diversity*. Bergen, Norway. 31 August 2002. Retrieved from http://www.angelfire.com/zine/kipworld/Kurosawa.pdf.

Jones, K. (2004). Thoroughly post-modern Mary: A biographic narrative interview with Mary Gergen. *Forum: Qualitative Social Research, 5*(3). Retrieved from http://www.qualitative-research.net/index.php/fqs/article/view/554.

Jones, K. (2006a). *The one about Princess Margaret* (film). Retrieved from http://vimeo.com/4339217.

Jones, K. (2006b). A biographic researcher in pursuit of an aesthetic: The use of arts-based (re)presentations in "performative" dissemination of life stories. *Qualitative Sociology Review* (April). Retrieved from http://www.qualitativesociologyreview.org/ENG/Volume3/QSR_2_1_Jones.pdf.

Jones, K. (2007a). The one about Princess Margaret (Script). *Forum: Qualitative Social Research, 8*(3). Retrieved from http://www.qualitative-research.net/index.php/fqs/rt/suppFiles/281/617.

Jones, K. (2007b). How did I get to Princess Margaret? *Forum: Qualitative Social Research, 8*(3). Retrieved from http://www.qualitative-research.net/index.php/fqs/article/view/281/617.

Jones, K. (2008). Rough talk and chocolate brownies. *Exploring Online Research Methods*. University of Leicester, U.K. Retrieved from http://www.geog.le.ac.uk/orm/futures/futuresperformance.htm.

Jones, K. (2009). How did I get to Princess Margaret? (And how did I get her to the World Wide Web?). In M. Srinivasan & R. Mathur (eds.), *Ethnography and the Internet: An exploration*. Nagarjuna Hills, Punjagutta, India: ICFAI University Press.

Jones, K. (2010). *Prime cuts* (film). Retrieved from http://vimeo.com/14824842.

Qikipedia. (2010). About 200,000 academic journals...Twitter, 22 June, 2010: 7:15 pm. Retrieved from http://twitter.com/qikipedia/status/16788883448_.

CHAPTER TWO

"People Get Tired"

African Australian Cross-Cultural Dialogue and Ethnocinema

Anne Harris & Nyadol Nyuon

People Get Tired is a part of an ongoing intercultural dialogue between a young Sudanese Australian activist and an American Australian writer/academic that looks at racism in Australia and intercultural collaboration in community arts and academic research. This dialogue is characteristic of the emerging practice of ethnocinema (Harris, 2009; 2010), which draws from its ethnographic documentary origins and yet goes beyond it. Combining ethnographic documentary methods (Rouch, 2003) with the principles of critical education (hooks, 2003; Kincheloe & Steinberg, 2001), ethnocinema uses the popular cultural forms of video and social media to address racial, gender, sexuality, and religious inequities and oppressions.

From mid-2007 to the present, what started as a high-school film project grew into doctoral research and additional ethnocinematic video collaborations between participants from different cultures in Melbourne, Australia. In the case of this project, the cultures can be reduced to binarisms such as Sudanese/American, black/white, young/middle-aged, teacher/student, gay/straight, middle class/working class, refugee/immigrant; but these would have been incomplete categorizations and so we resisted them. Thus, the research project known as *Cross-Marked: Sudanese Australian Young Women Talk Education* did indeed explore collaboratively through film the educational experiences of 15 Sudanese Australian young women, but it also explored the ways in which the researcher, a 40-something white immigrant from the USA, and the young women, 18- to 25-year-olds from South Sudan, were all building new lives in Australia, particularly in relation to the education system.

The project drew upon Giroux's notion of public and critical pedagogies (2004; 2005), Denzin's performative ethnography (2003), and arts-based research methods (Barone & Eisner, 1997; Bresler, 2007) to try to address the inequities between the co-participants and to recognize a need to honestly and collaboratively consult with Freire's (1970) so-called oppressed, even when the oppressed is in part ourselves. A history of ethnographic documentary (particularly Rouch's *ethno-fictions*) suggested a new development in the direction of eth-

nocinema, a more collaborative and mutually self-reflexive process, which extended the frac-
tured and multiple definitions offered throughout the past 20 years by various practitioners,
including Rouch (in Niger, 2003), Prins (in the US, 2004) and Gocic (in Europe, 2001).

Popularizing Critical Arts Education Research

A core tenet of the research is the notion that popular culture and media tools are increasingly at the centre of real education, especially for those from the margins (McLaren & Kincheloe,
2007). The internet, television, movies, music videos, YouTube, and other popular media are
accessible, often free, and still offer mainstream cross-over potential. This is one reason why ethnocinema (unlike its fuzzily named predecessors ethno-fictions, cine-ethnography, etc.) is a logical extension of the dynamic film-based work in traditional ethnography and anthropology that
has steadily grown and dynamically changed the face of research since the 1950s.

Ethnocinema plugs into 21st-century populist understandings that image can now become
existence, simulacra (Deleuze, 1983) becomes substance, and the virtual *is* real, just a different real. The *versus* has been, to a large extent, erased from these binarisms of bygone days;
instead of having to be this *or* that, contemporary theorists recognise how we are all this *and*
that, always already. Ever-changing positionalities and the transgressive and rhizomatic potential of electronic media mean that everyone can access documents or *presences* in these forums,
or in other words be multiple identities in multiple locations. Unlike the old days of dusting
one's doctoral thesis on out-of-reach shelves, or academic articles condemned to few specialist readers, today research must be increasingly popular to be relevant at all, and ethnocinema
is built upon this idea. It suggests that popular is not at odds with valid, as Ruby asserted as
recently as 2000 (p. 31). These definitions have gone out with Twitter, Facebook, and
YouTube, and are already having explosive and exciting repercussions for the popularization
of research beyond academic circles. Today, ethnocinema suggests ways forward that rhi-
zomatically blend academic/popular writing approaches in the same way that centre/margin
and researcher/subject are no longer able to be so easily distinguished, dismissed, or
dichotomised.

Some researchers and practitioners suggest Anne has all the power in these relationships
and these young women have none. When Anne tells Nyadol that she is gay, adopted, and frequently homesick for New York, some find in it an over-identification with Nyadol's margin-
alization in Western society and a diminishment of what she has been through; we call it respect
and recognition rather than a hierarchy of marginalized identities. Conquergood (1991) agrees
that true intercultural collaboration is both an intellectual and a bodily experience and demands
"understanding of the Self and understanding of the Other" (Banister, 1999, p. 13).

Cultural multiplicity continues to be, as Anzaldua (1987) showed us, layered and troubling,
and *People Get Tired* briefly demonstrates how true this still is. Nyadol reminds us in the film
clip that the experience of moving between cultures and emerging from painful pasts is often
about waiting, sometimes for acceptance that "you're probably never gonna receive" (Nyuon,
People Get Tired). Ethnocinema is one model for intercultural dialogue that rejects the "us"
/"them" impasse. Denzin (1997; 2003) encourages us toward a seventh-moment scholarship
in which cultural criticism is productively ubiquitous, and in which "the dividing line between
autoethnography and ethnography disappears" (2003, p. 224). Nyadol and Anne work (together and separately) within our own respective communities, but also together across cultural and

community boundaries, in order to speak multiple truths about "the tension of identity in motion" (Smith, 1993, p. xxxiv).

The film fragment *People Get Tired* that accompanies this commentary explores some points of view of both Nyadol and Anne in a conversational manner. It is composed of footage shot during the making of Nyadol's education film *Still Waiting* (2009), with some additional footage recorded by a stationary camera one evening while Anne and Nyadol were in conversation about the role of ethnocinema, and the nature of intercultural collaborations in Melbourne in late 2009.

In this film fragment, Nyadol does most of the talking, and we move through multiple subjects. The effect is like a visual/audio montage of perspectives and topics, the kinds of interrelated conversations that punctuate real relationships, especially across cultures. Viewers are also drawn to the interrelation between Anne and Nyadol, in the absence of a single narrative. This is the explicit intent of ethnocinema, and it can be productively used by researchers, artists, community workers and teachers.

hooks demands any site of education be "life-sustaining and mind-expanding, a place of liberating mutuality where teacher and student together work in partnership" (hooks, 2003, p. xv), and the mutuality of which she speaks inspires the ongoing ethnocinematic project. The troubling liminality of being a popular researcher for social change, yet one who challenges mainstream definitions of legitimacy within the academic scene, has been unpacked by others, including Conquergood (1991), Geertz (1988), and Richardson and Lockridge (2004).

So How Do We "Do" Ethnocinema?

These films were produced and distributed in collaboration: that is, we (researcher and co-participants) negotiated where the films would be shot, what they would contain (apart from the central theme of education), and how the films might be distributed.

While I (Anne) originally hoped to create the films in small friendship or family groups of young women, in the end most of them turned out to be solo affairs due to child-rearing, school, work, or cultural responsibilities of the co-participants. We usually met once or twice a week for a few months, and while they are all at least partly shot by both of us, most of the editing was done by me with critical feedback on each draft from my collaborators. For five of the six films, I used a personal-standard video camera from the media department at university; just before Nyadol's film (the last in the series), they purchased a high-end Sony HD camera and the difference is noticeable in the quality of the footage.

All seven videos (including my own, *EthnocineME*) were edited using Final Cut software on a Mac computer. All seven films were given a dust-up by a professional editor in the final stages, but otherwise the videos were completed solely by me and the Sudanese young women (see filmography). I had originally hoped to have more active collaboration in the editing and sometimes in the filming, but about half of the young women simply wanted to tell their story and were not overly interested in learning filmmaking.

The filmmaking itself was a learning process for me. Although I had done some music-video-style short clips with young people in previous collaborations, I was unprepared for the demands of documentary filmmaking. Some of the most difficult aspects were getting good sound quality (using poor microphones and filmmaking in chaotic locations); good lighting quality (I only tried using film lighting once, and the young woman immediately stopped talking as it was too hot, too bright, and completely changed the atmosphere); and good cinematography (I was "facilitating" as well as shooting for much of the time, and this limited my ability to vary the shots and angles). Nevertheless, when I tried bringing along a film crew, even a small one, the dynamics between me and my co-participants changed completely; I wasn't willing to lose the intimacy and one-on-one relationship, and our mutual commitment to this ethnocinematic style enriches, I believe, the content of the films.

Distribution was another surprise: when Achol suggested YouTube as the most appropriate public distribution channel, the other co-participants and I agreed. The decision demonstrated not only the public orientation of these collaborators from a younger generation, but unforeseen ways in which academic research can be of benefit to those involved: for Achol, it served her agenda to become an actress. For Nyadol, popularizing strategies like co-presenting and co-authoring helps build her resume. These are simple, free, and collaborative ways of popularizing research that immediately open up possibilities for all members of the research triad: "subjects" or co-participants, researchers, and scholar/viewers.

While the exegesis (textual) part of the PhD was written and will be published as a scholarly book, this is not the kind of document that is of interest to some of the co-participants (although it equally must be recognized that it *is* of interest to some). While a DVD of the six Sudanese films was produced and has been popular with secondary and tertiary teachers, it is even more convenient to log on to YouTube with friends or students and view our movies anywhere. Yet the "popular" aspects of this research take multiple forms: we can pop a DVD into the video player at home and show our families; we can give our parents copies of local newspaper articles written about us or the film launch where these films were made public. These are powerful research outcomes not only for academics (who benefit from research anyway), but for the co-participants and subjects of research, who often see no practical or personally beneficial result. By using methodologies like ethnocinema, the research can have a much wider audience; but more important, that audience can include those about whom this research is conducted. This is popularizing research in the truest sense of the term.

Throughout the two years of filming, the researcher and young women made videos about education and about their lives, but also began to work collaboratively in other ways in order to address some of what they commented upon in their videos. Achol and Anne have since made an audition tape for a mainstream Australian television program, which we shot and edited at Achol's home, improvisationally. This was easy and effective: Anne shot Achol reading a scene supplied by the show's producers, and they co-edited the footage in Final Cut software (as they had done with her *Cross-Marked* film). The audition process required Achol to post her audition piece on YouTube and then link to the show's homepage; when she did not get selected, Achol chose to delete the film clip and that was easily done by Anne.

Achol and Anne have been developing a reality show for YouTube based on her life as a Sudanese single teenage mother living in an all-white neighbourhood, called *Single Ladies*. Filming these five-minute segments is easy, and Achol loves the acting; it is difficult for Achol to improvise in English, though, and scripts haven't worked well. We are continuing to practice ways of maintaining the "reality show" feel in the footage, yet keeping the process simple enough to feel achievable for both collaborators.

Nyadol and Anne have co-written an academic article and this book chapter and co-presented at film festivals, conferences, and in university and secondary classrooms. Lina and Anne have also co-presented. Importantly, we have given to and received from each other community-based work in the arts and social action groups, demonstrating the power of personal relationships in popularizing arts and activist research.

Conclusion

The products and processes that result from ethnocinematic collaboration are usefully popularized in ways that extend the research but also deepen the relationship between researcher and researched. In keeping with other emerging rhizomatic research methods, ethnocinema is to some degree an anti-teleological practice in that it resists naming, limiting, and categorizing definitions. It is not meant to be one thing, or one way of doing ethnography. Denzin and other performative social scientists now agree that "dialogical performance is the means as much as the end of honest intercultural understanding" (Conquergood, 1985, p. 10), and this is apparent in the work between Nyadol and Anne in *People Get Tired*. The only central notion of the ethnocinematic project is a commitment to the principles of social justice through an authentic (not tokenistic) collaborative approach that values and interrogates both cultural collaborators from proposal, through development, execution to dissemination.

Both cultural collaborators bring different skills and knowledges, but both should be equally valued and included in the research process and products. hooks (from Freire, 1970) claims that "authentic help means that all who are involved help each other *mutually*, growing together in the common effort to understand the reality which they seek to transform" (hooks, 1994, p. 54), that both parties should benefit from the experience, and if possible from the outcomes. This does not mean that everything must be shared—that is impossible. Co-participants bring different skills, and so it would be illogical and tokenistic to imagine that both parties would equally participate in conceiving, writing, filming, editing, and marketing the resultant films and commentaries. We excel at different roles; for example, I ended up editing most of the videos, and the co-participants would advise on drafts; they structured (and sometimes restructured) the shape of their films and named them, and they chose who should shoot them. However, what this means is that all aspects should be approached critically, self-reflexively, and in consultation, with a view to benefiting both parties. This chapter and both authors invite readers to use this entry to comment upon our conception of ethnocinema, and to extend the project by extending these definitions or provocations into new and untapped areas. Ethnocinema is broad enough, contemporary enough, and welcomes innovation and anti-ownership.

References

Anzaldua, G. E. (1987/2007). *Borderlands/La frontera: The new mestiza* (3rd ed.). San Francisco, CA: Aunt Lute Books.

Banister, E. M. (1999). Evolving reflexivity: Negotiating meaning of women's midlife experience. *Qualitative Inquiry, 5(1)*, 3–23.

Barone, T., & Eisner, E. (1997). Arts-based educational research. In R. M. Jaeger (Ed.), *Complementary methods for research in education* (73–103). Washington, DC: American Educational Research Association.

Baudrillard, J. (1994). *Simulacra and Simulation* (S. F. Glaser, Trans.). Ann Arbor, MI: University of Michigan.

Bresler, L. (Ed.). (2007). *International handbook of research in arts education*. The Netherlands: Springer.

Conquergood, D. (1985). Performing as a moral act: The ethical dimensions of the ethnography of performance. *Literature in Performance, 5(2)*, 1–13.

Conquergood, D. (1991). Rethinking ethnography: Towards a critical cultural politics. *Communication Monographs, 58*, 179–194.

Deleuze, G. (1983). Plato and the Simulacrum. *October, 27 (winter)*: 45–56.

Denzin, N. K. (1997). *Interpretive ethnography: Ethnographic practices for the 21st century*. Thousand Oaks, CA: Sage.

Denzin, N. K. (2003). *Performance ethnography: Critical pedagogy and the politics of culture.* Thousand Oaks, CA: Sage.

Freire, P. (1970). *Pedagogy of the oppressed.* New York, NY: Continuum.

Geertz, C. (1988). *Works and lives: The anthropologist as author.* Stanford, CA: Stanford University Press.

Giroux, H. (2004). Cultural studies, public pedagogy, and the responsibility of intellectuals. *Communication and Critical/Cultural Studies, 1(1),* 59–79.

Giroux, H. (2005). *Border crossings: Cultural workers and the politics of education* (2nd ed.). New York, NY: Routledge.

Gocic, G. (2001). *The cinema of Emir Kusturica: Notes from the underground.* London, UK: Wallflower Press.

Harris, A. (2009). "You could do with a little more Gucci": Ethnographic documentary talks back. *Creative Approaches to Research, 2(1),* 18–34.

Harris, A. (2010, Nov. 1). Race and refugeity: Ethnocinema as radical pedagogy. *Qualitative Inquiry, 16,* 768–777.

hooks, b. (1994). *Teaching to transgress: Education as the practice of freedom.* New York, NY: Routledge.

hooks, b. (2003). *Teaching community: A pedagogy of hope.* New York, NY: Routledge.

Kincheloe, J., & Steinberg, S. (2001). *Multi/intercultural conversations: A reader.* New York, NY: Peter Lang.

McLaren, P., & Kincheloe, J. L. (Eds.). (2007). *Critical pedagogy: Where are we now?* New York, NY: Peter Lang.

Nyuon, N., & Harris, A. (2009). *Still waiting* (film). Unpublished thesis. Melbourne, Australia: Victoria University.

Prins, H. (2004). Visual anthropology. In T. Bilosi (Ed.), *A companion to the anthropology of American Indians* (506–525). Oxford, UK: Blackwell Publishing.

Richardson, L., & Lockridge, E. (2004). *Travels with Ernest: Crossing the literary/sociological divide.* Walnut Creek, CA: Alta Mira.

Rouch, J. (2003). *Cine-ethnography/Jean Rouch* (S. Feld, Trans. & Ed.). Minneapolis, MN: University of Minnesota Press.

Ruby, 2000. 2000. *Picturing Culture: Explorations of Film and Anthropology.* Chicago: University of Chicago Press. Original edition, 1975 article.

Smith, A. D. (1993). *Fires in the mirror: Crown Heights, Brooklyn, and other identities.* New York, NY: Doubleday.

CHAPTER THREE

Sturgis 2.0

Crafting a Filmic-Web Dialogue

Carly Gieseler

Sturgis 2.0 is the mixed-media result of my immersion in motorcycle rally culture. From my initial return to the legendary Sturgis Motorcycle Rally in my home state of South Dakota, through the compilation of a filmic retelling of the mobile culture experience, I used the voices within and around the rally culture to create a filmic experience that creates and recreates what Sturgis means to those passionate enthusiasts who journey across miles and years to participate in the annual rally. The film itself is a compilation of video clips and still photographs, mixed with songs and quotes lifted from my experience and from the generous donations and suggestions of those within the culture.

To get from my original material to the final film was a journey in itself; upon creating the original work, I visited various motorcycle websites and blogs, asking for suggestions and comments on my piece. In linking the extensive internet family of rally enthusiasts to my film site, I was able to create a filmic-web dialogue that furthered my commitment to the project and opened up the film to incorporate the impassioned voices of this mobile culture. Subsequently, I showed the final piece at a gallery in my hometown during the next Sturgis rally. This was meant to reassert the process of journeying through memories; at every showing I asked the attendees to fill out comment cards that responded to what they felt this film evoked in their memories about Sturgis. In this way, I hoped to create a tapestry of meaning and memory that captured the mythology surrounding this annual event for those inside and around the culture. In playing across various media and reaching out to multiple audiences, I created a film that was a multidimensional reflection on the devoted motorcycle rally culture.

My work on *Sturgis 2.0* became the locus of technology, media, and art. I believe that the increased use and access of internet sources allows us to invoke the complex and multiple identities and voices within our communities. My own reflexive ethnographic voice moves within the rally culture, and through my journey of memory helped grant greater representation to the film. Rather than simply crafting a piece recalling my own perspective and memory, the continuation of the dialogue through internet conversations and gallery showings created a sustained discourse crafted entirely through the memory process.

Above all, *Sturgis 2.0* became a film created by and for the rally community. The film offers an artistic retelling of the endless journey of mobile cultures; the conversations within the rally culture permit this journey to engage in questions of identity, performance, and memory. The participants whose voices shaped *Sturgis 2.0* provided the ongoing conversation of a cultural collaboration that allowed me to embody their recollections into the visual.

The Vision and the Journey

I needed to conceive of lived experiences within both the Sturgis rally and everyday existence to create a vision of identity and memory in rally culture. I interrogate how these identities might be "performed in 'spectacles'" (Robinson, 2008, p. 8) such as the nation's largest motorcycle rally. I constructed a reflexive ethnographic study of motorcycle culture, thus resisting the traditional pull of linear writing to weave between memories of my high-school self and my return to the rally as a grown academic. I wanted to step out of the self-surveillance that academic researchers and writers often commit; my solution was a return to a culture I once viewed with boundless wonder.

I re-entered the Sturgis rally from my new identity in the world, even as the memories of that South Dakotan teenager shadowed my every step. I created a filmic representation of my Sturgis return comprised of video and still images. I incorporated quotes from informal interviews, conversations, and my own personal narrative. The knowledge gathered through reflexive ethnography provides a unique frame for my understanding of rally culture; telling this knowledge through my film presents a firsthand account of my identity as performative within this experience. Using reflexive ethnography helps me play with the identities of insider/outsider within research. While I take a stance as a critical observer or ethnographic interviewer at times, I also position myself as participant. This brings emotional and physical insights to bear on my research that grant me an understanding of the embodied experiences and shifting identities produced and performed within rally culture.

In addition to my own work recording the rally experience through my own vision, I needed to encourage voices within the rally community to create a fully realized interpretation of that culture. Conversations with bikers and rally enthusiasts created a dialogue to complement the cultural productions of biker myth. As recollections often transfix our lived experience in suspended snapshots of memory, these voices gave my work movement. The filmic compilation emerged from seeking these voices in various ways: when motorcycle enthusiasts offered compelling thoughts about Sturgis, I embedded these quotes within the work or shifted the work to reflect these comments; when rally attendees offered their own photographs and websites to add to the project, I graciously accepted and incorporated their artistic visions; when Sturgis devotees offered specific memories, I tried to recapture the recollection through imagery and music. As I customized my film in response to the many voices and memories presented through the internet dialogue, gallery sessions, and personal recollections, the movement of the film became a reflection of the mobility of identity and memory within motorcycle culture. The project grew across borders of time and space, yet I realized that to further explore the Sturgis mystique, I needed and wanted the conversation to continue.

A Community Conversation

Popularizing research deepens and widens the conversation regarding how time, space, and memory surround motorcycle culture. A participatory dialogue on the internet provided commentary on my original filmic telling of Sturgis. The additional voices from those viewing the updated piece during the subsequent year's rally in the gallery space offered responses to the film and their own memories of Sturgis from inside the time of the rally. As these voices emerged in response to my project, my film reflected their memories and comments. This experience furthered understanding about how we engage in transformative cultures that permit us to perform, practice, and produce identity. In sharing my research of the rally culture with a broader audience, I hope to not only invite more voices to further my own knowledge, but also to foster discourse regarding memories and identities within our chosen communities.

Fusing reflexive ethnography with a creative and interactive work, I felt this project could sustain the interest of the biker culture it aimed to understand. In moments of meta-reflection, I realize that projects popularizing research can build a more extensive dialogue with a larger population about memory, liminality, and popular imagination. As empirical observations tend to dominate the academic tradition, we cannot neglect the potential for knowing through active participation, intimate connections, and embodied experiences. While much scholarly work demands the majority—if not all—of the individual author's time and efforts, the final result of my film was a product of a community of rally devotees and interested participants. This pulled me out of a self-centered, self-directed vision and brought in the multiple opinions, questions, and materials that shaped me and my project in this process.

Over the course of this project, I worked in collaboration with friends still living in South Dakota; they helped me recall the rally culture and stake out the original vision of my memories. After designing a plan to enter the culture, I interviewed more than 30 rally attendees in semi-structured conversations regarding what Sturgis evoked for them. I used these notes to craft the filmic structure; their words on the Sturgis experience helped guide what I included and excluded from the film. After compiling the embryonic film based on the initial experience, I was able to continue the conversation beyond rally borders of time and space. I visited various websites devoted to Sturgis, motorcycle rally culture, and mobile cultures in general. Through blog postings, I was able to inquire about the meaning of the experiences within the mobile motorcycle communities. I was also able to guide interested participants to view the film from my original site dedicated strictly to the film. At this point, those who commented on the work were often inspired not only to contribute their own suggestions or critiques, but also to provide additional materials. Thus, I adapted the film to embody all of these experiences, yet the project grew much larger than the finished film itself. *Sturgis 2.0* engendered a greater and continuing conversation about identity, memory, and performance within rally culture and across mediated screens.

The challenges in creating a filmic-web dialogue emphasized elements of practicality and creativity in the research process. My past experiences shadowed and forecast my return to Sturgis, offering a blueprint of the spaces I recalled along youthful travels. I relied heavily on the voices of the rally community to address the slippage of my own memory over the years. To share this cultural experience with a larger audience, I needed more memories to recreate the sense of energy surrounding the mobile culture. I achieved this in two ways: I expanded the scope of the documentation to incorporate conversations flowing from semi-structured interactions; and I expanded the conversation beyond the border of the event itself. Yet with each mediated sphere and additional voice, my focus continuously shifted as more knowledge, technology, and material expanded the project. Through these contributions, I found a greater sense of what the rally meant to these cultural members as individuals and as a community.

To document the nebulous aspects of identity and memory within the biker culture, I believed that a documentary would capture the colorful characters, liberated celebration, and general feeling of kinship. While I had no delusions of grandeur regarding my less-than-amateur filmmaking skills, I also recognized that a bare-bones operation was well suited to capturing the primal energy of this annual carnival of chaos. Language is the lifeblood of cultures, forging bonds of understanding and cohesion to legitimize cultural membership. This shifted my approach from structured questions leaden with academic jargon toward a more extemporaneous tone. Conversations along the road, on the street, and across the bar top taught me to immerse myself within the rally culture. In addition, as the issues of memory and identity seemed to create an almost artistic vision for myself and the rally enthusiasts, I chose to create something much more aligned with this vision. Thus, a documentary account shifted toward an aesthetic and musical retelling through my film. In this way, I felt that I best posited my own vision of Sturgis while artistically embodying the fluid energy and vivid retelling of the Sturgis community.

As greater access ensured multiplied voices that could reach a larger audience, continuing the conversation beyond the rally became necessary. I not only needed the voices at Sturgis but everyone intrigued by motorcycle culture to join the process. I opened the internet dialogue to individual memories of Sturgis; I solicited comments regarding the original documentation of my experience. My perceptions of this culture were opened up and the visual project was transformed by the internet blogs at various rally and biker websites and the posted comments reviewing my embryonic documentary on a temporary webpage. I was trying to package an academic commentary on time, space, and memory. It was a creative take on standard academic research; however, it retained a practiced distance. Striving for polish, I missed the essence of Sturgis. I might not have recognized this glaring fact if not for the contributions of my expanded audience. With each conversation, I began to see Sturgis clearly again. Even after my physical homecoming at the rally, the continued dialogue allowed me to continue returning and recapturing that frenetic movement that marks this culture.

In a study of time, space, and memory, I began understanding the importance of playing with all three to reflect this culture. While I originally conceived of the documentation of Sturgis culture as the move into liminal space, I found that the internet accomplishes a similar effect. The internet discussions become both suspended and pliable in accordance with our notion of time. The internet as a medium provides an intangible presence; it is a space we converse in and explore without ever actually knowing its borders. The resulting mediated interface of film, photography, interview, blogging, and film transformed the original project to encompass experience and embody memory.

Popularizing the Marginal

Initially, my research was popularized as a reflexive ethnography on temporal memory and liminal identity within the culture I knew as a youth. I wanted to reach edge-dwelling tricksters who embrace these mobile cultures. As the process expanded, spilling across the borders of Sturgis and into my film, I realized that communicating marginal cultures follows its own set of rules.

Challenging the cultural myth of motorcycle culture was another motivation in popularizing this research. Popular media often glamorize aspects of violence and danger inherent to biker myth. For those cultural edge-dwellers embracing this lifestyle, the myth speaks above and beyond their lived experience. Venturing into qualitative areas of ethnographic, interview, and personal narrative methods, I forged a path to capture the dynamism of lived experiences and identity negotiation. Thus, my work does not end at the representational surfaces. I move within the circles of biker culture to comprehend what media and myth often speak around; communicating with bikers and rally enthusiasts supplements what we know of representations with what we live through experience.

Expanding the dialogue of the film across the internet, I was able to recreate and re-imagine my own filmic memories through the eyes of others. As such, the process moved to a new stage of reflexivity, fluidly flickering from memory to present, my voice to others. My film reflects this extended dialogue, playing and shifting with the limits of time, space, and memory. In watching the finished film, I see how I retain my experience of the journey even as my conversations shape that initial memory. What remained was a rugged, chaotic, fleeting flight that marked something my expanded audience found most significant in their own memories of Sturgis—the journey itself.

What I Learned

Working with the undercurrent of movement within motorcycle culture, the process helped me not only to comprehend the culture I entered, but also to understand how that culture changed me once inside. Turner (1986) articulates "communitas" as magical togetherness, evidenced by heightened emotions, suspension of rules, and centralization of marginal figures and communities. Motorcycle culture thus draws participants and audiences toward the edge, creating that magical bond. My conversations with members of the biker community illuminate how rituals and performances produce messages about an entire culture. Across internet blogs and discussions, the recognition of rally locations or the description of one's motorcycle become strategies confirming cultural membership. Out of necessity for the project and to encourage community participation, I needed to entrench myself within rally culture and establish myself as a member of that community. The level of trust established through my mediated interactions engendered the flow of conversation that ultimately transformed the film itself.

While countless rally-goers reiterated the ruggedly haunting beauty of the Black Hills and embraced a familial camaraderie of the rally, most often it was the journey itself that sparked and sustained allegiance to Sturgis. My film thus shifted from something aiming toward scholarly ethnography toward an artistic vision of recalling and retelling that journey. The road remains functional in building our mobile nation and mystical in unleashing our cultural imagination. The road liberates us from the borders of time and place; our journeys free us of normative rules and roles of everyday existence. Once on the road, the scheduling demands of life slip away with the roar of the engine. The road dictates time; life becomes stripped down to the primal. In addition, the crucial need for play comes surging back. Play is typically stifled under the cloak of work and responsibility, yet the road reveals its necessity—there are sites to be seen, bypasses worth making, family and friends to reunite with along the way. As one enters this culture, time shifts back and forth across the years. Memory becomes peppered with details reflecting a temporal jigsaw rather than the linear timeline so imperative in our normative lives. Stripped of normative time constraints, we surface in communities of movement to find a temporal absence in which we often become most present. The original documentation of the road, the rally, and the reflection offered just one individual memory. However, *Sturgis 2.0* opened beyond my vision to embody the experiences and recollections encountered along every mile.

References

Robinson, V. (2008). *Everyday masculinities and extreme sport: Male identity and rock climbing*. Oxford, UK: Berg.
Turner, V. (1986). *The anthropology of performance*. New York: PAJ.

Part 2

VISUAL MEDIA AND GRAPHICS

CHAPTER FOUR

Cartoons as Praxis

Negotiating Different Needs in Adult Literacy Research Reporting

Frank Sligo & Elspeth Tilley

In 2007 we commissioned a series of cartoons to communicate the findings of a longitudinal research project exploring adult literacy. We agree with Marx's (1845/1969, p. 15) comment that "the philosophers have only interpreted the world, in various ways; the point is to change it." Thus we wanted to make our findings accessible to the communities we were working with. Also attractive was the prospect of challenging the assumptions inherent within governmental adult literacy policy—we felt that adult literacy policy tended to show characteristics of "experts talking to experts," but it could be enhanced if it showed strong awareness of the reality facing people with low literacy. However, we were also working within quite complex parameters. These included the postcolonial society of Aotearoa New Zealand, and the contested theoretical domain of adult literacy.

We fully accepted the need for strict participant anonymity and sought to communicate with diverse community and national audiences. Traditional, text-heavy scholarly research reporting seemed a poor fit. Cartoons, however, offered a novel way to navigate this tricky terrain. Therefore, we produced a series of cartoon-based posters (Massey University ALLR Group, 2007) and a book-style research report called *Voices* (Tilley et al., 2007). These contained large cartoon images on every page featuring verbatim quotations from research participants that brought to life key community perspectives. The visual material accompanying this chapter contains samples of those images. This chapter explains how the images were used and describes the feedback that resulted from the publication of *Voices*, both from community and policy audiences.

Background

The research, funded by the New Zealand Foundation for Research, Science and Technology, comprised a three-and-a-half-year community-based study in the city of Whanganui (population around 40,000 in a region [Manawatu-Whanganui] of about 220,000), with the aim of investigating connections and disconnections between literacy and employment. Our research would be built on local knowledge but would employ the university's research abilities in a coordinating role. This meant the research had to acknowledge and accommodate differing expectations and points of view.

One of the ways in which the research program aimed to capture varying perspectives was by involving the Whanganui community at multiple points. A lead role was taken by the Whanganui District Library, along with the Whanganui Community Foundation (a community development body), Literacy Aotearoa Whanganui (an adult literacy training provider), Te Puna Matauranga O Whanganui (an Indigenous educational authority) and a variety of other key local groups.

Another way in which the research aimed to incorporate plural perspectives was by taking a multimethod approach. The project used more than 20 methods, including a telephone survey, interviews with adult literacy training providers, one-to-one interviews then follow-up interviews with participants in adult literacy training, Iwi (tribal)-based research into indigenous ancestral literacy and bi-literacy, focus groups, interviews with employers, action research into family literacy within a prison setting, and case study research.

We recognized complex power issues inherent in any literacy research. Critics of adult literacy training point out how it may demean its participants by marginalizing the value of their other, non-print, capabilities. It can be used to co-opt them into questionable neoliberal discourses of participation. Literacy research may also comprise neo-colonization by privileging the colonizers' cultural values. Some commentators believe that when colonizers insist that the colonized must become literate (usually, and in Aotearoa New Zealand, almost invariably, in the colonizer's language), this comprises both a form of social control and a denigration of other kinds of cultural expertise (L. T. Smith, 1999; Shore, 2003). Literacy's power dynamic also has gender and class dimensions: as Le Guin (2008) recounts, "Literacy was not only a demarcator between the powerful and the powerless; it was power itself....Every literate society began with literacy as a constitutive prerogative of the (male) ruling class" (p. 34). We had, therefore, to be ever-mindful of this hegemonic "baggage" of literacy (Archer, 2002) in our research reporting.

Our data also showed that many of our participants were living with the consequences of widespread socialization of "deficit" models of literacy (Taylor, 1993), that is "simplistic understandings of literacy as a functional skill, or indeed something people don't have" (Shore, 2003, para. 1). Respondents frequently discerned a stigma around their literacy levels, feeling that they were being labeled as "the problem." Consequently, the word "literacy" invoked negative feelings. For example, comments from the interview transcripts included, "Literacy was that you were illiterate" and "I thought they're talking about dumb people...that's what it meant to me."

Nevertheless, it became evident to us that many research participants had been gaining a deep sense of empowerment through taking part in literacy training. Interviewees told us that, since undertaking a literacy course, they now had better interpersonal or family communication, or greater confidence, achievement, or motivation. Some had gained new or more rewarding employment, improved health or enhanced life skills, or were participating more in their community.

We wanted these multiple perspectives to come through in the research reporting, so that adult literacy learners' actual words would have a prominent place. Typically, research participants' own rich life-worlds were invisible in final reports, submerged under layers of governmental or scholarly discourse (Sligo & Tilley, 2009). Ironically, while literacy theory was starting to discover multi-literacies (i.e., the many non-print capabilities of reading the world around us), reporting of literacy research still largely privileged print. We wanted to differ, by giving the people impacted by adult literacy policy a vivid presence within our research reports. Using visual means to foreground interviewees' own words intrigued us, both to register their importance to readers and to signal the increasingly multimodal nature of literacy itself.

Why the Research Was Popularized

Although we needed to serve several goals, one important task was to properly acknowledge the people of Whanganui who generously gave us their diverse and rich stories. We were grateful to have learned from those who knew the issue best and lived it every day. The interview transcripts expressed powerful, poignant stories of vitality, diversity, intelligence, and skill, coupled with struggle, survival, strategy, resistance, and hope. We wanted other audiences to share what we had learned and felt that popularizing these stories would help to challenge stigma around low print literacy as equating with a "lack" (of ability, character, or motivation) and would display the multiple factors and human dimensions of literacy statistics to diverse audiences. Our policy reports thus had an interventionist aim for policy readers to see people with "low" literacy not as distant "other" objects but as present subjects—someone who might live next door.

Thus, with the thought in mind that "the very best research, no less than the worst, does and should 'speak' from particular, historically specific, social locations" (Harding, 2004, p. 4), we aimed to incorporate personal viewpoints, human stories, and the specific locale of Whanganui in our reporting. Communication standpoint theory (e.g., D. L. Smith, 1998; Harding & Hintikka, 2003; Harding, 2004) suggests that those who live within a situation can describe it more objectively than external observers and are more likely to suggest solutions that are effective as well as socially just. We wanted to embrace that idea and incorporate it into our reports to policymakers and opinion leaders. Hence we hoped to pay tribute to respondents' insights in their powerful original form: people's own words.

On the other hand, privacy was paramount. It was clear from our interviews that people considered to need print literacy training (often by government agencies that had referred them to training) frequently felt marginalized by the concept of a literate/illiterate divide. Few felt comfortable publicly identifying as participating in literacy training. All had been assured, through the research's ethics procedures, of total anonymity. Needed, then, was something non-print-privileging, yet incorporating respondents' own words. We wanted to give a sense of real people's struggles and challenges, and the actual communities within which people lived and worked, yet be anonymous.

How the Process of Popularization Worked

Some evidence from other research, including with people of low print literacy, suggested that carefully designed cartoons could more effectively communicate information content than print (e.g., Delp & Jones, 1996; Houts et al., 1998; Edmond & Tilley, 2002; Montoya et al., 2005). One study found that incorporating cartoons increased subsequent discussion about a topic, compared with using text alone (Moriyama, Harnisch, & Matsubara, 1994).

Our first experiment in representing participants' viewpoints in our research reports involved a pilot multimedia presentation. We used video to capture ad-lib statements from representatives of each of the research partners (not adult literacy training participants themselves at this stage). We then briefed an editor to compile those statements, along with a graphic designer's titles for each segment, into a summary narrative. The aim was to represent what the research partners wanted to achieve from the research.

At the first airing of this video among the research team, we immediately hit contested territory. One of the research partner representatives felt concerns at the publication of her statement after seeing it in the completed video. Other partners also felt uncomfortable seeing themselves speaking their own words. Video seemed to them a very unforgiving medium, too personalizing and too reductive. They felt that, during the specialist production phases of editing and design, they had lost control over the meaning of their words. While they did not necessarily disagree with what was being said, they no longer wanted their face shown speaking it. In light of these concerns, which we accepted as valid and important, the team decided not to make the video publicly available and not to use video for any other portion of the research reporting.

Ideally, we could have remade the video report from scratch, using participatory production processes—such as the examples of "sociocultural animation" described by Filewod and Watt (2001), in which workers were given video cameras and trained to script, film, edit, and produce their own audio-visual narratives of working conditions. This might have given consensus-based control to those whose viewpoints were reported, but it was not possible within our budgetary and reporting requirements. The important issue for us, though, was for participants' own words to be at the forefront of our reporting.

The failure of our video reporting attempt demonstrated to us the tension underlying our work between people's personal desire to be literate, yet their simultaneous awareness that literacy in English was and remains a tool by which elites exert power. We had not navigated that tension in the video but remained hopeful that some form of visual communication may help us mediate, or at the very least express, that tension better than printed words alone.

Our second attempt involved creating cartoons that quoted verbatim "voices" from the research participants. These voices came from three sets of interviews: first, almost 90 adult learners in 2005; second, many of the same people a year later; and third, a new group of adult literacy learners in 2006. In all, we interviewed almost 200 people in adult literacy training. The interviews ranged in length from 20 minutes to more than an hour.

From the dominant themes in these interviews, we created a series of graphics. Each graphic was intended to awaken the sense of these voices as coming from, and still connected with, speaking people. Each graphic used one or more quotations from the interview transcripts, depicted as spoken by one or more persons, against a de-toned photographic background.

The photographic backgrounds of Whanganui in these illustrations pictured actual places. The visuals of people speaking were Kerry Ann Lee's original creative artwork and did not relate to any particular individuals. Matching of faces with backgrounds and words was largely random or followed artistic imperatives.

Harper (2000) has observed that "the social power involved in making images redefines institutions, groups, and individuals" (p. 717). We knew that as researchers we were managing the process whereby the images were produced. And although as report facilitators we shaped how the comments were arranged, labeled, and presented, we wanted the bulk of our report to be, in essence, witness testimony. At the heart of this would be offering Whanganui adult learners' own experiences, priorities, concerns, and solutions. Bal (2005) has raised the question of whether "it is possible to deploy art not only as reflection, but also as a form of *witnessing* that alters the existence of what it witnesses" (p. 157; emphasis in original). We accepted that (assuming we had arrived at what could be construed as art) a political element was inherent in our intentions and that our form of witnessing shaped how our research participants might be seen. Specifically, we wanted to challenge deficit notions of literacy.

What Audiences Were Reached and How Audiences Responded

The reception accorded one research report in particular seemed to indicate that the images were seizing community readers' imaginations. This report, called *Voices* (Tilley et al., 2007), prompted more positive comments and a larger volume of feedback than any other. Community partners asked for additional copies to distribute in Whanganui, and described it as "the research equivalent of a best-seller" (Bob Dempsey, personal communication, 3 April 2008). Of all our outputs, *Voices* was the report with the fewest words and the greatest number of pictures. Although most of the reports had some images, *Voices* was the only report in which every double-page spread contained a half-page, cartoon-style, full-color image. It was also the only report, of 26, to require a second print run.

An anecdote from our illustrator suggested that we were making progress towards our aim of humanizing literacy reporting. She told us that after she had finished drawing the series of characters, which she did not base on any real human models, she suddenly "kept seeing them crop up in everyday places, like on the bus" (Kerry Ann Lee, personal communication, July 2007). To us, this implied that her created visual characters were indeed effectively normalized as ordinary and unremarkable, yet were still real and human in form.

We were fully aware of the sensitivities inherent in our situation as university researchers who were charged with producing reports on adult literacy within this community and knew that we had to find credible ways to reach out to the Whanganui people with whom we had worked so closely. Fortunately, we received strong support from community members for our venturing into visuality. Community collaborators told us that they valued our attempt to step aside from yet another proffering of dense academic prose in our reporting to them and to our government funders. Readers also liked our attempt at being open to risk-taking and creativity in depicting people with whom they could relate within actual photographed Whanganui street scenes. Government personnel also made complimentary remarks about the clarity of our messages.

However, we also learned that attempts to communicate visually offer more but demand more. We felt quite familiar with the routines of producing academic reports, but the nuances of communicating visually took us into a new zone. In this space we had to closely interrogate our own intentions and capabilities and to take fresh stock of the people in the community whom we wanted to reach.

References

Archer, D. (2002). The baggage of literacy. *Education Action, 16*, 41–43.

Bal, M. (2005). The commitment to look. *Journal of Visual Culture, 4*, 145–162.

Delp, C., & Jones, J. (1996). Communicating information to patients: The use of cartoon illustrations to improve comprehension of instructions. *Academic Emergency Medicine, 3*, 264–270.

Edmond, G., & Tilley, E. (2002). *Beyond role play: Workplace theatre and employee relations.* Australian & New Zealand Communication Association Conference, July 10–12, Gold Coast, 2002: Refereed Proceedings. Available at: http://www.anzca.net/download-document/374-beyond-roleplay-workplace-theatre-and-internal-relations.html

Filewod, A., & Watt, D. (2001). *Workers' playtime: Theatre and the labour movement since 1970.* Sydney, Australia: Currency Press.

Harding, S. (Ed.) (2004). *The feminist standpoint theory reader: Intellectual and political controversies.* London: Routledge.

Harding, S., & Hintikka, M. B. (Eds.) (2003). *Discovering reality: Feminist perspectives on epistemology, metaphysics, methodology, and philosophy of science* (2nd ed.). Dordrecht, Netherlands & Boston, MA: Kluwer.

Harper, D. (2000). Reimagining visual methods: Galileo to Neuromancer. In N. Denzin, & Y. Lincoln (Eds.). *SAGE handbook of qualitative research* (2nd ed.), pp. 717–732. Thousand Oaks, CA: Sage.

Houts, P. S., Bachrach, R., Witmer, J. T., Tringali, C. A., Bucher, J. A., & Localio, R. A. (1998). Using pictographs to enhance recall of spoken medical instructions. *Patient Education and Counseling, 35,* 83–88.

Le Guin, U. K. (2008, Feb.). Staying awake: Notes on the alleged decline of reading. *Harper's Magazine,* 33–38. Available at http://harpers.org/archive/2008/02/0081907.

Marx, K. (1845/1969). Theses on Feuerbach: Thesis XI. In *Marx/Engels Selected Works* (Vol. 1), pp. 13–15. Moscow: Progress Publishers.

Massey University Adult Literacy and Learning Research (ALLR) Group. (2007). *Research posters.* Available at http://www.massey.ac.nz/?r8f021611s

Montoya, J. A., Kent, C. K., Rotblatt, H., McCright, J., Kerndt, P. R., & Klausner, J. D. (2005). Social marketing campaign significantly associated with increases in syphilis testing among gay and bisexual men in San Francisco. *Sexually Transmitted Diseases, 32*(7), 395–399.

Moriyama, M., Harnisch, D. L., & Matsubara, S. (1994). The development of graphic symbols for medical symptoms to facilitate communication between health care providers and receivers. *Tohoku Journal of Experimental Medicine, 174,* 387–398.

Shore, S. (2003). What's whiteness got to do with it? Exploring assumptions about cultural difference and everyday literacy practices. *Literacies: Researching practice, practising research, 2* (Fall). Available at http://www.literacyjournal.ca/literacies/2–2003/practice/2/1.htm

Sligo, F., & Tilley, E. (2009). "Sort of set my goal to come to class": Evoking expressive content in policy reports. *Journal of Business and Technical Communication, 23*(4), 463–486.

Smith, D. E. (1998). *Writing the social: Critique, theory, and investigations.* Toronto: University of Toronto Press.

Smith, L. T. (1999). *Decolonizing methodologies: Research and indigenous peoples.* London: Zed Books.

Taylor, D. (1993). Family literacy: Resisting deficit models. *TESOL Quarterly, 27*(3), 550–553.

Tilley, E., Sligo, F., Shearer, F., Comrie, M., Murray, N., Franklin, J., Vaccarino, F., & Watson, B. (2007). *Voices: First-hand experiences of adult literacy learning and employment in Wanganui.* Department of Communication and Journalism, Massey University, New Zealand. ISBN 978-0-9582646-5-5. Series: Adult Literacy and Employment in Wanganui, 0605. ISSN 1176–9807. Available at: http://www.massey.ac.nz/massey/fms/Colleges/College%200f%20Business/Communication%20and%20Journalism/Literacy/Publications/Voices_First-Hand_Experiences_of_Adult_Literacy_Learning_and_Employment_in_Wanganui.pdf

CHAPTER FIVE

Rollin' and Dustin'

The Use of Graphic Images for the Dissemination of Study Results to Participant Communities

Jean J. Schensul, Colleen Coleman, Sarah Diamond, Raul Pino, Alessander Rey Bermudez, Orlando Velazco, Regina Blake, & Noelle Bessette

We are a collective of artists, anthropologists, and public-health popular educators working within a community-based research organization dedicated to using research in collaboration with community partners for social change (www.incommunityresearch.org). The goal of the organization is to use all of the tools of research to transform ourselves, our partners, and our communities. Rollin' and Dustin' represents an experimental/experiential approach to making the results of a ten-year research program on contemporary urban youth culture accessible to those who participated in it, their families, and the public.

The story of Rollin' and Dustin' began in 1998, when I (lead author) and others at In Community Research (ICR) discovered that young Latino and African American adults wanted an opportunity to tell their story to sympathetic listeners and in doing so to reflect on their lives and avoid future trauma. I was drawn to the idea of storytelling and embarked on a search for funding to involve young people in critical narrative and reflection. The U.S. National Institute on Drug Abuse supported three continuous research projects from 1999 to 2009. Much of the research respected the wishes of these young people by offering opportunities for sharing lives with young researchers like themselves, discussing issues, and even composing, recording, and performing their stories at CD release shows that they themselves organized (Diamond et al., 2009).

Our team membership shifted over time as young researchers moved on in their careers. But those of us who had worked together on the second study (2005–2009) wanted to narrate a larger tale for the public that went beyond our published articles (Diamond, Bermudez & Schensul, 2006; Schensul, Convey & Burkholder, 2005; Singer et al., 2005; Burkholder & Schensul, 2007). Our goal was to create a critical multimedia production that reflected the complex history of our area, the political shifts and trends that affected young people, and the many creative ways that youth found to navigate family situations, the challenges of school, community, drugs, and intimate relationships. Several team members—Orlando Velazco, Rey

(Alessandro Rey) Bermudez, Regina Blake, and Elsie Vazquez-Long—were of the same age and from the same urban cohort. In addition to their community research skills, Rey was a dancer, Orlando a hardcore punk musician, Regina a fabric artist, and Colleen Coleman, a socially engaged multimedia artist/curator. Together, as social scientists and artists, we struggled to transform a text-and-number-heavy study into what we viewed as "guerrilla" representations: materials that could be staged in settings where young people felt comfortable creating "actions" that provoked discussion and dialogue. Four young African American and Latino college students who had grown up in the area, Rashida Copes, Allan Wagner, and Bildade Augustin, and Kyle Young, a promising young animator and filmmaker, completed our team. The group was diverse in age, ethnicity, racial identity and complexity, skills and experience—reflecting the composition of the target audience.

We decided to convey the "Hartford story" through related and highly transportable "products": an installation consisting of a series of very large illustrated portable panels and accompanying audiovisual materials, a series of small media handouts, materials representing dance culture, and films on ecstasy and PCP, all of which complemented the two-dimensional and somewhat text-heavy panels. These products afforded the study teams an opportunity to become involved with members of the local community in data analysis and re/presentation. This was very important, since too often the production of knowledge for the science community does not include the voices of those who produce or interpret the knowledge. At the same time, study team members acted as guides and facilitators at installations, and their lived experience and technical knowledge enabled them to interact with audiences in a more authentic way.

The Project

The data on which our products were based were obtained during 1999 to 2009 from young adults of diverse backgrounds—primarily African American/West Indian and Puerto Rican/Latino—in the Hartford, Connecticut, region, an area confronted by economic decline, with few opportunities for young people. The studies addressed hard drug use, party culture, club drugs, and the culture of and risks associated with ecstasy use (Eiserman, Diamond, & Schensul, 2005; Diamond, Bermudez, & Schensul, 2006). Across all studies, we collected 2,000 surveys and more than 300 narrative interviews with young men and women from the study area as well as observations, photographs, and archival and audiovisual material on club drugs.

All three studies highlighted the widespread use of two relatively unknown or new drugs, ecstasy and "dust" (PCP). Urban youth in Hartford reported that ecstasy could produce a high level of sexual pleasure, and they had little concern about risks associated with the drug. It was only later, after the introduction of a government-sponsored anti-ecstasy campaign, that young urban users began to question the risks and benefits of use. "Dust" (a popular PCP-based locally prepared product often adulterated with dangerous substances like roach spray and nail polish) was described as contributing to emotional numbness and fearlessness in the face of potential violence, and consequences of use were severe. We wanted our audiences to understand these new drugs better so they could make informed choices about their use. Though our main goal was to provide enough information to enable observers to make good drug decisions, we also wanted to highlight the challenges facing minoritized youth struggling to achieve stable lifestyles in a marginalized urban environment and the function of drugs in their lives.

The Creation of Dissemination Products

The installation consisted of thirteen three-foot-by-nine-foot panels forming the centerpiece of a traveling exhibit. Each panel represented a chapter of our "graphic novel." Panels were accompanied by materials illustrating rave culture, such as ecstasy pacifiers, candy beads, glow sticks, Vicks Vapor Rub, inhalation masks, postcards advertising electronic dance club events, drug curricula, and documentaries on both drugs.

Summarizing ten years of research into a clear narrative was a daunting task. To develop the storyline, the entire production team divided the ten-year time period into three segments: 1994–1999, 1999–2003 (Study 1), 2003–2006 (Study 2), 2007–2010 (Study 3). Next we assembled data for each period that corresponded to three "levels" of influence: federal policies affecting local lives, significant events in the study community, and the study research results. We created six composite cartoon characters representing examples of lifestyle and ethnic/racial and gender-based diversity in the community, using situations culled from our narrative data. These characters appeared throughout the panels and "aged" appropriately in their appearance, clothing, and accessories over the ten-year period. Each panel included examples of quotations from narrative interviews narrated by a cartoon characters, charts and graphs, and photographs integrated in visually appealing ways to convey "standalone" stories related to one or both of the drugs.

Our statistician, Bill Disch, worked with the team to create simple bar-and-line charts that compared ecstasy and dust use with other substances. The youth team selected quotations illustrating an array of opinions about, experiences with, and consequences of use with respect to ecstasy and dust. Because we planned to exhibit the panels in public locations that might include young children, after much animated discussion about vernacular authenticity, we agreed to eliminate or replace expletives or inappropriate language with symbols. Despite our best efforts, and much to our dismay, we weren't entirely successful even after multiple readings, thus showing the extent to which local vernacular was embedded in our team's vocabulary! The panels also included headlines from newspaper articles on MDMA and PCP in Hartford, photographs of popular music DVDs containing ecstasy and "dust" as the theme, and the cover of NIDA's first national conference on ecstasy in 2001, to which we contributed with a panel presentation and poster.

Study team members also wanted the panels to dispel myths and stereotypes about urban minority youth, such as the myth that all urban youth sell drugs. To this, the data-based response was that ecstasy was first sold by white suburban young people to Latino youth frequenting downtown bars and restaurants, who then shared it with their friends (Schensul, Diamond, Bermudez, Disch & Eiserman, 2005; Eiserman, Diamond & Schensul., 2005). To the myth that all urban youth use multiple drugs, the data-based response was that unlike suburban youth in our studies who were in fact, polydrug users, most urban youth limited their substance use to alcohol and marijuana and tended to avoid other drugs including ecstasy and dust. Another typical myth promoted the idea that all African American young men earn substantial amounts through the sale of drugs. The data-based response showed that some youth across all ethnic groups, and both males and females did sell drugs, mainly marijuana, but that they sold these drugs irregularly and in small amounts, often to pay for their own use.

Once the materials were finalized for each of the panels, the artist, cartoonist, and study coordinator assembled the panels using Adobe Photoshop. This was an exceedingly painstaking process that involved first learning the program, then scrupulously designing each panel, and finally, working with the entire team every step of the way to ensure aesthetic quality, message clarity, representational concerns, and grammatical correctness. We caught critical errors even after the panels had been professionally printed and revised, and reprinted two of the panels the day before the installation's opening reception. The entire process took 13 months, involved more than 20 full- and part-time staff, and cost approximately $5,000 in panel printing to produce 13 completely portable retractable panels with attached overhead lights and hard and soft cases. Most of the other installation materials cost little or nothing or were donated.

The Installation and Film

The installation, first exhibited in the ICR Jean J. Schensul Community Gallery, included the panels, materials illustrating components of club/rave culture such as beads, glow sticks, pacifiers, face masks, Vicks, water bottles, and club fliers. Rounding out the installation were a collection of graphic novels and two video stations where visitors could watch the CNN program *Fried* (2002) based on the use of "dust" in Hartford and New Haven, Connecticut, and the national debate about the dangers associated with ecstasy entitled *Ecstasy Rising*, a 2006 ABC News documentary hosted by Peter Jennings. The opening reception was advertised on the ICR website, in the media, and through promotional materials, including a popular poster with images or cartoons from the panels. Each visitor received a brochure outlining the story that was linked to the panels and a numbered guide to the graphs. (*Ecstasy Rising* and other elements of the installation are available at www.popularizingresearch.net.) These materials allowed viewers to view specific panels of interest or follow the panel sequence independently. Members of the research and production team were available for questions, explanations, or dialogue and showed visitors through the exhibit.

The reception was a joyous occasion, in which the dedication of the research team, the artists, the young graphic artist, and the multimedia agency (Young Studios) that supported his work, were acknowledged with framed posters autographed by team members. Approximately 100 people, mainly youth and staff of agencies working with young people and drug users, celebrated the opening in the ICR gallery. Subsequently, the panels were exhibited at more local sites including the Trinity College International Hip Hop Festival, local libraries and colleges, Hartford Convention Center health expositions, and the University of Connecticut (Storrs and Medical School campuses). In the Hartford exhibitions, viewers were given LED toys and glow sticks, and study team guides pointed to main themes and images on the panels. Groups of young people were invited to participate in a treasure hunt to find the answers to specific questions on the panels and winners were acknowledged with prizes. When they could, the guides stood beside the viewers, waiting to discuss informally any aspect of the materials. Some viewers wanted to read the panel materials and took more than 45 minutes to do so; others preferred the photographs and cartoon captions. Small children examined the photographs at their eye level, while their caregivers offered their point of view to children. Most viewers found something to which they could relate.

Beyond Connecticut, the installation was shown at professional conferences (for example, the Campus Community Partnerships for Health annual conference, the Society for Applied Anthropology, and American Anthropological Association, and at the UCLA Graduate School of Education and Information Sciences). Later the panels traveled to community and gallery sites in five cities around the state of Connecticut. At each of these displays, one or more members of the study team introduced the ICR, the dissemination program, and the studies and guided viewers through the panels and accompanying materials.

The film was Noelle Bessette's student project done with the ICR study team in 2009–2010 to see whether youth in the study population would respond better to a video that reflected the voices and the language of other urban youth in their age cohort than to comparable visual and text-based materials via the panels. Due to cost and time constraints, the study team decided to focus on ecstasy only. Noelle selected quotations on ecstasy from interviews conducted during the third study, comparable to those already included on the ecstasy panels. She invited local young African American and Puerto Rican adults from an NGO serving the study population to record the quotations. With support, she produced a 20-minute film about ecstasy with photographs, quotations, and background music that she uploaded to YouTube (see website for link). ICR retained the sound files and images, and recreated the film in Windows Movie Maker for use with ICR's Windows-based computers. This version of the film is available from the lead author.

Final Reflections

To assess audience reaction to the installation panels, we utilized a Rapid Response Survey at several local events that included youth including a conference on violence prevention for youth workers and high school students; and a regional health and wellness exposition sponsored by NBC and attended by the general public. Of the 150 people who responded, 102 were young people ages 16–28. Responses to the installation and the panels suggest that the *Rollin' and Dustin'* exhibit has broad audience appeal. In large public events, it attracted our priority audience, African American and Puerto Rican youth and young adults in the 14–35 age group. Although the exhibit tended to appeal to minority viewers, it also attracted interest across urban and suburban areas, gender and age groups, and students and parents. Most viewers found the panels authentic, powerful, informative, and representative of the lives and challenges faced by urban youth, and accordingly, rated the exhibit highly. Some viewers connected less well with the graphic images, but still considered the representations accurate and real. Our concern that some of the images, language, or results might be viewed as stereotypic or as portraying young people in a negative manner was not borne out, although several African American males expressed concern that there were no white characters playing prominent roles in the panels.

In addition, approximately 35 young adults including college students and youth from the study population viewed and compared the film and the panels as ways of conveying research-based information using an informal group-discussion approach. In general they saw the benefits of both approaches, reporting that they could empathize with the film but that more substantive and accurate information was provided by the panels.

Our experience with the *Rollin' and Dustin'* exhibit plus film has demonstrated that the creation of an aesthetically attractive montage consisting of co-constructed history, discovered findings, storytelling, and collaborative assembly and presentation combined with film, is an effective way of disseminating social science data (and a prevention message) to a diverse set of audiences. The medium we chose is highly flexible, allowing for the addition of accompanying materials and rearrangements of the panels to accommodate the interests of different audiences. Though the products were geared to reflect the realities of drug use and a balanced view of associated risks and benefits, most viewers, when asked, suggested that drug use was a serious problem. Thus products such as these have promise for prevention programming.

Science results that reach the media are generally linked to benefits or liabilities to large institutions (e.g., pharmaceutical corporations, the military, hospitals, and international agencies). The results of local studies conducted with local partnerships rarely have wide public recognition. Through exercises like the *Rollin' and Dustin'* traveling exhibit, which combine aesthetic and mimetic representation and dialogue, study populations and scientifically disenfranchised people have the opportunity to interrogate studies, investigate meaning, and co-construct new findings that point to new directions for themselves and others. Such a process popularizes research by bringing a cultural production—the interpreted and re-presented results of basic social scientific research conducted by and with members of the study population—directly to the study community and opening methodology and results to community viewing, dialogue, and scrutiny in a safe, comfortable community environment.

Acknowledgments

We wish to acknowledge the students, participants, and many supporters of the *Rollin' and Dustin'* installation who helped us to organize it in Hartford, throughout Connecticut, and across the United States and Canada. We also express our appreciation to Christina Krawec, who went to great lengths to recreate the ICR Ecstasy short film for Windows-based software so that it can be shown at ICR and on ICR equipment.

References

ABC News. (2006). *Special Report: Ecstasy Rising*. (See website.)

Burkholder, G., & Schensul, J. (2007). Risk and protective factors for drug use among polydrug-using urban youth and young adults. *Journal of Social, Behavioral, and Health Sciences, 1*, 24–40.

CNN News. (2002). CNN presents: Fried (videotape). Lanham, MD: Federal CNN. http://www-cgi.cnn.com /CNN/Programs/presents/index.fried.html

Diamond, S., Bermudez, A. R., & Schensul, J. (2006, May). What's the rap about ecstasy? Popular music lyrics and drug trends among American youth. *Journal of Adolescent Research, 21*(3), 269–298.

Diamond, S., Schensul, J., Snyder, L., Bermudez, A., D'Alessandro, N., & Morgan, D. (2009). Building Xperience: A multilevel alcohol and drug prevention intervention. *American Journal of Community Psychology, 43*(3), 292–312.

Eiserman, J., Diamond, S., & Schensul, J. (2005). "Rollin' on E": A qualitative analysis of ecstasy use among inner-city adolescents and young adults. *Journal of Ethnicity and Substance Abuse, 4*(2), 9–38.

Schensul, J., Diamond, S., Bermudez, A. R., Disch, W., & Eiserman, J. (2005). The diffusion of ecstasy through urban youth networks. *Journal of Ethnicity and Substance Abuse, 4*(2), 39–71.

Schensul, J. J., Convey, M., & Burkholder, G. (2005). Challenges in measuring concurrency, agency and intentionality in polydrug research. [doi: DOI: 10.1016/j.addbeh.2004.05.022]. *Addictive Behaviors, 30*(3), 571–574.

Singer, M., Clair, S., Schensul, J., Huebner, C., Eiserman, J., Pino, R. (2005). Dust in the wind: The growing use of embalming fluid among youth in Hartford, CT. *Substance Use & Misuse, 40*(8), 1035–1050.

CHAPTER SIX

Focusing on Community

Photovoice, Local Action, and Global Public Engagement

Gregory P. Spira

People often say that a picture is worth a thousand words. However, in Chaicuriri—a small community located at 14,000 feet elevation in the Bolivian Andes—the photographic image was not meant to replace words. The photographs taken there were never intended to somehow stand on their own and tell the tale of a community. Instead their real usefulness was in the verbal descriptions of photographs taken, oral explanations, and critical discussions that flowed from the sharing of each image. Using a community-based research method known as "Photovoice" (Wang & Burris, 1997), 92 percent of Chaicuriri's residents over age nine took more than 2,000 photographs, and through them, spent dozens of hours discussing community development priorities. Their photographs, whether shared in a schoolroom in the Bolivian highlands or in a downtown Vancouver coffee shop, generated thousands of words.

The research and communication methods used show a fundamental respect for community-based research where both the process and results belong to and benefit the local communities involved. Within Chaicuriri, the primary objective of the *Chaicuriri Through the Lens* Photovoice project lay in supporting the efforts of residents drafting their own locally relevant blueprint for community development. Conducting this kind of community-wide participatory needs assessment (or Participatory Rural Appraisal—PRA) means getting local actors to actively participate in identifying issues of concern to them and to come up with locally inspired solutions. Focusing attention initially on the photographs helped further popularize this participatory research process and involve often-excluded groups of women and children as community planners.

Further popularizing the research, *Chaicuriri Through the Lens* also sought to take local understandings and concerns to wider audiences. This process began within the community itself through exhibitions. It continued by targeting specific audiences of NGO leaders and youth and social activists in Canada, the United States, and Latin America who attended multimedia presc..ations and discussion groups exploring both the issues and how to promote the inclusion and participation of diverse groups of people in shaping community development projects.

Opening the Shutter: Photovoice and Participatory Action Research

At its core, Photovoice is a research method that brings together community-based photography and social change, encouraging participation and stressing action. Project organizers give cameras to community members so that they can serve as researchers exploring and sharing their vision of the present and future. A project, usually structured by organizers to examine a pre-identified subject, can also be developed so that the community itself identifies the issues and determines the project's goals and objectives.

After photographing aspects of their lives, participants work together to analyze strengths, weaknesses, and opportunities present in the world around them. By discussing their images, community photographers assess and prioritize needs, draft plans, advocate for outside assistance, and evaluate programme effectiveness.

Academic researchers previously used the Photovoice method to assess a variety of issues affecting local communities, especially health concerns. In such projects, community members, receiving cameras and photographic instruction, normally aimed to capture their community's concerns relating to issues of specific interest to project organizers. Discussions of the images critically explored the underlying social, political, and economic contradictions. Participants then presented their views to governmental or non-governmental officials who were seen as the primary agents of change (Wang, Burris, & Xiang, 1996; Wang & Burris, 1997). The foci of previous Photovoice projects included maternal health in China (Wang & Burris, 1994), child health in the United States (Wang & Pies, 2004), and psychological trauma in Guatemala (Lykes, Blanche, & Hamber, 2003).

Straying from this model, *Chaicuriri Through the Lens* placed control over selecting the issues fully in the hands of local residents. This was done because "development" is a value-laden concept woven into the social fabric of each culture and development efforts flounder when the outsiders' values (governments, NGOs, etc.) do not respect the values of the communities they propose to "develop." Ultimately, development must be shaped, and judged, using the value-system of those benefited (Stohr & Taylor, 1981). Using the Photovoice method to conduct a community-based participatory needs assessment, or Participatory Rural Appraisal (PRA), the project's organizers believed that groups discussing images captured by their neighbours would be able to draw on their own distinct vision of development to produce a blueprint of local priorities.

By popularizing the research process and encouraging participants to take action and resolve their own concerns, the project drew heavily on the tradition of Participatory Action Research (PAR). This project also included Paolo Freire's ideas that fighting oppression and poverty requires that community members come together to critically explore the roots of social exclusion and discuss ways to change conditions that perpetuate poverty (Freire, 1970/2000). The marginalized and poor are seen as creative and capable—able to conduct their own investigations, analyses, and action plans. Outsiders enter the picture simply as facilitators, assisting marginalized individuals in gaining confidence in their knowledge and abilities. Locally crafted solutions are often more accurate and sustainable than those crafted by outsiders because residents themselves test their appropriateness (Chambers, 1994; Chambers, 2004; Rao & Woolcock, 2005).

Selective Focus: Methods Used

Fundación Kechuaymara—the Bolivian NGO partner organization coordinating the *Chaicuriri Through the Lens* project—chose Chaicuriri after selecting the community to host a field operations centre serving the region's remote rural communities. Fundación Kechuaymara also sought to spur on local development by encouraging local empowerment of marginalized groups—especially women and indigenous subsistence farmers.

Fifty-seven community members—women, men, and children ages 9–77—participated in the project's three phases. Participants were introduced to the Photovoice method and joined basic camera operation and photography workshops—necessary because 80 percent of participants had never taken a picture before. Participants brainstormed possible subjects to photograph and spent three weeks capturing their perceptions on more than 2,000 frames of film.

Unstructured gatherings saw participants informally share their photographs. Since most participants had never owned a photograph, these sessions proved key for bringing together individuals to support each other in analyzing their images. Participants then picked a few images that they believed best showed their views on a strength, weakness, or opportunity for the future.

Meeting in small self-selected groups, Chaicuriri's photographers described the photographs, analyzed their content, identified matters of concern to the community as a whole, and took charge of developing concrete plans for resolving these issues. The facilitator asked open-ended questions to help participants discuss why the subject of the picture was important, the underlying social context, varying perspectives, and how the community could address the issue or build on a local strength.

Participants participated in dozens of hours of group discussions. They critically explored the community development issues they considered to be of utmost concern—enhancing the viability of livestock rearing, raising agricultural productivity, protecting family bonds, correcting imbalanced gender relations, and maintaining communal traditions. These reveal the community's own priorities and outline means by which both internal and external actors could begin working on solutions. The project results strongly show how dialogues shape the method; project notes are full of varying viewpoints, priorities, and assessments of solutions. However, by critically exploring the issues, participants largely understood the rationales for the different opinions and incorporated them into integrated plans of action.

Capturing Audiences

Deciding to "popularize" this research process and its results was really no decision at all. Community-based research, at its very core, is a popularized process. This means results should not only be generated by the community, but also useful for it. The action orientation may have been lost had the research process ended with the discussion groups, and the results remained locked in the minds of each group's members. For participants, popularizing the research results meant sharing the diverse views and plans more widely—in the first instance with the entire community and with local decision makers. Members of each group shared their images and priorities at combined community meetings and photo exhibits. This helped to start community-wide discussions. Enthusiasm for the photographs overflowed, as many residents became judges in photography contests rewarding images that best captured both visual appeal and relevance to development planning. These exhibits, as well as informal gatherings in homes and in the fields, proved the primary means of spreading the reach of project activities to fellow community members and local leaders. Participants themselves organized the logistics of the events, arranged food and decided which photos to share.

Using community members' own images helped bridge some of the barriers previously blocking the participation of marginalized groups in political discussions. While male political leaders previously did not welcome women and children to share their views at most community meetings, these leaders had no problem with them sharing their photographs. Presenting images, rather than directly discussing contentious issues, can help remove initial barriers to marginalized groups' participation. As well, individuals not normally comfortable presenting their views in public, may feel more at ease talking about their photograph (Meade & Shaw, 2007). Therefore, the group discussions in Chaicuriri began as opportunities to share and talk about photographs taken by their friends, family, and fellow community members. Involving the majority of community members, including local leaders, as project researchers meant the lines between audience and community advocate were blurred. What started as photo sharing grew into forward-looking discussions that continued well after the project formally ended. For example, one woman described the picture she took in the following manner:

Photo by María R. This photo shows the death of a yearling calf. It died because it was too thin because there is not enough pasturage. This was a huge loss because it was a baby and represented a good investment. If they are to live, young animals need more support....The animal's owner did not take care of it and now he is very sorry. (María R.)

Discussion continued for about an hour after this single photo presentation, with children even talking about the difficulty of taking their herds to pastures located several hours' walk away. This led other participants to propose solutions, including Cansio C. who stated, "Livestock needs support in terms of access to forage. We can plant feed crops for the animals. My family and I are thinking of planting alfalfa." In a back-and-forth process, diverse residents voiced their viewpoints, presented their solutions, and ultimately agreed on the need to work together to expand feed crops.

Outside of Bolivia, meanwhile, popularization of project results took local understandings and concerns to global audiences. However, the residents were not interested in presenting their project to academic audiences. Instead, residents chose to share their research results with other communities around the world, entrusting project coordinators with this task. In Canada, efforts at popularization initially targeted local and regional newsprint and radio outlets in order to broadly increase awareness among Canadians of the challenges and opportunities facing Chaicuriri's residents.

Initial media outreach efforts—organized via personal connections, phone pitches, and press releases sent to local and regional print and radio outlets—led to interviews conducted before the project began. These aimed to build an audience already aware of the project's broad objectives. Shortly after the project began, the first of three feature-length newspaper articles (1,000–1,500 words) described the project to Canadians and shared the first images and perspectives raised by participants. Publication of this series continued after the project's completion. While primarily aimed at engaging Canadians in the project and issues, these activities also responded to funding requirements for "public engagement" activities to take place. While project funders appreciated the media exposure, it ultimately proved quite difficult to gauge how well these reached the extremely broadly defined audience due to the lack of accurate readership numbers available for community and regional newspapers.

In a more targeted manner, however, selected groups of NGO leaders and social activists in Canada, the United States, and Latin America attended multimedia presentations and discussion groups exploring both the issues identified in Chaicuriri and the importance of integrating community-led processes into development projects. Unfortunately funding limitations meant Chaicuriri's photographers could not be present. However, the project's results were used to initiate discussions with university students in Canada, the United States, Bolivia, and Colombia. Organized with assistance from other communication professionals and academics, promotion of these events occurred on campuses via posters, classroom announcements, conference programmes, and online calendars of events. Events in Bolivia and Colombia were also promoted by radio and student newspaper and appeared alongside already scheduled symposia on international development and communication for social change. Subsequently, Bolivian solidarity committee members in Vancouver and the membership of a council of Canadian international development organizations attended multimedia presentations that had likewise been promoted by word of mouth and via the council's e-newsletters.

Reaching out to these socially conscious and activist groups shared a common objective: to foment dialogues around participatory approaches, community empowerment, and development priorities. While audiences were already engaged in international development and social justice to different degrees, this was not simply "preaching to the choir" as the backgrounds of individuals and their approaches to development ranged considerably—including members of Rotary Clubs, undergraduate students, and members of faith-based and secular international development organizations. In all, approximately 500 individuals attended these presentations. More interactive discussions followed, maximizing the possibility for exchange and feedback.

Participants' photographs and the descriptions given by Chaicuriri's photographers formed the core of all presentations in order to more accurately convey the intention of the person who took the photograph. Many of the images that inspired hour-long discussions in Bolivia also generated considerable interest abroad. For example, in Bolivia, Canada, and Colombia, discussions around the following image filled hours:

Photo by Nelson B. This little boy's name is Vladimir. Alone in the morning, he has his little wheel. It is a wheel from a wheelbarrow. He is trying to escape from his brothers who hit him. He is always very sad and looks for toys to play with on his own. He is behind the wall of his house. Because his brothers go to school and his parents go to work, the boy is always left alone to play with toys that are not really toys. (Nelson B.)

Discussion in Bolivia focused on identifying the risks for younger children and eventually saw participants agree to create a community-run daycare to care for and begin the education of youngsters. In Canada and Colombia, these images led to discussions of child rights, echoed appreciation for community-based educational initiatives, and started discussions on ways to ensure education projects reflected the realities of rural communities.

At each event abroad, a multimedia slideshow, made up of images chosen by Chaicuriri's photographers and vibrant traditional music from a neighbouring village, brought the presentation to life (see www.popularizingresearch.net). This show, assembled using Apple Final Cut video-editing software, was complemented by several PowerPoint presentations adapted for the different audiences. Despite having 2,000 photographs to choose from, only those pictures that the groups in Chaicuriri actually presented were included. These images were grouped into the same themes identified by the photographers themselves, thereby helping to focus the discussions that followed around the issues of original relevance. Software limitations, however, meant that the images in the slideshow ran without the descriptions given by the photographers, thereby partially decontextualizing the pictures. Nonetheless, audience members reported that the visually engaging nature of the slideshow, when combined with other presentation material that put photographs and descriptions together, proved particularly effective at starting discussions while maintaining the original context. As well, demonstrating and discussing the Photovoice method prompted several in the Canadian audiences to seek out advice on planning similar projects in Canada, Mexico, Crete, Laos, and Cameroon.

In short, popularizing research need not simply focus on sharing the results and findings of a given project. Choosing participatory community-based research methods sets the stage for processes that involve community members not only as researchers, but also as knowledge-sharing advocates. Chaichuriri's photographers not only gathered and analyzed photographic data, but also actively determined how their insights would be shared. Together the community and project organizers collaborated on deciding on how the project's results would be popularized far beyond the towers of academe. Consequently, the images and perspectives they chose to share inspired thousands of words of discussion that flowed around the world.

References

Chambers, R. (1994). Participatory rural appraisal (PRA): Analysis of experience. *World Development, 22*(9), 1253–1268.

Chambers, R. (2004). Rural appraisal: Rapid, relaxed, and participatory. *Participatory rural appraisal: Methods and applications in rural planning (Essays in honour of Robert Chambers)* (2nd ed.). New Delhi: Concept. (Original work published 1995.)

Freire, P. (1970/2000). *Pedagogy of the oppressed* (30th anniv. ed.). New York: Continuum.

Lykes, M. B., Blanche, M. T., & Hamber, B. (2003). Narrating survival and change in Guatemala and South Africa: The politics of representation and a liberatory community psychology. *American Journal of Community Psychology, 31*(1/2), 79–90.

Meade, R., & Shaw, M. (2007). Editorial: Community development and the arts: Reviving the democratic imagination. *Community Development Journal, 42*(4), 413–421.

Rao, V., & Woolcock, M. (2005). Mixing qualitative and econometric methods: Community-level applications. In D. Narayan (Ed.), *Measuring empowerment: Cross-disciplinary perspectives*. Washington, DC: World Bank.

Stohr, W., & Taylor, F. (Eds.). (1981). *Development from above or below?: The dialectics of regional planning in developing countries*. Chichester, NY: J. Wiley.

Wang, C., & Burris, M. A. (1994). Empowerment through photo novella: Portraits of participation. *Health Education Quarterly, 21*(2), 171–186.

Wang, C., & Burris, M. A. (1997). Photovoice: Concept, methodology, and use for participatory needs assessment. *Health Education and Behaviour, 24*(3), 369–387.

Wang, C., Burris, M. A., & Xiang, Y. P. (1996). Chinese village women as visual anthropologists: A participatory approach to reaching policymakers. *Social Science & Medicine, 42*(10), 1391–1400.

Wang, C., & Pies, C. (2004). Family, maternal, and child health through Photovoice. *Maternal and Child Health Journal, 8*(2), 95–102.

White, S. (1994). The concept of participation: Transforming rhetoric to reality. In S. White, K. Sadanandan Nair, & J. Ashcroft (Eds.), *Participatory communication: Working for change and development*. New Dehli: Sage.

Part 3

EXHIBITS AND INSTALLATIONS

CHAPTER SEVEN

Mixed-Media Storytelling Installation

Embody

Brigid McAuliffe & Bryce Merrill

Embody is a mixed-media—new and traditional—gallery installation inspired by oral histories of dance. Audio and video from interviews with women who perform percussive dance—jazz tap, Spanish flamenco, Mexican folkloric, Fancy Shawl, and West African dances—are projected onto four gallery walls and through panels of embroidered cloth. Looped with this video footage are animated thread drawings of silhouettes of the dancers. A live cinema and flamenco performance also accompanies the show. *Embody* was created as part of a residency at an art organization where artists work with children from secondary schools that lack substantial opportunities for artistic engagement. The installation includes photographic "flip books" created by a group of middle-school girls.

The first author of this chapter, Brigid McAuliffe, a new-media artist, directed *Embody*.[1] My work lies at the confluence of art, technology, and interpretive social research. I am inspired by ethnographic techniques that encourage a grounded understanding of people's lived experiences. I commonly employ interviewing and participant observation to create a foundation for aesthetically engaging works. I value technology less for its intrinsic or novel qualities, and more for the ways it can enable captivating representational forms. Technology and ethnographic methods are merely tools I use to portray social worlds with empathetic, creative, and aesthetic sensibilities.

Embody is a community-focused and produced artwork. It was created at PlatteForum, an arts organization and venue in Denver, Colorado. According to its mission, "PlatteForum gives hope and direction to underserved youth who collaborate with master artists from around the world. This experience transforms the lives of the youth, the artists and the community" (http://platteforum.org). Seven girls from Clear Lake Middle School, along with their art teacher, joined me in creating the work. The girls interviewed, filmed, and photographed the dancers, and spent time with each dancer learning a few steps and dancing. Volunteers from the community and PlatteForum employees also contributed to the project in a number of creative and logistical ways. The dancers featured in the work are also from the community: Amanda Bishop, Spanish flamenco; Jeanette Trujillo and dancers from Fiesta Colorado, Mexican Folkloric and Spanish classical; Cathy Phelps and dancers from Baba Joda and Friends, West African dances; A. J. No Braid and daughter, Lara, American Indian intertribal dances; and Jan Sherman and dancers from Jan's Happy Tappers, jazz tap. *Embody* tells their stories with their help and that of their community.

The work engages in a multisensory fashion with questions of cultural identity, gendered bodies and memories, and generational empowerment. The dancers weave together stories of their social and artistic lives, and with a collaborative community, I cast these tales into aesthetic auditory and visual shapes. *Embody* is a public artwork inspired by qualitative research. Some of the challenges encountered in the process of creating *Embody* are considered here. However, the visual record of the artwork that accompanies this chapter is the focal point.

Concept and Process

Conceptually, *Embody* is a project to celebrate and represent generations of female dancers who find empowerment, identity, and *flow* through percussive dance. The term "embody" can be defined as "giving body to a spirit." Dancers who participated in this project articulated a unique experience or spirit found in dance: it is one that arises when they are wholly immersed mentally and physically in what Csikszentmihalyi calls "flow." He writes that

> [f]low experiences provide…flashes of intense living.…When goals are clear, feedback relevant, and challenges and skills are in balance, attention becomes ordered and fully invested.…Self-consciousness disappears, yet one feels stronger than usual. A sense of time is distorted. Hours seem to pass by in minutes (1997, p. 31).

Although the dances featured in this work are importantly distinct, the commonality expressed in *Embody* is the experience of flow when immersed in rhythm, movement, and the physical and mental challenges of dancing. When experiencing flow, many dancers I worked with describe feelings of levity and clarity as if nothing else exists and their problems and self-consciousness disappear when they dance. Jan Sherman, an elderly tap dancer and leader of Jan's Happy Tappers, describes dance as a meditative retreat. "When you dance," Jan reveals, "you have to forget about all your problems to focus on the steps. It's total relaxation." Cathy Phelps, a member of Jan's troupe, also chimes in: "It's a groove. It's a flow. It's a power and a spirit. I've heard runners say they get into a zone and can just run and run. It's the same for me with dance. I can dance for hours and hours." A. J. No Braid, a dancer of Native American Fancy Shawl, describes a similar experience. "When I dance," A. J. says, "if it's a really good song, I kind of lose myself in the moment. I get a light, happy feeling. It takes me to a different place."

In *Embody*, I focus on percussive dances including jazz tap where the dancers respond to rhythm with their steps or dances where the rhythm and counter rhythm are actually produced by the dancer's feet. I worked with dancers from five percussive dances: Spanish flamenco; Mexican folkloric and Spanish classical; West African dances; American Indian intertribal dances; and jazz tap.

I presented the research on these dancers as a multichannel video/audio installation, featuring each woman's dance and dialogue within a dynamic mix of projected images and sound. The audio fluctuates between sounds of dancing and the dancer's voices. Video and animation allow me to share and preserve important stories through a mix of audio and visual elements. These are also time-based media, which are important for expressing moving art forms.

Desiring to express the ephemeral quality of dance, I incorporated some light material, such as thread, paper, and transparent fabrics. Starting with video stills, I isolated a dancing figure from its surroundings by tracing a simple contour of the form. This reflects a simplicity and clarity that many of the dancers articulate when in flow. After tracing the figure onto plain white paper, I then retraced it using a needle and thread. Both sides of the thread drawing hold importance conceptually. The front of the drawing is somewhat clean and contained. The back of the drawing appears unraveling and free. These two sides can reflect the two sides of a dancer. The contained, self-conscious side before the movement, and the opposite side that lets go, experiencing a freedom, clarity, and an unraveling when immersed in a dance.

Upon realizing how the use of thread reflected my concept, I decided to incorporate many of these drawings into the installation. The thread drawings took place in three ways throughout my exhibit. They took form as drawings on paper and on large fabric panels and as transitions in my video work. I made a digital photograph of both sides of the final thread drawings and then created transitions using these threaded depictions of the figures. The drawings slowly evolved between the two sides of thread and then finally transformed into the moving figure featured in the video. I made similar thread tracings upon large panels of transparent fabric (five feet by nine feet). Volunteers helped to trace these lines with stitching. These panels created an intimate viewing space for the audience. I projected video onto these surfaces. With people moving throughout the space and from the help of small fans, the light fabric took on a movement that reflected the movements being projected upon them. Finally, I selected 36 of the thread drawings on paper, and we stitched them into a grid, forming a quilt.

I also incorporated a live cinema performance into the body of work as a way to express the fleeting nature of dance, the energy and the flow that is only experienced through performance or intense practice. I collaborated with flamenco dancer Amanda Bishop to create this performance that incorporated three important genres of flamenco: Soleá, Escobillas, and Bulerías. These genres are personally significant to Bishop, showing the different emotions and gender roles a woman can express through flamenco. I created custom video clips and thread drawings of Bishop dancing that correspond with her live movements. In addition, I set up a live camera feed to narratives by Bishop and also translated *cante* (lyrics) to the first section. I had the clips, the audio, and the live camera set to specific channels on a mixing board. As she danced, I mixed in video or written statements that reflected or responded to her movements.

Creating a Collaborative Artwork

Collaboration was an important and complex part of this project. There are many interpretations of what makes a work collaborative, and Sara Diamond's (2008) guidance can be helpful. She writes that:

> [c]ollaboration can be understood as a process between two or more individuals that blurs roles, can confuse authorship, and can create new forms of identification and cohesion. At the same time this process inevitably leads away from the lucid single voice to work that is either explicitly or inexplicitly process driven and multivocal (2008, p. 136).

Embody was not completely collaborative in the sense that all participants shared equal engagement and authorship. Serving as director and main author, I dedicated much more time and energy than any other contributor. However, this project was heavily participant driven, leaving room for multiple voices, opinions, and surprises to emerge and influence me throughout the process.

I worked with 17 dancers and seven young artists, the middle-school girls, in addition to the volunteers and staff at PlatteForum. The girls, dancer, and the volunteers all influenced my process in different ways. By helping me stitch and set up the installation, volunteers helped me achieve a body of work I could not physically complete on my own. The dancers contributed their life histories, visual expressions, and specialized artistic knowledge to the project; without their devotion and experiences, this project would not exist.

For the schoolgirls, I directed workshops where we discussed cultural identity, memory, and empowerment embodied in dance. I shared my work, inquiries, and explorations as we researched the dances, brainstormed questions, and as I taught some audio/visual techniques. The dancers participated by coming to PlatteForum and giving the young artists a chance to ask their own questions, film some dancing and also learn some basic steps (and the meaning behind these steps). The participatory dance was an important part of the process. Rather than being passive observers, we were actively participating. Through this ethnographic approach, we were able to gain a greater understanding of the challenges and feelings experienced while dancing.

The students used Flip video cameras at PlatteForum, a simple consumer camera that allows easy, automatic filming with instant access to files. The cameras are equipped with a USB port for quick downloading. I chose to work with these cameras because they are inexpensive and simple. I wanted to show the girls that a continuation of this kind of work is within their means, and I did not want the girls to be intimidated by complicated technologies. The simplicity of the cameras allowed them to focus more on composition, aesthetics, and conversation, than struggling with technical challenges. After filming, I helped the girls select video clips based off of aesthetics and what movements they were most drawn to. We discussed filming techniques and what makes a video visually dynamic. We discussed movement, sound, color, and angles that best suited each form of dance. Time-based media were crucial for this study of movement. With the selected clips, I taught the girls how to export stills using QuickTime Pro. We printed the stills as individual photos and then bound them into flip books. Through this process, the girls were able to study the movement of the dancers in slow motion as they selected stills. They learned that just as dances are made up of many movements forming a whole, animation and video are similar. When broken down, one can see individual frames. When viewed all together, the frames create a fluid movement. We also filmed each other dancing, combining movements we learned from the dancers as well as our own. These videos were transformed into stop-motion animations, again focusing on the individual frames forming a whole.

The challenges to creating this collaborative work were considerable. The focus of the project shifted continuously as the dancers contributed more knowledge to the project and as I gained a greater personal sense of the physicality and meanings of their dances. Interesting conversations with dancers, or filming a great performance would tempt me to focus on one particular dancer or aspect of a dance. For example, when working with senior tap dancers, I was tempted to do an entire project on age and dance, the physical, social, and mental benefits as well as the challenges. Working with the girls also brought a different perspective because of their age and place in life. They would often ask questions that forced me to think from a new angle. During a workshop with A. J. and Lara No Braid, an Arikara mother and daughter, the girls asked Lara if she ever gets made fun of for dancing or wearing her regalia. It made me uncomfortable when they asked the question. I was tempted to divert the conversation from a potentially sensitive or offensive topic. However, I was ultimately glad they asked because Lara's response was telling. She responded, "Yeah, sometimes people make fun of me, but I don't care. This is who I am and what I do. This is my culture and my family. I'm proud of it." The importance of dance to cultural identity might not have been addressed if I were the only one asking questions and interacting with the dancers.

It was also quite difficult to be assertive in my vision while maintaining a high sensitivity to participants' comfort levels. I originally planned to have all the dancers look straight into the camera while talking. I wanted to edit the work on multiple screens and have the projected dancers looking out at the viewer and each other. The dancers felt much more comfortable looking at me while talking and occasionally looking at the camera. I quickly had to adjust this plan to accommodate this issue. I had to forfeit my original aesthetic vision to accommodate the comfort of the participants. I also thought it would be best to have the dancers wear their dance clothes for filmed conversations, but decided to leave this choice up to them. Most decided to wear their regular clothes, but I still was able to record them in dancing clothes when performing and during the workshops. In the end I was happy with this decision, as seeing them in everyday attire and then performing in dance attire became a visual manifestation of the transformation all of these dancers experience when they dance.

Challenges to Popularization

Embody is a project, performance and gallery exhibition that incorporates new and traditional media to celebrate and represent generations of female dancers. These women find a unique experience or spirit in dance, and *Embody* conveys this sensation and their stories of finding it. The sensory and aesthetic fabrics of this work are woven together by first-person accounts of cultural identity, history, gender, and empowerment. It is inspired by qualitative research on women in a particular community, but it was always intended to be a public work of art. In other words, it was popularized from the outset.

One significant challenge to creating popular qualitative research in this way is the unique way audiences experience ethnographic work in art galleries. With *Embody*, the layered narrative and sensory accounts of the women—and of the entire process of creating the work evident in the installation—invite a focused and sustained viewing. On one hand, it was difficult for audience members to experience this immersive installation while chatting with other patrons and sipping on wine. The work competes for attention in ways that monographs do not. However, the presence of the audience *in* the installation and the ways they react to it create an additional representational layer. The "live" reading of the work adds an authorial dimension—in the manner of Foucault (1977)—but it also changes its aesthetic. During *Embody*, the shapes of audience members blended and contrasted with the animating shapes of the dancers. Their voices recounting their own tales of dance mixed with the dancers' pre-recorded accounts. The challenge, then, to this type of work is to the experience of it.

Note

1. The first-person pronoun singular refers McAuliffe; Merrill, an ethnographer, contributed to the essay and was a consultant to the project.

References

Csikszentmihalyi, M. (1997). *Flow: The psychology of optimal experience.* New York, NY: Harper Collins.

Diamond, S. (2008). Participation, flow and the redistribution of authorship: The challenges of collaborative exchange and new media curatorial practice. In C. Paul (Ed.), *New media in the white cube and beyond: Curatorial models for digital art* (pp. 135–164). Berkeley, CA: University of California Press.

Foucault, M. (1977). *Language, counter-memory, practice: Selected essays and interviews by Michel Foucault* (Donald F. Bouchard, Trans.). Ithaca, NY: Cornell University Press.

CHAPTER EIGHT

Producing Multimedia Exhibits for Multiple Audiences at the Hokkaido University Museum

Guven Peter Witteveen

The year 2009 marked the tenth anniversary since the national government in Tokyo directed that science education should be more accessible to citizens. As a result, at the Hokkaido University Museum (HoUM), the small collection of artifacts and campus history was given a prime location, with staff and programming to engage the public in subjects rooted in the expertise of the faculty and stories local to the island of Hokkaido. In recognition of ten years of special exhibits as well as ongoing refinements to the permanent collections, the HoUM decided to find ways to present its materials online, thereby expanding its potential audience.

With financial help from the Hokkaido University Museum in central Sapporo, I was invited to produce multimedia material between March and June 2009, together with my host researcher of informatics, Dr. Yuuki Komata. In those weeks, we demonstrated ways to present the exhibit-hall stories visually online, we taught faculty and students how to continue making more digital content of their own research subjects, and we produced sets of panorama views, online albums, audio tours, and short introductory audio slideshow movies for playback online or at gallery kiosks on-site to extend the informal learning.

Museums have come a long way from being "cabinets of curiosities" (Karp, Kreamer, & Lavine, 1992) to being hybrid learning communities of online engagement or experience with original materials on-site (Costello & Bliton, 2009). This essay discusses digital mediation at the Hokkaido University Museum in Sapporo, Japan, in order to distill lessons for making the exhibit subjects more accessible to the public. Beyond artifacts and galleries, these same methods for presenting words and images may be of use to authors seeking to streamline their materials for wide appeal through the internet.

Background and Principles

The connection of people to a subject, to a key message, or to a new concept can be summarized in the word "see." First, a learner can readily see the subject in his or her field of view. Second, the level of difficulty is apparent, too: neither too hard nor too easy to see what is meant. Finally, the form in which the idea appears will allow the person to see how it can be used or applied to one's own purposes. In other words, popular audiences can best be served by materials that are readily visible, easy to understand, and in a usable form. By this measure, the visual rendering of the HoUM offers a good way to attract and engage a general audience as well as to serve specialist researchers. Website visitors can quickly see the overall arrangement of exhibit spaces and elements (panorama views). They can linger over details in the close-ups (online album), and they can push the playback button to hear and see something of each exhibition.

Another part of this popularizing approach comes from the entrepreneurial mindset (Kauffman Foundation, 2010). Mindset means both a working outlook that sees valuable resources and possible applications for these, as well as a set of skills that support what some have dubbed *edu*preneurship, the enterprising, project-oriented, practical application of an educational idea. Examples of skills for edupreneurs include pattern recognition (recognizing analogous functions or structures from diverse contexts), relational thinking (seeing connections or relevance that others do not see), persistence, written and visual communication experience (including software and internet tools available to disseminate an idea), subject-matter expertise, and knowledge of one's target audiences. In the HoUM multimedia project, my mindset consisted of an outlook shaped by six years of directing outreach projects for the Asian Studies Center (Michigan State University) and then for the Center for Japanese Studies (University of Michigan). So the HoUM faculty's research areas, the campus events, and the exhibits both permanent and temporary, both current and archived, were all potential sources for multimedia production.

The skills of my edupreneurial mindset consisted of photo, video, and audio editing abilities, including panoramic image stitching, making online photo albums, and producing audio slideshows (see www.popularizingresearch.net for useful resources on these and other tools). It's said that the man with only a hammer in his toolbox sees his world only in terms of nails to be hammered. This also holds true for the edupreneurial mindset: the more tools one has at hand, the more solutions present themselves. More skills make for better projects. Given the aim of the HoUM for wider access to its stories online and the principles that guide the design of popular outreach, one can ask about the subjects chosen for production, the methods, and the actual deployment of the multimedia in the overall museum plan and the assessment of these efforts.

Specific Projects

Between March and June, there were three stages: introducing the multimedia approach and menu of possible products, actual production, and establishing the products online and in the galleries of HoUM. After meeting museum colleagues and conferring with my host researcher, I began by making sample products to illustrate what was possible. These included gallery panoramas, photo albums to show exhibit detail, and a short movie made from a combination of video clips and still images using a digital camera. By placing both still and moving images into Windows Movie Maker (MM) and adding a narration, the resulting movie faithfully introduced viewers to the entry hall and exhibit space of the museum. The work was recorded in English: my native language, useful for internet audiences, and a script from which Japanese and additional languages could be written to change the movie audio track later.

With the approval of the museum director and board, we proceeded to digitally photograph and record short video clips for all three floors of exhibit space. Later we documented the two special exhibits that came and went during the time of my stay at HoUM. Ancillary projects included collections affiliated with HoUM: the *Botanical Garden* (housing separate collections on the grounds), the open-air agriculture park (*Model Barn* and out buildings), and a three-part traveling exhibit that documented the university history through photo panels. In each case, the digital photos were the basis for the same three-layer approach taken at the HoUM: panoramas to simulate the angle of vision natural to human sight, albums for rapid view of details taken from the subject, and narrated slideshows to give a linear playback experience built up from scripted remarks.

Various free and paid software allows one to "stitch" a panorama at the points where image elements overlap, thus forming a continuous, lengthy field of view. Based on the online discussion of a user group at flickr.com, I found Autostitch well suited to the work. It's free, lightweight, rapid, and reliable. With or without tripod, I rotated the view at the nodal point of the lens, where the image focuses onto the photo sensor. With the camera base parallel to the ground, there was little danger of converging lines at the top or bottom of the finished stitch. By stitching two to five adjacent frames into wide views, I could gather wide sections of exhibit rooms or individual displays up close. One variation was to begin with a panorama and narrate the caption on an audio track. This so-called Ken Burns Effect (panning across a photo) is available in iMovie (free on Mac computers) and Photo Story 3 (Windows PC free download at Microsoft.com). The result is a long, continuous view that rolls across the screen, thus giving the sensation of looking around.

Software allows one to select images for display with captions online. The photo editor and organizer Picasa is popular and includes a function called "Export as HTML." Pressing this button produces a self-contained set of photos, thumbnails, captions, folders, and navigation links that one can then move in toto online. Alternatively, one can directly upload to the free storage at Picasaweb. This service allows the images to be marked private or public, and visitors can leave comments or questions. The images marked "public" are searchable, too. For the HoUM project, though, they hosted the content on their own servers. The plan was to have English as well as Japanese versions of the photos. Displayed in album form, one can move through the collection at any pace, examine details at length, and download images. The multimedia is onsite in kiosk form.

Compared to online albums, setting the images into a narrated slideshow limits a user's control to pause, replay, and resize the display. However, what's lost in user control is regained as convenience: the play button gives an armchair tour of the subject. The Windows operating system with its video and audio editor (Windows Movie Maker) as well as its playback software (Windows Media Player) is pervasive. So it makes sense to use these utilities to produce multimedia for museum visitors and to encourage museum faculty and students to present their own work this way, too. I also used Photo Story 3 in order to pan across the photos. The video file that results (*.wmv) can be interspersed in Movie Maker (MM) with other images or clips.

The complete workflow for a narrated slideshow begins with clean photos: corrected for color contrast, cropping, and horizon tilts in the Picasa photo organizer. A basic decision about the structure of the movie's visual and sound elements must be made early on: will the words follow the string of images in a supporting role, or will the narration be primary and the images simply illustrate the points being made verbally. If photos are primary, then they can be imported into MM and clumped by related subsections by dragging and dropping them around the timeline view of MM. On the other hand, if text is primary, then it should be recorded on computer or onto a digital voice recorder to transfer to the computer. In the case of HoUM, both were developed: matching label text to suitable illustrative visuals, and the reverse—composing new scripts to suit the set of gallery details photographed.

Once inside MM, it is possible to divide the narrated audio file into segments to position at the right moment in the timeline. That way, the image playback duration will match the audio. Unlike the audio silences between images, the visual elements must be contiguous, allowing for no gap in the playback material, even if that image is just a black background inserted to fill the timeline. This working project file of MM is worth saving because it allows one to change individual elements of a playback file later (screen text, narration language, and so on). When "publishing" any given version of the movie file, all the elements become locked into place for optimum playback. That is why one needs the original movie project file in order to make edits.

A word about producing movie files: the higher the data rate (kilobits per second, kbps), the better the quality and the bigger the resulting file. When uploading to a free host like blip.tv, vimeo.org, or Youtube, the source file is compressed for best web distribution. So the original file size will not affect viewers too much. For direct distribution to viewers, the source movie file size can be reduced by changing the audio from stereo to mono (50 percent data savings) and changing the dimensions of the movie from full-size (standard definition at 640 pixels by 480 pixels) to 320x240 pixels, for instance. Moreover, a word of advice: individual movies should be two to three minutes for single-subject stories. For wider topics, eight to twelve minutes is best. Taking a cue from eyeball tracking studies of the dominant skimming behavior online (contrasted to the careful reading of printed text), the multimedia products should not linger more than four to five seconds per image, much like TV and cinematic conventions for pacing.

Uses for Multimedia

With so many products in hand, the question arises about how best to use these in service of the HoUM mission of engaging its publics. Digital products can be economically copied, circulated, excerpted, cross-linked, or interwoven to form new fabric altogether. Either in their finished file format (JPG for panorama, WMV for moving panorama, HTML for photo album, WMV for audio slideshows), or in a derivative format, these products can be published online, distributed by email, incorporated in a PowerPoint-type of presentation, or appended to existing CD and DVD-ROM products of the HoUM. Because the accompanying text or narration track can be substituted with foreign languages, different editions can be released for the convenience of the numerous visitors to the museum, as well as for the users of its website.

From an institutional point of view, there may be a couple of immediate concerns about providing a digital facsimile of the museum displays online. One is a standard for style or brand: at the highest level of production value, the museum or university may wish to have a consistent look for anything that is associated with the institution. My no-frills visual communication lacked those high production values. Another concern is of setting precedent and the time or financial burden this could entail. For example, it can be politically sensitive to provide multimedia of one event or collection, but not of another event, or to show two of the special exhibits, but none of the older ones, or future ones. This could be viewed as less than professional. And if some researchers provide brief multimedia introductions to their projects past and current, the others could feel compelled to do so, as well. Finally, even the permanent displays are not immutable, since they are revised as better data or more complete syntheses emerge. So unless the museum was prepared to update the multimedia version of the gallery revisions, too, the eventual inconsistencies of on-screen and on-site experiences could lead to an impression of unprofessionalism. Production value by staff or contractors may be the same, but gaps over time may detract from the public perception of the museum.

My intention was to supplement the museum experience by offering a preview of the spaces, selected details, and audio slideshows for overview. Visitors could return to the digital resources to collect souvenirs, too. And in the future they would be able to relive their museum visit by browsing the digital materials. However, without precedent or prior experience to form any internal motivation and without top-down pressure to form any external motivation, the potential uses of multimedia were not fully appreciated by most faculty, staff, and students. Instead the status quo prevails: printed exhibit guides, frenetic production of special exhibits, along with touch ups to the permanent exhibits.

There are several sorts of lessons learned from conceiving, designing, and producing digital excerpts from the gallery displays. These range from the practicalities of workflow, to project team dynamics, to the possible deployment and ongoing engagement with the digitally visual and audio media. Multimedia for collections that are actively curated should be regarded as something akin to a quarterly magazine or digest rather than a daily newsletter or something with the bulk and authority of a monograph. This means the content should be amended or revised periodically, with budget set aside for this living cycle. Earlier versions could be viewed in an archive area.

Conclusion

Evaluation is the most delicate part of the presentational cycle that runs from author to audience to responses and then back to the author. Advertising analysts, market observers, and social critics have many assessment tools available, but seldom has there been a satisfactory evaluation of the full impact of an article, video, or other story on real people. In other words, while multimedia material is vivid, creative, and closely derived from its source subjects, it is still unclear what the "return on investment" for multimedia online galleries is, say, when compared to the value from on-site engagement, memories, attitudes, or curiosity. Specifically, what makes multimedia better or worse than earlier forms of presentation?

My 2009 experience at HoUM reaffirmed my earlier experiences of multimedia: that a person gets different sorts of information through visual channels. Verbal handling of a subject gives precision and allows an author to draw careful distinctions. And while both text and voice/image can be published online, the ease of viewing or listening compared to reading on-screen text is likely to attract a larger audience.

The literal meaning of "popularize" is to "spread among the populous" at an easily digested level of complexity. For this reason, I conclude that the HoUM project was successful for initiating researchers and graduate students to become multimedia authors. Tracking their progress six months later, one in four actually produced multimedia for conferences, experiments, or their websites. Reflections by my host researcher agree that the four-month span limited the uptake by museum faculty. Individual coaching would have yielded bigger results. The ability to substitute various languages was trialed but was never released in final form. As of the summer of 2010, the museum took a conservative first step by positioning the audio slideshow introduction to the galleries on kiosk-type stations in the museum. But the full capacities for engaging domestic and foreign visitors online had not yet been fully realized.

In sum, the project resulted in more accessible content (easy to find, easy to grasp, easy to obtain for subsequent uses). The coverage included panoramas (immersive interior views), online albums (close-up aspects selected and annotated from the gallery), and short movies (playback convenience). Perhaps most valuable of all was the expanded mindset of the scholars to regard themselves now as multimedia producers-to-be: a new standard of practice can emerge. While the researchers began by playing with the multimedia idea and tools, they may soon apply this experience to work subjects to disseminate online. Whether it is the wider accessibility to content, the wider functionality that viewers have, or the wider scope for professional presentation online, multimedia offers a powerful way to popularize and engage with one's audiences.

References

Costello, R., & Bliton, D. (2009). Assessment of educational visual storytelling at the Smithsonian. Presented at the annual Interservice/Industry Training, Simulation, and Education Conference (Orlando).

Karp, I., Kreamer, C. M., & Lavine, S. D. (Eds.). (1992). *Museums and Communities*. Washington, DC: Smithsonian Institution Press.

Kauffman Foundation. (2010). *The Entrepreneurial Leadership Initiative*, http://elientrepreneur.ning.com and http://buildastrongeramerica.com.

CHAPTER NINE

Using Multimedia Artworks to Disseminate Psychological Research on Attacks on Firefighters

Vivienne Brunsden, Joe Robinson, Jeffrey Goatcher, & Rowena Hill

The phenomenon of abusive and violent behaviour towards emergency workers is a problematic issue within the UK. An analysis of British Crime Survey data suggested that employees working in protective service occupations are the most at risk of experiencing violence at work (Webster, Patterson, Hoare, & O'Loughlin, 2008). It is unclear exactly how often firefighters experience violent attacks as the UK government does not publish the data they collect on this, even though they require the formal reporting of these events. However, they have claimed that attacks are falling, citing a decrease from 1,300 in 2005/6 to 400 in 2006/7 (see Labour Research Dept., 2008) and have declared an intention to see rates fall further by 2018 (Communities & Local Government, 2008). These figures are however disputed with the Fire Brigades Union (FBU) long being critical of government figures on attacks (see Labour Research Dept., 2005). FBU-commissioned research suggested attacks were actually rising, suggesting figures such as 2,030 in 2005/6 and 2,098 in 2006/7 as more accurate with attacks occurring around 40 times a week and six times a day (Labour Research Dept., 2008). Regardless of whose figures are more accurate, it is clear that this is a serious issue for the Fire & Rescue Service (FRS), with negative implications not only for the health of FRS personnel but also for public safety.

This issue is starting to gain some media attention and the government has responded by passing the Emergency Workers (Obstruction) Act (2006), which makes it an offence to obstruct or hinder any members of the emergency services in the performance of their duties. Despite this, the general public remains largely unaware that attacks occur and can be incredulous once made aware. Firefighters are held in high regard by the community (CLG, 2008), and many find it unfathomable that anyone could wish to attack them. Aggression towards firefighters can range from verbal abuse to physical attacks, which can be directed at the fire appliance or at the firefighters themselves. However firefighters are not the only FRS personnel to be abused. Control staff—whilst they do not experience physical aggression—are subject to subtler aggression through abusive calls which can include hoaxes and sexual harassment.

Physical attacks occur in particular areas, usually areas of extreme economic deprivation. Most often the perpetrators are children and adolescents, generally acting in groups, and it is unclear how intentionally malicious the motivation for attacks is. The physical effects of violence towards appliances and personnel are often clear, but the psychological effects of aggression are more subtle and can be extremely debilitating. The interaction between socioeconomic deprivation, the highly developed public service ethos throughout the FRS, and these attacks presents a complex sociological and psychological picture. Generally, however, this issue of aggression towards FRS personnel is a phenomenon that has received little attention from the research community.

The intention behind our research was to explore the impact that attacks (physical and verbal) have on the FRS personnel who experience them. The academic team conducting the research consisted of two psychologists and a sociologist. From the outset we were convinced that a different way of disseminating the findings was needed, rather than just the traditional peer-reviewed articles/conference presentations route. We were aware of the relatively low readership that empirical research articles receive (see Loke & Derry, 2003), but even if readership of these were high, the audience would inevitably be rather restricted. Journal articles are read primarily by other academics or by students, but for this research we felt it was important that the findings be available to the UK FRS who suffer the aggression; in order to contextualize and assist in validating their experience. Even more importantly, we felt it was crucial that the findings reach the communities that the FRS served. In particular, we felt that those communities where attacks occur should have the opportunity to see the findings. This meant that we needed a dissemination strategy that was not only accessible but also was in some way attractive and engaging to lay audiences. We chose to do this through an exhibition entitled "Brick, Ball, Hoax Call" which reflects the types of missiles thrown at, and psychological terrors inflicted on, FRS personnel. This chapter and its accompanying web-based material show and discuss the outcomes of our research and this dissemination strategy.

Our Project: "Brick, Ball, Hoax Call"

A mix of ethnography and semi-structured interviews were used, with the interview data and field notes then being subjected to an interpretative phenomenological analysis (IPA). IPA is concerned with trying to understand lived experience and how participants themselves make sense of their experiences (Smith & Osborn, 2003). The findings enabled the formation of a typology of abuse wherein the perceived nature of the attacks (for example, malicious versus panic driven) interacted with the possibility of attributing explanations to attackers' motivations and resulted in differential psychological impact. For example, if an aggressive attack could be explained in terms of distress during the high emotion of an emergency situation, or could be attributed to normal adolescent behaviours, then the detrimental psychological impact would be negligible. However, if those attacked saw the aggression as malicious, and could not ascribe an understandable motivation, the resulting bewilderment generated psychological distress.

Reaching FRS personnel was relatively easy—there are a number of FRS relevant conferences (e.g., Brunsden, 2007a), and there is a trade publication that is read by almost all UK FRS personnel (see Brunsden, 2007b). However, reaching the general public and specific communities needed a different strategy. To address this, a professional artist was included as a member of the research team from the very start of the project.

Our idea was relatively simple; the artist would be part of the research team and access and use the data and analytic findings as a source of inspiration, in order to create artworks in a variety of media. These artworks would then be displayed in public spaces alongside more traditional research posters which contextualized the research project and detailed its methods and key findings. Artistic representations such as sculptures and pictures offer immediate impact. Harnad (1991) notes that pictures can be read at a glance by many people simultaneously, whereas reading the many words that would be needed to convey the same information requires a considerable investment of time from isolated individuals. Viewing pictures can thus become an embodied, communal activity. Further, artworks can provide powerful metaphors which can convey abstract states of mind, such as emotion, which words may struggle to articulate. The incorporation of imagery into research may bring significant benefits to the quality of the understanding of social and psychological phenomena (Brunsden, Goatcher, & Hill, 2009). In encountering images, people are free to determine what is significant to them and together with the image's originator (whether researcher, participant, or artist) can subsequently negotiate a verbal interpretation of that significance.

This is similar to what Gadamer (following Heidegger) called the "fusing of horizons," central to any and all acts of reaching understanding (Gadamer, 1979). The intention for our dissemination strategy was not merely that artworks and analytic findings be presented alongside one another, but instead that the research and art production became fused, integrated into a holistic art-science process to facilitate richer understandings. It has been suggested that synthesized analyses integrating both visual and verbal understandings can produce unpredictable information and perspectives (Hurworth, 2003) and thus offer new and richer insights into how people make sense of their worlds (Brunsden & Goatcher, 2007). The IPA did not therefore merely drive the artworks, but in turn the artworks informed and reframed those aspects of the IPA which introduced the subjective interpretations of the analyst; with this interrelated process of negotiation between art and science continuing iteratively. In dissemination too, a fusing of horizons will always take place; even with positivistic social science the meanings given to, and the perception of, data and analysis is inevitably interpretative and subjective at some level. Through our art-science process, this audience reception hermeneutic is overt, deepened, and broadened. The art-science works also went beyond mere passive verbal and visual representation. Some of the artworks contained elements of interactivity, they could be played with like children's toys, allowing an embodied reflection on the player's actions rather than communicating through passive consumption of information.

The resulting art-science works formed the basis of an exhibition which lent itself to being taken to the wider community and shown in public spaces such as libraries, market places, community halls, etc. The exhibition could be taken both to areas where attacks are commonplace (to raise awareness of their human impact), and where they do not occur (to raise awareness of the phenomenon's existence). Thus the exhibiting of art-science works would become part of an action research strategy that also served to democratize the research process (Brunsden, Goatcher, & Hill, 2009).

Throughout the production of the art-science works, a constant dialogue was maintained between all four members of the team. Frequent meetings took place before, during, and after data collection. Preliminary cartoons and sketches detailing ideas for the artworks were discussed before final creation started. The IPA approach used in this research is underpinned by a realist ontology (Flowers, Smith, Sheeran, & Beail, 2002), and the academic team members were keen that, even with the inevitably subjective and interpretative nature of the artworks, there remained a viable connection between these and the data, creating art-science works as opposed to mere artworks. In practice, however, achieving an accommodation between art and social science proved to be more challenging than we had expected. During our structured discussions about how to visually interpret and represent the data and analytic findings, it quickly became apparent that the social scientists and the artist initially had different stances in attempting to represent the realities we were examining. A particular difficulty centred on the status of the participants' testimony and their consent, in terms of what was deemed suitable material for use in the artworks.

Ethical Considerations

Empirical research relies upon the cooperation, time, and lives of its participants: social actors, individuals, and groups must give of themselves to enable social science to have the data from which to draw reliable and representative knowledge of society and its workings. Social science research is generally based on fundamental principles of participant privacy, whereas the basis of creative art is centred more on individual creative license. This proved a fascinating area of discussion for our project in bringing these particular understandings of representational veracity to a shared standpoint. The team needed to ensure that the artworks kept faith with participants and did not misrepresent them, or exploit their experiences beyond the boundaries of consent that they had given. This constrained and limited some of the artist's creative ideas. For example, one of the initial suggestions involved photographing a series of actors who would be made up to indicate physical injuries, wearing t-shirts bearing quotes from participants' data. The social scientists were concerned that viewers could construe that the actors were actually those FRS personnel who had made the statement or alternatively would realize that these were actors but might be misled as to the seriousness of the injuries suffered by the research participants (with the exception of one person who had been hospitalized following a stabbing, participants' physical injuries were all minor). The key concern for the social scientists here was that these images could in some way potentially create misperceptions about both the participant and the context of their data, thus diluting the veracity of the testimonies given by the FRS personnel, in a rather exploitative way. At the same time the team did not wish to constrain creative imagination or art production. A form of working compromise between disciplinary approaches and ethical stances was needed.

To inform our decisions, we turned for guidance to the various ethical codes and codes of practice by which our different disciplines were bound. The British Sociological Association (BSA, 2004) statement of ethical practice highlights that sociologists enter into personal and moral relationships with those they study and that researchers should strive to protect participants' rights, interests, and privacy. It further states that researchers have some responsibility for the use to which their data may be put and how the research is to be disseminated. The British Psychological Society issues various ethical guidelines which all proceed from the basis of "the dignity and worth of all persons, with sensitivity to the dynamics of perceived authority or influence over clients, and with particular regard to people's rights including those of privacy" (BPS, 2006, 10). However, we could find no such overarching code for artists to derive guidance from.

There are a few codes available for particular subsets of artist or art organisations, however these tend to either focus on customer relations (e.g., that of the Fine Art Trade Guild, 2008) or refer to ethical practice in terms of the *use* rather than *production* of art, particularly in relation to protecting the artist's work (e.g., that of the Association des Illustrateurs et Illustratrices du Québec, AIIQ, n.d.). Indeed rather than protecting those whom an artist portrays, it appears that the artist instead has complete freedom to represent whatever they so choose, in whatever way they judge appropriate. The contemporary artist Georg Baselitz expresses a similar sentiment: "The artist is not responsible to anyone. His social role is asocial; his only responsibility consists in an attitude to the work he does" (Gablik, 1993, p. 61). This is of course entirely legitimate for "Art," but did not feel appropriate for social science or for a synthesized art-science.

An exception to this joint "commercial"/freedom approach appears to be the codes of artistic professions which are in some way connected to science and involve necessarily realistic representations. For example, the code for medical illustrators sets the profession's aim out as depicting and clarifying scientific information and making it understandable through visual media "using the fidelity of the scientist and the skills of the artist" (AMI, 1991). Similarly the code of ethics for forensic illustrators states that after thorough investigation to make factual determinations, "These findings of fact and their conclusions and opinions should then be reported with all the accuracy and skill of which the artist is capable" (IAI, FA, n.d.). These are positivistic, fact-based approaches to illustration, in service of the master science. Although we felt that these scientifically oriented codes had more resonance with the social science paradigm of our research than did other artistic codes, these went too far towards literalism for our methodological approach. The phenomenological and hermeneutic paradigms mentioned above commence from the conviction that knowledge and understanding of reality/ies are socially constructed or negotiated. Therefore the whole project strove to use interpretation to convey a multilayered, stratified understanding of the realities of the FRS personnel, the researchers, the artist, and the viewers/interactors of the joint work. The most useful artistic codes came from the arena of film and photography, where a range of professional codes did offer some more robust practical guidance and addressed issues such as privacy, confidentiality, and image manipulation. The consideration of a wide variety of disciplinary codes, and the continued discussion around both these and our various intentions for the research, were incredibly helpful in allowing the team to negotiate a position where all were happy with the resultant art-science works and with the process which had led to them.

Once the artworks had all been developed, a further problem emerged in terms of funding the costs of the exhibition. The team managed to secure a small amount of money internally at their university (from a scheme co-funded by the Higher Education Innovation Fund and the East Midlands Development Agency), and this provided materials to make the artworks and enabled some small-scale exhibitions (e.g., Robinson, Brunsden, Goatcher, & Hill, 2007; Brunsden, Robinson, Goatcher, & Hill, 2009), but the costs of exhibiting on a wide scale became prohibitive in terms of staff time. The exhibition is still available for those who are willing to host it, but it was felt an alternative strategy was merited to enable wider access to the materials. The artist therefore developed a short film about the project which included some of the artistic works. This film, along with contextual documentation about the film and the original research, is available to each of the UK's 58 Fire & Rescue Services for them to use however they wish. In particular, it is anticipated that it could be used in support of the various schemes run by the FRS throughout the UK (for example LIFE, Phoenix, Bendigo) for those youth who exhibit antisocial behaviours.

Conclusion

As research continues to be popularized in various ways, the ethical issues governing the different actors involved in these popularizing processes are likely to come to the fore. This has already been seen even with the more traditional dissemination reports of publishing in journals which then get picked up by journalists who may fail to fully understand findings and therefore, perhaps unintentionally, misrepresent these (Goldacre, 2009). This has led, for example, to Dorothy Bishop, a professor of developmental neuropsychology at the University of Oxford instigating the "Orwellian Prize for Journalistic Misrepresentation" (Deevybee, 2010). There is possibly the need to develop ethical guidance to govern popularizing endeavours, however it is highly unlikely that one code could address all situations encompassed under this heading (journalistic and artistic behaviour, for example, would inevitably need to attend to very different behaviours). For popularizing activities that involve artistic interpretations, a code would need to keep faith with both the original participants and researchers' own disciplinary codes; but would also need to allow the artists' creative expression to flourish and bring the benefits of emotional impact to the dissemination. It is clear from our own attempts at unpacking these issues that this is no easy task, but also that it *is* possible.

References

AIIQ. (n.d.). Code of ethics. *Association des Illustrateurs et Illustratrices du Quebec*. Available from http://www.illustrationquebec.com/en/code-of-ethics.

AMI. (1991). Professional ethics. *Association of Medical Illustrators*. Available at http://www.ami.org/about-the-ami/professional-ethics.html.

British Psychological Society. (2006). *Code of ethics and conduct*. Leicester: British Psychological Society.

British Sociological Association. (2004). *Statement of ethical practice for the British Sociological Association*. Durham: British Sociological Association.

Brunsden, V. (2007a). Violence at work: Experiences of fire and rescue service personnel. *Fire Research and Related Developments (RE07)*. Moreton in the Marsh, Gloucestershire, November 2007.

Brunsden, V. (2007b). Award-winning research reveals truth of attacks on firefighters. *FIRE, 100 (1229)*, 41–43.

Brunsden, V. & Goatcher, J., (2007). Reconfiguring photovoice for psychological research. *Irish Journal of Psychology,28 (1–2)*, 43–52.

Brunsden, V., Goatcher, J., & Hill, R. (2009). Photographic methods: An under-used approach. *Social Psychology Review, 11(1)*, 45–50.

Brunsden, V., Robinson, J., Goatcher, J., & Hill, R. (2009, May 13–14). Raising public awareness of the phenomenon of attacks on firefighters. *Fire Brigades' Union Annual Conference 2009*, The Spa Complex, Scarborough.

Communities & Local Government. (2008). *A survey of current and ex-firefighters in England*. London: CLG.

Deevybee. (2010, June 1). Orwellian prize for journalistic misrepresentation. *BishopBlog*. Available at http://deevybee.blogspot.com/2010/06/orwellian-prize-for-journalistic.html.

Fine Art Trade Guild. (2008). Guild code of ethics. *Fine Art Trade Guild*. Available at http://www.fineart.co.uk/Public/Code_of_Ethics_Public.aspx.

Flowers, P., Smith, J., Sheeran, P., & Beail, N. (2002). Health and romance: Understanding unprotected sex in relationships between gay men. In D. F. Marks (ed.), *The health psychology reader*. London: Sage.

Gablik, S. (1993). *The re-enchantment of art*. London: Thames Hudson.

Gadamer, H. G. (1979). *Truth and Method*. London: Sheed and Ward.

Goldacre, B., (2009). *Bad science*. London: Harper Perennial.

Harnad, S. (1991). Back to the oral tradition: Through skywriting at the speed of thought. Available at http://eprints.ecs.soton.ac.uk/7723/1/lyon.html.

Hurworth, R. (2003). Photo-interviewing for research. *Social Research Update, 40.* Retrieved August 28, 2010. Available at http://sru.soc.surrey.ac.uk/SRU40.html.

IAI, FA (n.d.). Code of ethics. *International Association for Identification, Forensic Artists. Forensic Artist.com.* Available at http://www.forensicartist.com/IAI/ethics.html.

Labour Research Department. (2005). *Attacks on firefighters.* London: The Fire Brigades Union.

Labour Research Department. (2008). *In the line of duty.* London: The Fire Brigades Union.

Loke, Y. K., & Derry, S. (2003). Does anybody read "evidence-based" articles? *BMC Medical Research Methodology, 3,* 14.

Robinson, J., Brunsden, V., Goatcher, J., & Hill, R. (2007, Nov.). Using art to raise awareness of the phenomenon of attacks on firefighters. *Fire Research and Related Developments (RE07).* Moreton in the Marsh, Gloucestershire.

Smith, J. A., & Osborn, M. (2003). Interpretative phenomenological analysis. In J. A. Smith (Ed.). *Qualitative Psychology.* London: Sage.

Webster S., Patterson A., Hoare J., & O'Loughlin, A. (2008). *Violence at work: Findings from the 2005/06 and 2006/07. British Crime Survey,* HSE.

CHAPTER TEN

Geographies of the Imagination

Engaging Audiences and Participants in Collaborative Interdisciplinary Gallery Installations

Lydia Nakashima Degarrod

Geographies of the Imagination is a multimedia and interdisciplinary installation that I designed and created with the collaboration of nine political exiles living in the Bay Area of San Francisco, California. The installation, shown at the Oliver Art Center Gallery from October 27, 2008, to November 23, 2008, aimed at depicting internal images of exile after 30 years of the immigrants having resided in the United States. I made the installation over a period of 16 months while I was Artist in Residence at the Center for Art and Public Life at the California College of the Arts from June 2007 to October 2008. The project was funded by the California Story Fund of the California Council for the Humanities and by the Center for Art and Public Life of the California College of the Arts.

The public exhibit of *Geographies of the Imagination* was successful in terms of audience attendance and by the demonstrated public engagement with the installation. The greater effect of this form of popular research occurred among the exile participants themselves throughout the making of the installation and through their viewing of it at the public exhibit. In both of these processes, the immigrants engaged in reflections on identity, exile, and belonging.

In this chapter, I will present the process of making this form of popular research by starting with the methodology used and its background, followed by the production of the installation, its public display, the reactions of the audiences, and ending with my reflections on the findings.

Ethnographies and Visual Art

Interdisciplinary works that combine both ethnographic research and visual art are rare among cultural anthropologists, with the exception of ethnographic film. They are less rare among visual artists who have been incorporating research techniques, in particular ethnographic techniques, in the development of their artistic projects (Coles, 2000; Schneider & Wright, 2005, 2010). In the last decade, there has been a growing interest among cultural anthropologists to explore the possibilities of using the fine arts as part of doing ethnographic research (Schneider & Wright, 2005; Coles, 2000; Grimshaw & Ravetz, 2005).

I designed the installation of *Geographies of the Imagination* using both my knowledge and skill as a visual artist and as a cultural anthropologist, following some of the same interests and concerns that have guided my interdisciplinary work for the last 14 years. I use visual art to express aspects of the research that tend to be eluded by traditional textual ethnographic representations. These include emotional climates and experiences that defy textual representation. I have learned, as have other ethnographers, that words alone cannot fully represent all aspects of the ethnographic experience (Nakashima Degarrod, 1998, 2010; Ravetz, 2005). In this case, the traumatic aspects of the migratory experience of the Chilean exiles, which included memories of torture and imprisonment, challenged representation.

I made use of mono-prints, a technique that gave me the freedom to express emotional textures through colors and shapes and at the same time incorporate image photo transfers. I incorporated video in the installation to convey some of the aspects unique to the experience of migration and exile, including the perception of the immigrant of inhabiting several imaginary and real places as the Chilean exiles simultaneously maintained an emotional existence in three places: the idealized homeland of their memories, the homeland that expelled them, and the host country. I made the work available to a general audience by showing it in a gallery. The use of the gallery also alters the quality of the interaction with the work in that the viewers can see and interact with objects socially and publicly and share their subjective experiences instead of the more solitary experience of reading a book (Heller, 2005). I designed the installation to honor the memories of the exiles whose stories were silenced by the 17 years of the dictatorship of Augusto Pinochet and to provide the exiles with a public arena for the expression of their memories of and reflections on exile.

Production of the Installation and Exhibit

The nine Chilean participants were recruited from La Peña Cultural Center, a community center located in Berkeley, California, which served as the community partner for the California Story Fund Grant. Since its creation in 1975, La Peña Cultural Center has been a meeting ground for the Chilean exile community in Northern California. All of the participants in this project had departed Chile either as voluntary exiles or as forced exiles from 1974 to 1982, within eight years after the 1973 military coup d'état in Chile that deposed the government of Salvador Allende and placed General Augusto Pinochet in command of the country. The Chilean participants arrived in the San Francisco Bay Area as part of one of the major waves of migration in the history of Chile when approximately 2 percent of the country's population either fled the country or were expelled by the regime of Augusto Pinochet (Sznajder & Roniger, 2007). Five of the exiles had left voluntarily because of well-grounded fears of being arrested or killed. The rest of them, who had been incarcerated and tortured prior to their exile, had been officially expelled from the country and the letter L had been stamped in their passports indicating that the bearers were on a list of those forbidden from returning to Chile.

The participants were selected for the project based on their willingness to share their stories of migration. For most of them, this multimedia art project was the first opportunity to publicly share their memories of migration. They had tried previously to erase all memories associated with their migration as a way of coping with the difficulties of adjusting to life in the United States. All of them expressed a desire to remember and to bring their stories into the public sphere for their own children and for younger generations who had not experienced the events of the coup in Chile.

My work on this project as both as an artist and as an ethnographer was facilitated by my Chilean background. While I am not an exile, I was born and raised in Chile and have lived in the United States almost the same amount of time as the exiles. I shared with the exiles commonalities in history and cultural sensitivies that helped in my understanding of their experiences.

Making the installation involved both ethnographic research and collaborative art making. In my role as ethnographer, I conducted individual ethnographic interviews with the exiles, participated in many social events of the Chilean exile community, and conducted background historical and social science literature research on the Chilean coup d'état and dictatorship, and on the experience of exile in general. As the lead artist, I designed the installation, created the images for the mono-print banners, and directed the video-taping. The exiles collaborated by providing their memories of migration and exile. They also collaborated in the selection and editing of the images of the banners and of the videos.

Making the installation involved three phases. The first was collaboratively making maps that represented the exiles' recall of their journeys. This involved a series of steps that oscillated between interviews and image making. I conducted the interviews and consultations privately with the participants about their memories of migration and their images of their journeys. Using their suggestions, I made two or three images in the form of mono-prints, which included etching image transfers of photos selected by the participants and other images that I selected. These etched images were shown to each participant and changes were made based on their recommendations until the final approved mono-prints were completed. The process was not unidirectional, going only from memories to images, as the images I made brought out more of the exiles' memories and reflections. During this process, the exiles, aware of the public nature of the project, addressed much of their memories and reflections to imaginary audiences, which guided their selection and editing of images. These imagined audiences varied from their immediate families and friends in the United States and Chile, to the Chile they loved but whose government had expelled them, to contemporary Chile. In my role as the maker of the mono-prints, I also created imaginary audiences in reference to whom I judged the aesthetic value and ethical importance of the images.

The second part of the project consisted of videotaping in their homes, and in local places that the participants chose because they brought back memories of their homeland. Making the videotapes involved a similar process of interviewing, taping the performance of the participants' reflections at places that bring or used to bring nostalgia to the exiles, and collaborative editing.

The last part of the project was the installation itself, which included 23 banners that were each 36 inches by 46 inches, and nine seven-minute videos. The banners were divided into three types: nine affective maps that portrayed the journeys of the Chilean exiles as they were recalled today, seven banners representing the actual geographical movement of the exiles, and seven banners representing their current identities. In the nine videos, the participants discussed their migration to the United States and the places in their current location that bring back memories of the homeland, as well as reflections on their identities. For each participant, there was one monitor on a pedestal playing her or his video. Above it was each participant's set of three banners hanging from the ceiling. The monitors on the pedestals and the maps were arranged in a V shape at the gallery. The exhibit was presented in three rooms of the gallery. The first room had large displays explaining the exhibit and a digital projector displaying different maps of the world. The installation was displayed in the main room. The third room had several tables with blank maps where the viewers were invited to trace their own journeys of migration in outlines of maps of United States and the world.

The installation's opening, on October 29, 2008, was attended by more than 400 people. All but one of the participants attended the opening reception with their families and friends. The La Peña Cultural Center Choir performed during the opening. The show continued for one month, and it was attended in all by over 600 people.

Audience Responses

There were two types of audience responses to the installation that I was able to observe and document. One came from the general audience at the exhibit. The other came from the participants in the project both during the making of the project and during its exhibit.

The general audience participated in the exhibit by responding to the invitation to trace their own journeys of migration in at the exhibit. Almost a fourth of the attendees traced their journeys. I observed several families with their children where the parents and in some cases grandparents were showing their journeys of migration on the maps. Half of the people traced their journeys within the United States, whereas the other half were from abroad. Many of them wrote reflections about their journeys. One woman tracked her journey from southern India to the United States: She wrote "I came in 1980 in an arranged marriage. I had never seen my husband before."

The most visible reaction to the exhibit came from the exiles themselves who reacted quite emotionally during the opening, which triggered more reflections on their conflicting views about their identities and their places of belonging. For all the participants, the opening of the exhibit was the first opportunity they had had to view the artwork in its completed state and hear the memories of migration and exile of the others. All of them, with the exception of one, knew each other, but they didn't know the details of each other's stories. This new awareness led the participants to spontaneously create a group to meet periodically to share and talk about their experiences. All of the exiles came to see the exhibit several times, some as many as five times during the entire run of the exhibit. They came alone and with friends and relatives. They told me of their emotional reactions and reflections during the opening and during meetings and social gatherings afterwards. All of them expressed amazement about the commonalities of their experiences, and felt much compassion and sorrow for the suffering that they observed by listening to the others' stories.

They also reacted emotionally as spectators of their own stories. Jaime, one of the exiles who had been arrested and tortured before being expelled from Chile, expressed compassion, pride, and sorrow for himself:

> I was almost in tears when I saw my map. Also seeing myself on the screen made me feel a combination of pride and admiration at seeing myself surviving and being strong, but also of sadness for

the pain that I experienced. I didn't want to be weak in the past, so I didn't allow myself to dwell on my suffering. Sometimes I feel sorrow. I feel it now. Before I was angry. I had so much anger in myself. In spite of everything I went through, I did what was best.

Viewing the exhibit also brought about reflections on identity. For example, during the reception, Jaime and Rosita commented about their identity as Latinos in the United States and as descendants of the Mapuche indigenous people of Chile. As Latinos in the US, they commented on their accents and the relief that both experienced when listening to themselves in the videos, because their English pronunciation sounded good to them. "I was worried that nobody would understand my English," Jaime said. He expressed at times feeling inadequate because of his accented English and limited vocabulary, and the social barriers created by the limitations of those who are not born and raised in the United States. He commented with Rosita about their shared ethnicity and the discrimination that they felt in Chile as members of an ethnic group that is looked down on by members of the white elite that rules the country. Both of them commented how their experiences in the United States as dark-skinned people and with *mestizo* features were different than the experiences of European-looking Chilean immigrants.

The exiles also reflected on their places of belonging. For example, Eliana, who had spent much time during the making of the installation pondering her identity and her place of belonging, said that she became aware that she belongs a to a country and that country is the United States. She said:

> I don't want to say that I am going to live here forever, but this idea of going through the world with my suitcases trying to find my place is over, and I was able to confirm this idea when I had to speak about it and tell my experience. This is my country. I made this place my country. The rest is very beautiful, but they are just my memories. It's just the past. I believe that every time I go back to Chile that I am going to feel that Spanish is my language, that in Chile is where my people are, that my education comes from Chile. My friends there are not replaceable. The years are not coming back. The past remains in the past. It's an idealization. I am never going to be 17 again and neither am I going back to the Chile of my memories. Talking with you forced me to think about these issues. I know that I had inside me all these thoughts and ideas but the project made me think of them. It gave me a state of peace to realize that this is my place.

What I've Learned

The most important thing that I've learned about *Geographies of the Imagination* as a form of popular research is that it had the most visible and profound effect on the participants or collaborators of the project, and that this effect was visible not only at the end, but it was manifested throughout the process of making the installation. The making and the display of this installation were a catalyst for the exiles to recall repressed memories of migration, to reflect on their identities as exiles and as immigrants to the United States, and to contest past images and narratives about themselves that had been created by the dictatorship of Augusto Pinochet that expelled them from Chile. The collaborative nature of the project in which the exiles and I worked together in making the art, and the awareness brought to the exiles by the public display of the installation contributed to making the production and the exhibit become sites for the formation of memories, reflections, and the feeling of having received social justice.

References

Coles, A. (Ed.). (2000). *Site specificity: The ethnographic turn.* London: Black Dog Publishing.

Grimshaw, A., & Ravetz, A. (Eds.). (2005). *Visualizing anthropology.* Bristol: Intellect.

Grossman, A., & O'Brien, A. (Eds.). (2008). *Projecting pigration: Transcultural documentary practice.* London: Wallflower.

Heller, R. (2005). Becoming an artist-ethnographer. In A. Grimshaw & A. Ravetz (Eds.), *Visualizing anthropology.* Bristol: Intellect.

Nakashima Degarrod, L. (1998). Landscapes of terror, dreams, and loneliness: Explorations in art, ethnography, and friendship. *New Literary History, 29*(4).

Nakashima Degarrod, L. (2010). When ethnographies enter galleries. In S. Dudley (Ed.), *Museum materialities: Objects, engagements, interpretations.* London: Routledge.

Ravetz, A. (2005). News from home: Reflections on fine art and anthropology. In A. Grimshaw & A. Ravetz (Eds.), *Visualizing anthropology.* Bristol: Intellect.

Schneider, A., & Wright, C. (Eds.). (2005). *Contemporary art and anthropology.* Oxford: Berg.

Schneider, A, & Wright, C. (Eds.). (2010). *Between art and anthropology: Contemporary ethnographic practice.* Oxford: Berg.

Sznajder, M., & Roniger, L. (2007). Exile communities and their differential institutional dynamics: A comparative analysis of the Chilean and Uruguayan political diasporas. *Revista de Ciencia Politica, 27*(1), 43–66.

Part 4

AUDIO

CHAPTER ELEVEN

Radio

Engaging Communities through Grassroots Media

Kevin Howley

In this chapter, I use the term "grassroots media" to describe a set of social relations, political attitudes, and cultural practices associated with community-based media production and distribution. I do so at the risk of glossing over significant conceptual distinctions between grassroots media and equally useful designations, such as "alternative," "citizens," "community," "participatory," and "radical media" (e.g., Downing, 2000; Atton, 2001; Gumucio Dagron, 2001; Rodriguez, 2001; Howley, 2005a). Despite, or perhaps because of, the use of these different terms, scholars have produced an impressive body of research that enhances our understanding of the critical and decisive relationship between grassroots media, democratic communication, and evolving notions of citizenship (Rodriguez, Kidd, & Stein, 2009; Howley, 2010).

Savvy and politically committed as it is, this scholarship rarely explores the potential of grassroots media for popularizing research. This situation is a bit surprising given that academics frequently work alongside, and in support of, grassroots media (Halleck, 2002; Day, 2009). Indeed, for scholars, cultural critics, and public intellectuals whose work is unapologetically out of step with so-called conventional wisdom, grassroots media provide an outlet for research and analysis that receives scant attention in mainstream media. Drawing on my personal experience with community and independent media across the United States, this chapter considers the possibilities for engaging communities in research efforts within and through grassroots media.

Early Inspiration and Personal Engagement

An early inspiration for my efforts to popularize research through grassroots media is the US-based video collective Paper Tiger Television. Since 1981, Paper Tiger has featured research and analysis from leading American academics including political activist Noam Chomsky, sociologist Stanley Aronowitz, and feminist media critic Judith Williamson. Taking a low-budget, "do-it-yourself" (DIY) aesthetic to television production, Paper Tiger invites academics and cultural critics to address contemporary social, economic, and political issues (Halleck, 1984). Likewise, syndicated radio programs such as *Alternative Radio* and *Making Contact*, both staples of the US community radio sector, feature the work of scholars, independent journalists, and public intellectuals. Each week, contributors offer critical perspectives on public policy—from education reform and environmental regulation, to labor relations, economics, and health care—that are routinely marginalized by dominant media organizations.

My personal engagement with grassroots media began in New York City, where I worked as a public access television (PATV) producer, facilitator, and trainer. Significantly, my experience with PATV led me to pursue a career in academia and develop a research agenda on alternative media and community communication. In the years since, I have volunteered with community radio and the alternative press in Bloomington, Indiana—a college town with a rich tradition of independent media. More recently, my video critique of US President George W. Bush's infamous "Mission Accomplished" speech, *Victory at Sea? Culture Jamming Dubya* (Howley, 2005b), had its broadcast premiere on Free Speech TV, an "independent, publicly-supported, non-profit TV multi-platform digital media pioneer" (Free Speech TV, n.d.). All of which is to say that I have a keen appreciation for the capacity of independent and grassroots media to popularize research.

The balance of this chapter discusses an audio documentary I produced for Pacifica radio's weekly news magazine, *Sprouts: Radio From the Grassroots*. I begin with a consideration of the theoretical and practical implications of popularizing research through the medium of radio. Following this I discuss the impetus behind an oral history of the life and times of Russell J. Compton (1909–2007), a beloved professor of philosophy and religion at DePauw University. Finally, I discuss the production and distribution strategies employed in the making of *Hard Times Come Again No More: A Tribute to Russell Compton* (Howley, 2007).

Radio from the Grassroots: Rethinking Research, Methods, and Products

In a thoughtful discussion of radio's potential in and for research, Christine McKenzie observes: "although radio is ideal for knowledge creation, the power struggles over whose knowledge is developed through the airwaves continues to be a central issue" (McKenzie, 2008, p. 338). The history of US broadcasting reveals the contours of this struggle in radio's formative years. As Robert McChesney (1995) has shown, from the mid-1920s to the early 1930s, noncommercial broadcasters—trade unions, civic and religious groups, as well as colleges and universities—battled commercial interests over the regulatory framework that would govern the nation's airwaves. For their part, college and university stations were eager to exploit broadcasting's accessibility and popular appeal to provide educational opportunity to mass audiences. Sometimes referred to as "universities of the air," educational broadcasters played a significant, but largely forgotten, role in shaping early American radio.

Over time, commercial interests won out and US radio assumed an all-too-familiar approach to the art and craft of broadcasting; one that puts a premium on entertainment and consumerism at the expense of educational programming, let alone the production and dissemination of research. In the intervening years, college radio has all but abandoned educational outreach, opting instead to uncritically mimic commercial radio formats. This is not to suggest, however, that commercial broadcasting's dominance has eradicated the impulse to leverage the medium's unique characteristics for producing and distributing research. Public service, community, and grassroots radio continue to develop inventive ways to popularize research.

Before proceeding, we should first consider what popularizing research means in actual broadcast practice. On one hand, popularizing research refers to disseminating new knowledge to geographically dispersed audiences by way of radio broadcasting. Thus, radio relays knowledge produced by academic researchers in the natural sciences, social sciences, and humanities. Moreover, radio publicizes research taken up by any number of fields and institutions including government agencies, the medical and legal professions, consumer and market research firms, as well as the military and intelligence community. On the other hand, popularizing research refers to collaborative, community-based approaches to knowledge production—approaches that not only invite "popular participation" in research processes, but also facilitate the creation and dissemination of "nontraditional" research products designed to address general audiences. As McKenzie argues, "the medium of radio enables innovation, both artistically and *in terms of what constitutes research*" (p. 338, emphasis added).

What constitutes research is, of course, a matter of form as well as content. Moreover, popular participation in research projects raises important issues over research legitimacy and authority. Here, we can detect the ideological distinctions between US public radio (NPR) and its grassroots counterparts in terms of popularizing research. That is to say, NPR's approach to popularizing research is constrained by the network's institutional arrangements with (some might say dependencies upon) political and economic elites. In contrast, grassroots radio operates with greater autonomy and editorial independence than NPR and its affiliates.

Put differently, grassroots media tend to be more receptive to research and analysis that challenge conventional wisdom. Consider, for example, Pacifica radio's flagship newscast, *Democracy Now!* Billing itself as a "daily, grassroots, global, unembedded, independent, international, investigative news hour," *Democracy Now!* routinely features a roster of academics and public intellectuals—founder of peace and conflict studies Johan Galtung, investigative journalist Naomi Klein, and Pan-Africanist scholar Ali Mazrui, to name but a few—who rarely appear in US public broadcasting.

Equally important, grassroots media are well suited to facilitate audience participation in program production and development. That is to say, unlike their counterparts in public radio, whose adherence to bureaucratic structures and professional ideologies limits listeners' participation in program production, community and grassroots radio workers embrace participatory production practices, effectively "rupturing the barrier between audience and broadcasters" (McKenzie, 2008, p. 338).

This rupture between producers and listeners has enormous possibilities for popularizing research through grassroots radio. From a methodological perspective, radio production invites an ethnographic approach to data collection. Indeed, field recordings and other sound elements—ambient sound, musical performances, storytelling, interviews, as well as all manner of "found sound" such as archival recordings and the like—challenge commonplace definitions of what constitutes "data." As for distribution, radio represents a flexible alternative to traditional research publication in books and journals: one that not only makes research more accessible to nonspecialists, but also, quite literally, preserves the voices of research subjects in an intimate and engaging fashion.

Thus, popularizing research through grassroots radio has consequences for researchers and research subjects alike. As Daniel Makagon and Mark Neumann observe, "audio recordings can provide qualitative researchers with opportunities to more fully engage the people and places being studied while functioning as an alternative to a written representation of cultural life" (Makagon & Neumann, 2008, p. 2). All of which is to suggest that radio is uniquely suited to popularizing research in terms of its production and distribution, its form as well as its content. The rest of this chapter considers all of this by way of some reflections on the making of *Hard Times Come Again No More*.

Chatting with Russell

DePauw University is a liberal-arts institution located in Greencastle, Indiana. Not long after joining the faculty in 2002, I began hearing stories about the much beloved and admired Dr. Russell J. Compton. By all accounts, Compton's reputation for "engaged pedagogy" (hooks, 1994) and his commitment to social justice endeared him to generations of faculty, students, and staff. Compton remained a fixture on campus well into his nineties. He was a frequent visitor to classes and was invariably in attendance when guest speakers arrived at DePauw. An attentive and respectful listener, Russell Compton was a walking, talking advertisement for "lifelong learning." And yet, apart from recognizing his name from the campus Peace & Justice Center, incoming students and newly hired faculty and staff were largely unaware of Compton's legacy.

In my capacity as faculty advisor for DePauw's student television, I seized upon the idea of producing a video profile of the university's "elder statesmen." However, during our initial recording session, I became aware of the shortcomings of my medium of choice as well as my overall approach. For instance, lengthy video interviews under hot lights would be physically demanding for the elderly Compton. Equally important, Russell was a bit reluctant to talk about himself in a one-on-one interview. He was more lively and forthcoming in small-group settings. Finally, in the absence of still photographs and moving pictures documenting Compton's career, a video would be visually limited to a series of "talking head" shots of Compton and other interviewees. In sum, I began to question whether or not video was a suitable medium for this project.

I soon turned my attention to radio documentary. Specifically, I decided to produce an oral history of Compton's life and times. This approach had several benefits. First, audio recording complemented Compton's teaching philosophy based on dialogue and active listening. Over the course of our interviews, I came to appreciate the significance of Compton's "dialogic" approach to teaching and learning. My assistant producer, Amira Kokor, and I adopted this conversational approach to our interviews with faculty, students, and staff—all with impressive results. Second, audio recording was less time and labor intensive than video production. This gave us greater flexibility during the production phase of the project. For instance, I could sit down with Compton and a few colleagues while recording conversations in an informal fashion. Third, as I hadn't produced a radio feature since the days of analog recorders and reel-to-reel editing, this project gave me the opportunity to acquaint myself with radio production in the digital realm.

Over time, I also came to recognize the "therapeutic" dimensions of this project. During one memorable conversation, Compton recalled an occasion, prior to his arrival at DePauw University, when his activism got him in "hot water" with college administrators. As it happened, this painful incident had faint echoes with my recent experience at DePauw—an episode that, among other things, derailed the Compton documentary for nearly a year. Suffice it to say, chatting with Russell reaffirmed my commitment to engaged pedagogy at a decisive moment in my teaching career. More important, the production of this oral history unearthed a tradition of social-justice work at DePauw University, a legacy of activism and dissent that is rarely acknowledged on an otherwise conservative campus. As student co-producer Amira Kokor observed: "Not only does [the documentary] very respectfully honor Dr. Compton, but it also sheds some light on the noteworthy progressive activities and hardworking students at DePauw, which we know don't get much, if any, press."

In short, the medium of radio proved an exceptional vehicle to capture, and to some extent enact, Dr. Compton's teaching philosophy. What's more, the documentary created a legible history of progressive campus activism at DePauw University: a tradition that was uncovered through the process of popularizing research. As we shall see, the grassroots production and distribution of this project likewise helped popularize research, insofar as new knowledge was generated by program producers and interview subjects in a collaborative fashion.

Production and Distribution

In his later years, Russell Compton met once or twice a week with two dedicated DePauw University staff members, Sarah Ryan and Valerie Rudolph, to review campus activities, discuss current events, and socialize a bit. Sarah and Valerie invited me to sit in on these weekly meetings, a Marantz field recorder at the ready, and join their conversations. These freewheeling, roundtable discussions yielded a great many details of Russell Compton's personal and professional life: his childhood in rural Indiana, his upbringing in a Quaker faith community, and his teaching and activism. More often than not, Compton's thoughts returned to the relationship between speaking and listening, education and social justice. In doing so, Compton articulated his teaching philosophy: a pedagogy deeply influenced by the deliberative model of public speaking associated with the Quaker meetinghouse tradition.

Finally, in a bid to keep things "in-house," I enlisted the help of my colleague in the Department of Communication & Theater, Ron Dye, to record Stephen Foster's "Hard Times Come Again No More." This tune was selected for several reasons. First, the song echoes Russell Compton's lifelong commitment to social justice. Second, since much of Foster's work is in the public domain, using this song avoided the costs and logistics associated with obtaining copyright clearances. Third, in keeping with the project's DIY aesthetic, Ron Dye's subtle yet evocative guitar and vocal performance contributed to the "grassroots" character of this program.

If the production of this documentary developed organically over time, the distribution of the finished program was largely a matter of good fortune. I first learned about *Sprouts: Radio From the Grassroots* while attending the 2007 National Media Reform Conference in Memphis, Tennessee. At that meeting, I discussed my plans for the Compton project with the program's outreach coordinator. A few months later, *Sprouts* contacted me with a tentative airdate for the documentary. The prospect of nationwide distribution through the Pacifica network spurred me to complete post-production in a timely fashion. The documentary was edited using Audacity, an open-source, cross-platform audio editing program. As the airdate approached, the staff of *Sprouts* provided constructive criticism on several rough cuts. The completed program had its broadcast premiere on September 6, 2007, and has since been archived, along with hundreds of very fine grassroots radio programs, on the *Sprouts* website.

Conclusion

The significance of Pacifica radio's distribution of this audio documentary was not lost on Russell Compton. Despite the network's relative obscurity—a factor that limited the audience for *Hard Times Come Again No More*—Compton was well aware of Pacifica's history. Founded in the late 1940s by San Francisco Bay Area conscientious objectors, Pacifica aimed to reinvent broadcasting as a mechanism for promoting peace and justice through radio communication (Land, 1999). What's more, the Quaker traditions of witnessing and deliberative democracy that informed Compton's teaching philosophy likewise influenced the founders of Pacifica. In this respect, I could not have found a more appropriate venue to distribute a program about Russell Compton's life, times, and legacy.

In terms of the present discussion, I hasten to add that Pacifica endeavored (with mixed results) to overcome the "ivory towerism" (Land, 1999, p. 38) of scholars, public intellectuals, and political dissidents during the early years of the Cold War. In the years since, the Pacifica network's radical politics, countercultural aesthetics, and internecine struggles have limited its ability to reach popular audiences. Nevertheless, Pacifica's iconoclastic approach to broadcasting was, and remains, an effort to popularize research as well as dissent.

References

Atton, C. (2001). *Alternative media*. London: Sage.

Day, R. (2009). *Community radio in Ireland: Participation and multiflows of communication*. Cresskill, NJ: Hampton Press.

Downing, J. (2000). *Radical media: Rebellious communication and social movements*. Thousand Oaks, CA: Sage.

Free Speech TV. (n.d.). About. Available at http://www.freespeech.org/about.

Gumucio Dagron, A. (2001). *Making waves: Stories of participatory communication for social change*. New York: Rockefeller Foundation.

Halleck, D. (1984). Paper Tiger Television: Smashing the myths of the information industry every week on public access cable. *Media, Culture & Society, 6*, 313–318.

Halleck, D. (2002). *Hand-held visions: The impossible possibilities of community media*. New York, NY: Fordham University Press.

hooks, bell. (1994). *Teaching to transgress: Education as the practice of freedom*. New York: Routledge.

Howley, K. (2005a). *Community media: People, places, and communication technologies*. Cambridge: Cambridge University Press.

Howley, K. (Producer). (2005b). *Victory at sea? Culture jamming Dubya* (video recording).

Howley, K. (Producer). (2007). *Hard times come again no more: A tribute to Russell Compton* (audio recording). Available athttp://www.pacificanetwork.org/radio/content/view/309/47/.

Howley, K. (Ed.). (2010). *Understanding community media*. Thousand Oaks, CA: Sage.

Land, J. (1999). *Active radio: Pacifica's brash experiment*. Minneapolis, MN: University of Minnesota Press.

Makagon, D., & Neumann, M. (2008). *Recording culture: Audio documentary and the ethnographic experience*. Thousand Oaks, CA: Sage.

McChesney, R. W. (1995). *Telecommunications, mass media and democracy: The battle for control over US broadcasting, 1928–1935*. Oxford: Oxford University Press.

McKenzie, C. (2008). "Radio in/for research." In J. G. Knowles & A. L. Cole (Eds.), *Handbook of the arts in qualitative research*, (pp. 337–349). Thousand Oaks, CA: Sage.

Rodriguez, C. (2001). *Fissures in the mediascape: An international study of citizens' media*. Cresskill, NJ: Hampton Press.

Rodriguez, C., Kidd, D., Stein, L. (Eds.). (2009). *Making our media: Global initiatives toward a democratic public sphere* (Vol. 1). Cresskill, NJ: Hampton Press.

CHAPTER TWELVE

Music of the Streets

Bringing Local Rappers to the Ivory Tower

Hinda Mandell & Carol M. Liebler

Everything seemed to be in place: the rappers had arrived on campus at Syracuse University and sound-checks for the afternoon hip-hop symposium were well underway. One hip-hop artist, known as Cream da General, was testing the microphone with his song about aspiring wealth accumulation. "Get them stacks [of cash]," he rapped.

Other rappers were clustered around pizza boxes. We were all wolfing down a few slices of pizza nourishment just before the 2 P.M. curtain call, going over last-minute stage instructions for the event. After our semester-long research study involving in-depth interviews with 31 Syracuse rappers, we were about to commence a campus symposium that stemmed from this research at the S. I. Newhouse School of Public Communications. But in the short time leading up to the event, we were just a group of four graduate students and seven rappers hanging out together.

By now we've come to know these local artists. Their cell phone numbers were keyed into our mobile phones, and an unexpected encounter at the local grocery store would result in chit-chat about school or work or kids. We didn't think this relationship—a new take on the standard "town and gown" interaction—was all that unique. But rewind to the fall of 2008, a few months prior to the symposium, and we were more than a little apprehensive about how a group of 20-something graduate students could possibly woo city rappers to participate in a school research project. What was in it for them? Yet on December 5, 2008, as people from across campus *and* across town began to file into the auditorium for this first-of-its-kind event, it was clear there was interest in the rappers and what they had to say. People from this private university were curious, as were members of the community. That much was clear. How in the world did we get here?

The Research Project

Good teaching prompts students to step outside their comfort zones and to pursue research questions beyond what they may already know or think they know. Indeed, the four of us in our research group would never have made an effort to learn about what it means to be an aspiring, small-city rapper—light-years away from the craved international limelight—if it weren't for Carol Liebler's class "Media and Diversity." At the core of this graduate-level course is a group project that engages with a qualitative method, such as interviews or focus groups, to answer questions about the media environment and the less heard voices, or misrepresented voices, that circulate within it.

The aim of this class research project is for students to engage in diversity work that is anchored outside the classroom. As part of the course requirements, each master's student is expected to conduct seven in-depth interviews on the group's research topic, each interview lasting about 45 minutes. Each PhD student conducts ten interviews on the topic. Students then transcribe the audio-recorded interviews and analyze them according to established qualitative data-analysis guidelines. A key goal of this research is for students to have the experience of interviewing people across lines of race, ethnicity, class, sexual orientation, (dis)ability, and/or age.

Our group became interested in the Syracuse rap scene after one student, Hinda Mandell, noticed a hip-hop recording studio down the street from her apartment. The brightly decorated studio with colorful graffiti tags piqued her curiosity about the people who rent it out by the hour and the type of music they produce there. The other group members agreed that interviewing rappers would place them in an interviewing space they've never been before.

None of us previously had any interactions with rappers from Syracuse or anywhere else. In fact, three of the students in our group had just arrived in the US to begin their graduate work. Adeniyi Amadou is from France; Arushi Sen is from India; and Kris Alcantara from the Philippines. Hinda Mandell is from the Boston suburbs. The four of us were adept at navigating international cities, and most of us were fluent in more than two languages. But when it came to interacting with and interviewing Central New York hip-hop artists, we wondered if we'd be able to speak the same language. In other words, we had preconceptions we'd need to overcome in order to engage meaningfully with this type of work.

We embarked on this journey one night in the fall of 2008. Hinda drove Adeniyi and Arushi in her red Corolla to the recording studio, hoping to speak to a few hip-hop artists and present them with our pitch as to why they should become our research participants. We were nervous. After all, we were putting ourselves on the line and keenly aware that our pitch would likely end in outright rejection. And then there was the matter of Hinda's dog, the miniature, white fluffy kind that screams upper-middle-class. At least that's what worried Adeniyi. Nigel, Hinda's retired show-dog champion, was strutting alongside us in the gravel parking lot by the recording studio. We were trying to be cool, not over-eager grad students clearly exhibiting social-class markers that might turn the rappers against us before they even got a chance to hear our pitch. Adeniyi was worried that Nigel was ruining our slim chance of wooing rappers to the research project.

That's when we met Runnamuck, a hip-hop artist and Syracuse entrepreneur who runs More Than Music, a retail outlet adjacent to the recording studio. At first we were taken aback by his name. Runnamuck? Who goes by Runnamuck, we thought? Having never met rappers before, we didn't realize that they would be known by their rap name and not the name on their birth certificate (for Runnamuck, that would be Dwayne). But it makes sense, since rap superstars such as Jay-Z, 50-Cent, T. I., and Lil Wayne, go by their "nom de rap." So why not

Runnamuck? He is, after all, working toward hip-hop success. He also grew up in the Brooklyn, New York, projects close to where 50-Cent came of age.

We made our research pitch to Runnamuck and he seemed outright interested—happy to help, even. And he seemed to care less about the small canine, Nigel, panting at his feet. Runnamuck introduced us to other rappers we could interview for our project. We used this "snowball method" to meet more and more Syracuse recording artists until we met the required number for our group: 31.

The rappers' stories of hardship and perseverance left us, as interviewers, vacillating between feeling sad and uplifted. Yet there were also challenges to conducting this work. One such challenge was a cultural one. However, it is first necessary to provide a brief description of rap music in order to ground it culturally, in the gritty city environment from which it was born. As Rose (1994, p. 2) describes it, "rap music is a black cultural expression that prioritizes black voices from the margins of urban America […and] a form of rhymed storytelling accompanied by highly rhythmic, electronically based music." The genre emerged in the 1970s in the South Bronx of New York as part of a larger hip-hop culture. In rap music, stories of and from "the street" form the backbone of its content. Forman (2002) compares the centrality of "the street" in rap music to the importance of pickup trucks and bars in country music. Therefore, it's clear that rap is a cultural artifact.

It's also reasonable to assume that those unfamiliar with it and its associative elements may face a learning curve when encountering it, just as we'd expect the same learning curve for any other cultural experience. Hinda experienced firsthand this cultural challenge as a result of a linguistic misunderstanding when interviewing one of the rappers, Cream da General. She was unfamiliar with the slang he used. Here is an excerpt from the October 2008 interview at an off-campus eatery known as Funk 'n Waffles.

> CREAM DA GENERAL: I got a song called "my life" that's basically about like the past few years of my life and in the song I start talking about everything going good. And everything going good in the beginning of the song go bad at the end. I talk about how I don't have no job . . .
>
> HINDA MANDELL: But you do have a job.
>
> CREAM DA GENERAL: Now I do. Now I do. But how I didn't have a job but I still have money in my pocket; my ride or die—which is my son's mother . . .
>
> HINDA MANDELL: His mother died?
>
> CREAM DA GENERAL: No, "my ride or die," my soldier, my everything.
>
> HINDA MANDELL: Who died?
>
> CREAM DA GENERAL: Na (laughs). It's called—they say my "ride or die." Basically a female that is down for you or whatever.
>
> HINDA MANDELL: I have no idea what you're saying.
>
> CREAM DA GENERAL: They have a term called "ride or die." And it is basically a significant other basically—she's down to ride with you through whatever.

It's clear from this brief exchange that Hinda, a suburbanite who only sporadically listens to rap music on the radio, didn't possess the language skills to understand her research participant's experiences with his girlfriend (his "ride or die"). While the confusion only lasted for a couple of minutes—and in fact acted as a bonding experience for them after Cream da General settled the confusion—it was enough to briefly derail the interview and reinforce the cultural differences between the two.

A second challenge to conducting this research was finding a suitable "payoff" for the participants in this student project. The rappers did not receive any financial compensation from us. Besides any personal enjoyment they may have taken from sharing their experiences with graduate students, the only other benefit they received was a courtesy cup of coffee or donut that the student interviewer purchased for them at the time of the interview.

Popularizing Our Research

It quickly became clear to all of us in our group that these research participants were not only taking the time out of their day to meet with us—to help us, really—but that they had talents and experiences to share with a broader audience beyond our group of four and our professor. It was this motivation to give back to the rappers, by providing them with a large venue to perform, that prompted us to create House of Rap.

Before we explain how we popularized this research, we will first outline some of our research findings. As a result of 31 individual interviews, spanning upwards of 40 hours of research data, we found that the local rappers do not think of themselves in small, localized terms. They see their talents as absolute, and they exhibit clear confidence that they are "going places." The artists also articulate that their music represents authentic rap, while the rap of their local competition is fake and amateurish. Finally, many of our interview subjects acknowledge their long road to stardom but say they know they'll get there eventually because of their work ethic and talent. This will distinguish them from their competitors.

When we first came up with the idea of holding a hip-hop symposium at our school, we approached Carol Liebler. She was immediately enthusiastic about the idea and about students extending research beyond the confines of a classroom setting. Liebler directed us toward school staff who could help us in everything from booking the auditorium to helping with publicity to ordering post-symposium dessert refreshments. Liebler brought notice of our planned event to the school's diversity committee, which sponsored the symposium along with the Newhouse communications department. The sponsorships provided us with a stipend that covered printing and refreshment costs. The school administration paved the way for the symposium by letting us book the event in the wood-paneled auditorium, and the public-relations staff helped edit the press release.

Meanwhile, Syracuse photographer Diana Ecker donated her skills by organizing a weekend photo shoot with Runnamuck and Herizon, two of the rappers who would be attending House of Rap. Diana captured photos of them, with the recording studio and a chain-link fence as the backdrops. After visits to a copy center, we mounted the large posters of local rappers onto tripods and placed these posters as event advertisements throughout the three-building Newhouse complex.

Outcomes of Popularizing Research

The effects of the symposium involved significant press coverage and even an award from a national journalism educators' association. House of Rap drew nearly 200 people from the

Syracuse area. The event included a rapper roundtable, musical performances, and a rap battle with a journalism student (who almost won but succumbed to the rapper's lyrical advantage). Students in the audience had the opportunity to ask rappers about how they handle pressure to look and act in a certain way. Rappers spoke from their own experiences about paving a path they hoped would set them apart. The *Syracuse Post-Standard*, the daily newspaper with a print circulation of nearly 170,000 readers, jumped on the House of Rap story. It selected the symposium as the paper's "Best Bet" for Friday, December 5, 2008. A newspaper videographer captured highlights from House of Rap, and placed the video on its website. And the *Post-Standard*'s music critic wrote a glowing review of the event. "It was quite a show," he wrote. "The…rappers answered questions from the heart and rapped from their soul." Liebler and Mandell also earned an honorable mention in the contest "Best Practices in Teaching Diversity," sponsored by the Association for Education in Journalism and Mass Communication.

While the news coverage helped popularize the research to the greater community, and while the honorable mention was a nice pat on the back, the symposium allowed for more personal interactions that may have a lasting effect. After House of Rap, professors went up to the rappers and exchanged contact information with them in hopes of bringing the local artists into the classroom as guest speakers. And the rappers connected with students majoring in film production who offered to produce music videos for them. In the Newhouse lobby immediately following House of Rap, the classic town-versus-gown tension was eased and replaced with a spirit of collaboration. It was clear from House of Rap that the unusual pairing of academics and rappers turned the tables on the traditional conception of education. The rappers schooled us. They also were excited at having the opportunity to make connections with a new audience at the university. After the symposium, Hinda received a number of text message "thank you's" from the rappers, who said they had a blast at the event. (Unfortunately, her cell phone crashed months later and the text messages were irretrievably lost so it's not possible to directly quote from them.)

House of Rap, as a months-long culmination of relationship building, research, planning, and writing, brought home the notion that music has the potential to jumpstart research. In the past, music—as an object of research inquiry—has taken a backseat to academe's primary interest in fine and theatrical arts (Bresler, 2008). Yet a medium that has the potential to literally get people up out of their seats and sway to the beat music can also help popularize research. As an artistic form, music has the rare potential to reach people, lift or lower their moods, even if they do not understand the harmonics of the composition or the lyrics of the song. After all, an upbeat pop song with German lyrics has the same potential to bring people to the dance floor as one written in English. The power of music is its ability to reach people in a way that they can feel and be moved by the beat. (In some cases, individuals with hearing loss are also able to feel the reverberations of a composition's deep base notes.)

Since music can reach its audience in a visceral and emotional way, researchers may want to consider disseminating their findings to the public using music as a backdrop. This can be done in a number of ways. First, findings can be expressed via a spoken-word performance. Second, music can be incorporated into PowerPoint or Keynote research presentations. Third, video or Soundslides productions of research highlights can incorporate music. Finally, a public event featuring a research presentation can use music to help punctuate the opening and closing of the symposium. Research doesn't have to be about music in particular in order for researchers to leverage its power. Instead, music can act as a bridge between the researcher and her audience. This may help the audience understand key findings in a visceral way by matching the tone of the findings to an appropriate musical score. Clearly, some research topics lend themselves to these practices more than others, but we feel a broader audience may be brought to the research table through the use of music.

Back at Syracuse University, the hip-hop artists' beats at House of Rap had much of the audience bobbing their heads. The music helped forge a connection between those on stage and those in their seats. There was synergy. From the researchers' perspective, it might be a bit uppity to say that giving the rappers a chance to perform at a large university is the researchers' way of saying thank you. On the other hand, if researchers work closely with informants and develop a regular interaction with them, it's important to think reflexively about the ways in which researchers can provide a space to let the informants showcase their talents with minimal framing from the researchers. Qualitative research instructs us to let the informants speak for themselves as much as possible (Bogdan & Biklen, 2003). Additionally, while researchers have more power than the informants in qualitative research, it is necessary to make attempts to balance this power by allowing the informants a venue to exercise their own voice and agency.

References

Bogdan, R. C., & Biklen, S. K. (2003). Qualitative research for education: An introduction to theory and methods (4th ed.). Boston, MA: Allyn & Bacon.

Bresler, L. (2008). The music lesson. In J. G. Knowles & A. L. Cole, Handbook of the arts in qualitative research: Perspectives, methodologies, examples and issues (pp. 225–238). Thousand Oaks, CA: Sage.

Forman, M. (2002). The hood comes first: Race, space and place in hip-hop music. Middletown, CT: Wesleyan University Press.

Rose, T. (1994). Black noise: Rap music and black culture in contemporary America. Hanover, NH: Wesleyan/University Press of New England.

CHAPTER THIRTEEN

Audio Documentary

Hearing Places and the Representation of Sonic Culture

Mark Neumann

One time when I was recording sounds on the streets of New Orleans' French Quarter, a tourist stopped to ask what I was doing. I always packed my recorder, headphones, and stereo microphone when traveling. Compared to other tourists with cameras and video recorders, I stood out. I was a little self-conscious about wearing the gear and receiving curious glances, but I liked to walk city streets wearing headphones—using the microphone as a kind of divining rod, amplifying certain sounds and filtering out others, depending on where it pointed. I followed specific sounds coming through the microphone. The microphone oriented me to the city's soundscape, gave me direction, and ultimately revealed a map of the streets' sonic culture. I tried to explain this to the tourist in the French Quarter that afternoon, and he seemed to understand.

"We visited South Africa and we've got hundreds of pictures," he said, "but I wish I had a recording of the sound of the rain in the forest. That's something that the photographs don't give you."

Anyone making or listening to such recordings knows this is true. Sound recordings evoke visual images that can recall and represent a sense of places and people that are conveyed differently than in written form. Even now, when I listen to the tapes of my "soundwalks"[1] from years ago, I remain intrigued by how they call forth images of specific cities as a series of scenes brought to life as sound. Listening to my tapes from the French Quarter, I hear street musicians playing Sticks McGhee's "Drinkin' Wine Spo-Dee-O-Dee" and Louis Jordan's "Caldonia," but I also hear tap shoes clicking a rhythm on pavement as two teenage boys dance for tips on Bourbon Street; clinking plates, cups, spoons, and the random conversations of a busy Café Du Monde; and New Orleans resident Tyrone Bowie standing on the banks of the Mississippi River playing "Somewhere Over the Rainbow" on his sax, harmonizing his instrument with the horn of a passing barge. These tapes were made in 1994, more than a decade before Hurricane Katrina devastated New Orleans, and they are full of details, voices, sounds of a city—like any recording—that are specific to the time of their making. While my own recordings initially started as a personal passion, I easily connected the virtues of sound recording with its possibilities for doing ethnographic work. This chapter and its accompanying audio documentary detail a project I conducted to document interaction at Jim Morrison's grave at Père-Lachaise Cemetery in Paris.

Historical Background

Clearly, audio recording is not new to ethnographic fieldwork. Since the late 19th century, folklorists and anthropologists have employed the technology in their work. For example, J. Walter Fewkes (1890) recorded Passamaquoddy tribal stories and songs on the St. Croix River using wax cylinders. These recordings were the basis for his published work. Fewkes' experiments with the Passamaquoddy eventually continued in New Mexico by recording Zuni songs. In the 1920s, Robert Winslow Gordon recorded hundreds of wax cylinders of American folk songs from sailors, stevedores, hoboes, and the people of Appalachia. He published transcripts of these songs in *Adventure* magazine. By 1928, Gordon was the nation's expert on collecting folk music and named first director of the Library of Congress Archive of American Folk Song.

Fewkes and Gordon exemplified the same impulses toward a practice of "salvage ethnography" motivating many anthropological field studies at that time. They aimed to rescue disappearing cultures from erasure by the engines of modern progress through documenting, recording, and thereby saving the language, songs, and stories. For the most part, sound recordings served as the basis for textual transcriptions, incorporated into academic journals or, in Gordon's case, as a popular magazine. Gordon held a faculty position at the University of California, Berkeley, but few of his colleagues appreciated his fieldwork with recording folk songs and, as Debora Kodish (1986) points out in her biography of Gordon, "many expressed the wish that he would spend his time on more orthodox academic pursuits." In a similar vein, Norm Cohen (1974) admired Gordon's prolific collection of more than 3,000 folk songs, but wondered, "why did Gordon never publish a case study based on his research?"

For those invested in the traditions of academic research as published journal articles, sound recording was typically viewed as an avenue for conducting fieldwork and interviews, but not a medium for displaying that research on its own. The primary vehicle for sharing academic research was (and still is) the printed word. David Morton's (2000) history of sound-recording technology notes that even academics who have been invested in oral history relegated their actual sound recordings to a secondary status in their research. "Partly for practical reasons, almost all oral history archives sought to transcribe taped interviews into typewritten documents," observes Morton (2000), recalling, "through the early 1960s Columbia University among others routinely destroyed the original recordings following their transcription."

The ethnographic potential of audio documentary work is not new. Although sound recordings have typically been given a back seat to written ethnographic texts, I am reminded that radio producer Tony Schwartz used a tape recorder in 1948 to begin documenting the migration of Puerto Ricans to New York City. Schwartz recorded over an eight-year period, taping immigrants learning to speak English, the sounds of airports, neighborhoods, and children playing in the streets, interviews with people who arrived and interviews with people who saw their neighborhoods changing from the new population. Schwartz edited the recordings together as *Nueva York: A Tape Documentary of Puerto Rican New Yorkers*, which was released by Folkways Records in 1955. These recordings have mostly been forgotten. In the following decades, anthropologists and cultural critics would begin to consider how a "crisis of cultural authority" and an examination of the representational politics found in ethnographic texts, among other things, would engender calls for new modes of representation. While these critiques enlivened ethnographic discourse, actual experiments in ethnographic work came at a much slower pace.

I took to heart the ideas of influential critics who called for new representational forms. James Clifford's conception of a "dialogic" approach to "writing culture" is, perhaps, one of the most convincing critiques for rethinking ethnographic practice. Clifford's views were heavily influenced by the dialogical conception of the novel developed in the critical work of Mikhail Bakhtin. For Bakhtin, the novel is an arena of multiple voices and discourses engaged in dialogue with each other; these discourses animate the novel through their differences as they respond to each other in the text. Clifford expanded Bakhtin's dialogic approach as a way of thinking and writing about culture. It is a polyphonic view of culture and entails an ethnographic practice of listening to a multiplicity of voices in dialogue with each other. Although such a conception of culture (and ethnographic work) has primarily remained a textual endeavor, a dialogic approach is a useful metaphor for using sound recording in the production and dissemination of ethnographically based work.

The Research Project

My interest in Jim Morrison's grave at Père-Lachaise Cemetery in Paris emerged as I was completing an ethnography of tourism at the Grand Canyon (Neumann, 2001). While working on that book, I had initially used a tape recorder for interviews, as many ethnographers do, but increasingly found that recorded sound served me well in other ways. Recording conversations, tour guides, the ambience of trails, campgrounds, visitor centers, parking lots, and hotel lobbies all provided me with a rich source of "notes" that allowed me to write about the canyon's scenes and events in detail. As I was finishing the canyon project, I was invited to Paris to lecture about ethnographic methods. I visited Père-Lachaise cemetery and began to record the sounds of the cemetery. I eventually found my way to Morrison's grave and was surprised that the normally quiet and somber atmosphere of the cemetery was, by comparison, full of vitality. People stood around the grave speaking openly and enthusiastically about their passion for Morrison. Some sang songs and played guitars. Others carried boom boxes and played music by The Doors, Morrison's band. Hardcore fans and curious tourists mingled in the carnival-like atmosphere.

I had spent several years watching tourists wander around the rim of Grand Canyon, gazing and hiking into the empty chasm. Here, among the cemetery's crowded tombs, people huddled around a very different space of absence, performing rituals, making sense of Morrison's legacy, and reflecting on their own reasons for their pilgrimages. Initially I thought I might write an interesting article about fan culture in Paris, and I responded by recording interviews with people at the grave and making photographic portraits of those who came to stand over Jim's bones.

Through the generous invitations of my Parisian colleague, I was able to make annual trips to teach in Paris, and I kept going back to Père-Lachaise for more photographs and sound recordings. I thought I might use these recordings for some kind of audio documentary, and I strived to make good recordings. In many ways, my recordings were field notes that would eventually help me in writing about Morrison's grave. But I also knew that I would need clear recordings that could be edited together to create a self-standing audio work.

Getting good sound recordings is a challenge. At Père-Lachaise, I used a Sony PCMM1 DAT (digital audio tape) recorder and an Audio Technica 835b shotgun microphone. This microphone is excellent for focusing on a sound source, particularly amidst competing sounds. At Morrison's grave, groups of people are frequently in conversation, playing music, laughing. The shotgun mic is exceptional for focusing on a single sound source. It works well for conducting interviews, too. When I record, I try to collect a mix of sounds and interviews that will give me a variety of choices when it's time to edit. For example, one person brought a cassette-tape player with an external speaker to the cemetery and was playing "Strange Days" from a cassette tape. The batteries in her player were running out and the song sounds distorted. I recorded the music from her cassette player because it sounded different, worn out, and it added a new dimension to the final sound portrait. In addition to specific sounds and interviews, it's a good idea to record several minutes of the space where the action and the interviews are taking place. Such recordings serve as sound bed that helps when editing interviews because the background sound remains the same.

The equipment I used (a DAT recorder, shotgun mic, and headphones) when I recorded at the cemetery cost about $700 when I purchased it in the mid-1990s. Today, I use a Zoom H4n digital recorder (approximately $300) and a Rode NTG2 shotgun mic (approximately $275). It is a relatively small investment considering the high-quality digital recordings such equipment allows. Regardless of the recorder, I always recommend using an external mic because it allows for better control and sound quality. And I always wear headphones so I hear exactly what the microphone is picking up.

After assembling a wide variety of recordings, I shared them with independent radio producer Barrett Golding, who in addition to producing numerous audio-documentary works for public radio, is also the founder of HearingVoices.com, a collection of audio works created by some of the best independent radio producers working today. Golding listened to my recordings and edited them to create a sound portrait of Jim Morrison's grave, incorporating sounds and interviews I made over various visits to the Parisian cemetery. I had tried to edit a sound portrait from some of my recordings, but it relied too heavily on The Doors music and bootleg recordings of Morrison's rants. Working with Golding was a collaboration. I had the recordings, and he had a level of editing experience I greatly admired. Working with someone who had never visited the site and who had not made the recordings was an asset to the development of the piece. Golding was focusing purely on the sounds and interviews that appeared most interesting to him. He took the lead editing and together we made decisions about the final version of the work. Having someone who was neither attached to the recordings, nor had a reference point for their origin, was considerably beneficial to this project.

The concept of a sound portrait involves the creative layering of recordings that allows the listener to become "transported" into the sonic environment of the recording. As with the writing of ethnographic scenes, the sound portrait blends sounds that are descriptive of the place and provide evidence of what it feels like to be there. These sonic scenes can be amplified and made meaningful through the use of interviews that offer narration and self-reflection about what people are doing there. Producing a sound portrait is a highly creative endeavor that requires recognition of how sounds can be used to give a sense of place as well as how moments of silence, and the fading in and out of sounds, can signal transitions to new scenes.

Interviews are equally important in that they allow for a narrative to develop that guides the listener through the sonic "space" of the sound portrait. For example, in the sonic portrait of Morrison's grave, the listener hears an improvised blues song performed by a visitor who sings

"I went to Paris, I went to see the Lizard King's grave . . ." In addition to his guitar and voice, we hear the voice of someone speaking in French. These sounds fade and the voice of another visitor says: "What I did while I was at the grave? I just smoked a cigarette with Jim Morrison." All of this happens within the first minute of the sound portrait and it serves to locate the listener in a specific place through the unique sounds recorded in that place but also through cues ("I went to Paris," the sound of the French language). Including the visitor's reiteration of the question ("What I did while I was at the grave") provides an entry point for beginning a section of the sound portrait where interviews provide the description of the ways people ritualize their visits to Morrison's grave. His description of lighting two cigarettes, placing one on the grave and smoking the other is then followed by an interview with a photographer who often visits Père-Lachaise. She offers her observations on the many visitors she's seen pay their respects to Morrison. Through the editing of these sounds and interviews, the sound portrait embodies a dialogic quality where a sense of scene and action unfolds as an audio composition. The voices and sounds respond to each other to create a whole that puts the listener in the space of the scene, surrounded by music, environmental sounds, and the narration of visitors describing what is happening, what they are doing there, and why they have made the pilgrimage.

The sound portrait is an audio work that does not rely on a single authoritative narrative voice. Instead, it works in concert with the imaginative participation of the listener. To some extent, this idea echoes the "theatre of the mind" that has always been part and parcel of radio drama. In this case, the listener is making sense out of the multitude of voices and sounds—what Bakhtin called "heteroglossia"—that are woven together to create the sonic fabric that becomes a holistic representation, an acoustic world that exists entirely of sounds and voices knitted together.

I was fortunate to work with Golding on the creation of this sound portrait. He is a skilled sound editor who can tell a story with voices and sounds. My experience in doing fieldwork and conducting interviews provided a range of strong recorded material he could draw from when producing the layered composition of this sound portrait. Although I initially considered this work an ethnographic experiment, the finished work found a more popular audience through its broadcast on American Public Media's radio program *The Savvy Traveler*.[2] Working with Golding, a longtime radio producer, provided us with a network of people in public radio. He sent the project to several of them and ultimately *The Savvy Traveler* picked it up. This sound portrait was initially broadcast on the program that aired during the week of February 6, 2004, under the title "Communing with Jim Morrison's Spirit." Although a lack of funding resulted in the end of *The Savvy Traveler* radio program, its programs still exist in the form of a web archive.

Golding is at the helm of HearingVoices.com and he is continually putting programs together under different themes. Repurposing existing stories in new thematic packages is a way to get different venues to broadcast work, and different audiences to hear them. In addition to *The Savvy Traveler* broadcast, the sound portrait about Morrison's grave is also part of the HearingVoices.com website as a single story and as a contribution to self-contained program, "Fans and Bands: Groupies, Gravediggers, and Rock 'n' Roll Singers" that aired several times as part of the *Hearing Voices* radio-series broadcast on National Public Radio. The sound portrait also received a Silver Reel award from the National Federation of Community Broadcasters in 2005.

Conclusion

All of these venues seem to exist at a distance from those worlds where academic work typically circulates. The sound portrait of Morrison's grave shares more with radio journalism than the kind of text one might find in an academic journal. It does, however, display many of the same principles driving contemporary ethnographic work. It strives toward representing people and places in a manner that allows people to speak for themselves; it conveys a dialogic approach to understanding cultural life through a juxtaposition of sounds and voices mutually informing each other; and it is an open text inviting multiple interpretations among listeners. Audio-based documentary illustrates what ethnographic work might take as model for achieving a sense of dialogue between researchers, subjects, and audiences. One difficulty in grasping the potential of audio work as a medium for ethnographic inquiry is that it has been the province of the recording industry and radio. Both are forms of popular entertainment and have thrived at some distance from academic inquiry.

My own work with sonic representation, however, has been infused by the work being done by so many radio producers who use sound in the spirit of understanding and representing cultural life to reach broader audiences than those of academic publishing. Collaborating with Barrett Golding on this sound portrait was an education in how to use sound innovatively and imaginatively, and still accomplish some of the same goals achieved in ethnographic writing. Audio-documentary work need not be confined to the broadcast signals of radio stations. Internet websites have become an avenue toward disseminating all types of documentary work. Because of this, the conventions for creating sonic representations are not bound by those of broadcast traditions. Websites offer new venues for finding new audiences for ethnographic work, for experimenting with the use of sound, and perhaps enlarging the ability of people to understand people and places through new forms of representation.

Notes

1. Hildegard Westerkamp first used the term "soundwalking" in 1974. I discovered her essay many years after I started making my own recordings. Westerkamp's essay was an invitation for people to recover the quality of sound in their surroundings. It was not so much an effort to record, but to tune in and appreciate the sonic environment.
2. The chapter page at www.popularizingresearch.net provides a link to the sound portrait.

References

Cohen, N. (1974). Robert W. Gordon and the second wreck of "Old 97." *The Journal of American Folklore*, *87*, 12–13.

Fewkes, J. W. (1890). A contribution to Passamaquoddy folklore. *Journal of American Folklore*, *3*, 257–280.

Kodish, D. (1986). *Good friends and bad enemies: Robert Winslow Gordon and the study of American folksong*. Urbana: University of Illinois Press.

Morton, D. (2000). *Off the record: The technology and culture of sound recording in America*. New Brunswick, NJ: Rutgers University Press.

Neumann, M. (2001). *On the rim: Looking for the Grand Canyon*. Minneapolis: University of Minnesota Press.

Schwartz, T. (1955/2004). *Nueva York: A Tape Documentary*. First released in 1955 by Folkways Records. Available as MP3 download released by Smithsonian Folkways Recordings.

Westerkamp, H. (1974). Soundwalking. *Sound Heritage*, *3* (4), 18–27.

Part 5

PERIODICALS

CHAPTER FOURTEEN

The Relevance of Relevance

Why and How I Write Op-eds

John Llewellyn

I am no academic "lifer." I earned my PhD after having a career in communication positions in state and local governments in the American South. In all candor, my earlier career has proven to be a genuine bonus for teaching and research, but an actual handicap in my conformance to the special logic that inhabits campuses and the people who run them.

My pre-doctoral background has everything to do with how and why I write op-eds. This is a term of art that reflects the article's position "opposite the editorial page." These 700-word essays are essentially guest editorials; they are sometimes sought by the newspaper, but most often they are written as speculative pieces and then offered to the paper. I sometimes think I could place one op-ed a week if I worked at it and varied the targeted outlets. That is the pace of a columnist though, not of a teacher/scholar. For me, op-eds are a satisfying alternative to the teaching and research that occupy the majority of my professional time. I have engaged in this practice for at least a decade, doing as few as one and as many as four in any given year.

Why Write Op-eds?

In rhetoric, my academic specialty, analysts focus on what Aristotle called "invention," the process of selecting a speaking topic. When I look at my process of invention regarding op-eds, I find I have covered a wide array of topics. What central theme organizes those topics? Every one of these issues was a topic I felt strongly about and I thought my perspective would enrich the public discussion on each topic.

Do you have to be a scholar to identify important topics and write about them? Of course not, but you need interesting ideas, some expertise that makes you a credible source, and the ability to express those ideas clearly. Scholars do have special advantages in preparing op-eds. We work with ideas all the time and recognize patterns and anomalies. We can convey a great depth of knowledge in the realms we study. Writing, albeit sometimes in a turgid academic voice, is how we make known our research findings. The label "professor" carries a lot of clout in society at large and with the media. We often do not recognize this fact because we live in a world thoroughly populated by professors and we know that the quality of opinions in that world varies widely.

As scholars, we are equipped to do the careful thinking and writing that an op-ed requires. That leads us to the larger question: Why should a scholar write op-eds? As a group, we are accused of residing in an "ivory tower" and being completely disconnected from common sense. You may think that judgment is misguided and nonsensical, but you should ask yourself what basis an average citizen would have for any other opinion. The "absent-minded professor" is a cliché, but just barely. This ill-fitting reputation has sprung, in part, from the fact that scholars rarely interact with the communities in which they live. You may be the world's leading expert on subject X; that expertise may be recognized by fewer than 100 specialists scattered across the globe. The insights and talent needed to rise to that professorial stature surely can be useful to our neighbors and fellow citizens, but only if we decide to reach out to them. The op-ed is one effective outreach device.

Most scholars operate in a world where teaching, research, and service are primary values. A well-conceived op-ed is a genuine public service to the readership of the publication and the broader community. In order to embrace that claim, you must first appreciate the give-and-take of popular politics and value the intelligence of the average citizen. Surely, as scholars, we are above the norm in intelligence quotient; we can take that conclusion as a given without falling into the delusion that we are the only smart people in town. Our talent obliges, or at the very least invites us to make messages that promote our view of the public good and to share those messages with our neighbors. An op-ed is an investment in what argumentation scholars call "bilaterality." That term acknowledges the fact that when you argue, you also open yourself to the opposition's arguments and give them serious consideration. The public interest benefits when there is a clash of strong arguments.

When I write and promote an op-ed to a local newspaper it is because I think I have a novel perspective: either to identify an issue that has not been recognized in public life or to explore a new angle on an issue of public concern. In either case, newspaper editors are jealous guardians of their product; they want quality on their pages, but they also want a diversity of perspectives and an involved community. A professor's well-conceived and well-executed essay on a timely topic should have a better-than-average chance of success.

Following these principles has given me a better than 90 percent success rate in placing op-eds. Why is there 90 percent acceptance? The primary value in the news media is timeliness; the news is a rolling account of social life. Issues rise and fall in public awareness. The editorials that I write and place deal with topics that are current and therefore news: Michael Vick's apology, the consultant's public attack on Andy Griffith, the NCAA Final Four, or President George W. Bush's endorsement of tort reform. My op-eds are a sort of counterpunch, so I have to write and place them promptly while the initial news account is still in the public mind. This process means that you have to pay close attention to the news, which for learned people should be no burden, and then react quickly when an issue takes shape. I have stayed up all night writing a piece where I felt my perspective needed to be aired; I could not rest until I had woven my insights into a coherent argument. If the essay gives a current issue a productive twist, most editors will easily see its news value.

So what explains the 10 percent failure rate? Sometimes I perceive a certain topic as a burning issue, but I'm the only one who smells the smoke. Sometimes my novel perspective is too idiosyncratic; in those instances, my insights do not succeed in reaching a threshold of public understanding. Occasionally, I stew over an issue too long so that by the time I figure out what I want to say, there is no longer an audience for the message. When I have failed with op-eds, it's due to one of two errors: I have not been clear enough within myself about what I want to contribute to the public dialog; or, if I have the clarity, I have not been fast enough in putting those ideas into a coherent argument. Like so many other things in life, propitious timing—what the Greeks called *kairos*—is the key to success with op-eds.

How to Write Op-eds

How do I decide what I will write about? What research seems suited to being popularized? I have no specific rule, but what I respond to are issues where I find myself saying, "The public needs to understand this." Then I try to tell that story in 700 words. Two formative experiences help me in that process. My first doctoral course, one on rhetorical criticism taught by my eventual mentor, required us to write four-page analyses. The principle was that, in four pages, you could either make a salient point or stumble around, but you could not do both. So the premium was on clarity with brevity. The second advantage came from reading a useful article by Murray Davis (1971) titled "That's Interesting!" which explains how to craft a compelling academic essay by juxtaposing it to "what everyone knows."

Davis offers a template for building an interesting argument. He answers the question: What are the rhetorical features that hook readers? He provides a listing of 15 *topoi*, or topics, which will assure attention. For instance, if everyone thinks two processes are unrelated, say the crime scenes of a serial felon and where that felon will choose to live, you can craft a compelling case if you can show that the two are related. That relationship was, in fact, proven by a doctoral student whose day job was with the Royal Canadian Mounted Police. The innovation is now known as geographic profiling. Similarly, if everyone thinks a social trend, say teenagers' extensive use of video games, is negative, you can catch readers' attention by asserting that it is positive. In both cases, you still have to prove your claim, but you have captured public attention for your argument.

Examples

Each essay has an essential message that I want the public to understand. Writing an op-ed is best driven by a clear desire to get across a message as a form of public service. The standard length is roughly 700 words; determine the paper's standard and write to that target. I also have a target publication in mind because the message is often place-specific. So my piece about the NCAA was pitched to the *New Orleans Times-Picayune* while the Final Four was there. The piece on the McDonald's hot-coffee case was directed to the *Albuquerque Journal*, since that city was the site of the original trial. Many of my op-eds treat city and state issues, so they appear in the papers in major North Carolina cities: Winston-Salem, Raleigh, and Greensboro. Unless I know the editors first-hand, I call on the university's public-affairs office to pitch the essay.

After a submission is made, if an editor asks for a revision of some sort, I'm not troubled. That inquiry means we're on the road to getting published and that is the purpose of the exercise. I have never been asked to do violence to my argument; these suggestions come from professionals with decades of experience whose writing has to be understood every day. I always profit from their recommendations.

Here are snapshots of the op-eds that accompany this essay and the core information I intended to impart in each of them.

"Poll conducted on a frothy topic fails to convince." This column was written overnight. A political polling firm produced dubious data to suggest that North Carolina TV legend Andy Griffith was massively unpopular. I simply did not believe that claim and decided to investigate. I went to their website, examined the survey questions, and found that they had tortured their data to reach the desired result. The op-ed explained what the firm had done and how it misrepresented the facts. I used the piece to point out how media often relay, but do not check, assertions by interest groups and thus harm their own credibility and the public interest.

Once this piece was in print, I emailed the editor of the *Outer Banks Sentinel*, the newspaper that serves the town of Manteo and Dare County in the northeastern coastal portion of the state. This is the area where Andy Griffith lives in retirement, and he is not just a celebrity but a respected neighbor. I thought the paper's readers might have seen the news accounts disparaging Griffith and would be interested in knowing how bogus those charges were. The editor was delighted to know of the piece, contacted the *Winston-Salem Journal* editor and got permission to reprint it. So the essay did double duty. This incident underscores a key principle: once you have written something like an op-ed, think of all the possible outlets for the information. You do not want to submit the same piece to more than one media outlet without the agreement of all parties. However, do think of all the media that might be relevant; for instance, an op-ed could be posted to the website of a concerned organization so that the ideas have greater reach and durability.

"What about Garber-Gaines Field?" This essay was written to propose that the field at the city's new downtown baseball park be named for two civil-rights pioneers: a legendary coach at a local HBCU and a groundbreaking female sportswriter. The naming rights to the stadium have been bought by a local bank, despite the fact that the public has funded the vast majority of the project's costs. This is a common practice in modern stadium naming, and to me, it is tantamount to misappropriation of public funds. The public pays 95 percent of the costs and a bank or an airline makes a small payment and then names the stadium. This process makes the public facility seem like a private shrine, since the bank claims the identity of the stadium as its own. The naming of the field was suggested as a way to reassert the public ownership and purpose of the facility and to honor two local sports and civil-rights legends who smoothed the community's path to integration. This essay was intended to reawaken this issue of social and racial justice.

"Reflections of an Early Voter." When the 2008 presidential election was winding down, I decided to vote early and to do so at a predominantly African American voting site. I wanted to experience the social climate at that time and among that community. I reflected on a life begun in the segregated South and the social progress achieved by fits and starts in the intervening decades. I was attempting to describe and understand the local angle on a watershed moment in national history. I publish op-eds with some frequency in the *Winston-Salem Chronicle*, the local paper concerned with issues of minority rights and social justice. The community needs more interchange of ideas and these essays are a modest step in that direction.

"Professional or Political; Officers Decide." There was a major scandal over public-information officers in North Carolina state government and whether they were complying with state open-records laws. Reports showed that these officials were subverting the letter and the spirit of the law and compromising the public's right to know at the direction of political higher-ups. As someone who had worked in that profession for a decade, I weighed in to explain the situation to the wider public and to suggest an outcome that served the public interest. At the political level, I thought the issue was being poorly explained by all sides, so average citizens would be hard-pressed to identify genuinely sound positions and arguments. As a scholar of organizational processes and a veteran of more than a decade in that specific bureaucracy and profession, I thought I knew better than almost anyone how to explain what was really going on and what was at stake. Whether I was right in my assumptions, I felt compelled to offer an informed, but somewhat dispassionate, explanation.

"Art of Pubic-Figure Apology: Michael Vick's Statement Seems Formulated to Move Focus from Fault to Forgiveness." When Vick was convicted of the dog-fighting charges he issued a public statement as an "apology" that was transparent in its goal to minimize and excuse his actions. I took the message apart in order to show readers why it failed as an apology and how it revealed persistent issues with Vick's character, even as he was attempting to evoke a sympathetic reaction. I found this public ritual of apologia (speech of defense of one's character) so transparent and so badly done that I wrote and submitted this analysis while 8,000 miles away teaching in New Zealand.

"What Imus can learn—and teach." When radio host Don Imus insulted the women's basketball team from Rutgers University, the standard hue and cry went up for him to be removed from radio. In public responses to such situations, there is a tradition called "sacrificing the official racist." The person who has uttered the offensive words is banished from the public stage. The premise is that some statements are so horrific that no repair is possible. After decades of applying this logic, we find no improvement in the quality of behavior. Obviously, the ritual banishment has not ended racist discourse. My op-ed suggested that, in lieu of banishment, Imus and the students be brought together in a form of constructive engagement. The plan was not adopted, but I did get a personal email from the president of Rutgers thanking me for the comments. As a public-relations theorist, I was impressed with that level of responsiveness and took it as a sign that Rutgers was carrying out a well-considered plan, even if it was not mine.

"How One Verdict Grew to Myth Status" The piece ran in the *Albuquerque Journal* because the case it addressed, *Liebeck v. McDonald's*, had originated there 11 years earlier. The column was written in response to inaccurate comments from President George W. Bush regarding tort reform. This case is one that I have become expert on and use in my scholarly work. In 2004, in recognition of the verdict's tenth anniversary, I organized a panel at a scholarly convention. It included the judge, a jury member, the local newspaper reporter, and one of the plaintiff's attorneys. The group was meeting for the first time since the trial and spoke to a gathering of scholars about their experiences and reactions to the public misunderstandings of the case.

"When Vietnam Vets Came Home." I targeted this column for Veterans Day 2004. I wanted to explain the spitting accounts in terms of urban legends, which I had researched in depth. The spitting story had been used throughout history to indirectly express frustration from inconclusive wars. Without disputing any individual's account of their experience, the larger point being made was that, whatever our differences, we are not a nation that disrespects the sacrifices of the troops. Whatever our national way forward, I asserted, it can only succeed if we are clear about fundamental character issues. Dealing with this topic and challenging the prevalent myth will result in a lot of what can only be called hate mail. On the other hand, several veterans wrote to say that they had always had their doubts about the stories they had heard. When you write op-eds, especially on sensitive topics, you should be aware that a segment of the population will express their disagreement through hate mail, angry telephone calls to your home, and pillorying you on sites like freerepublic.com. On the other hand, at least they are paying attention; you cannot try to elevate discussion in this manner if you are thin skinned.

"Beyond Victory: Losing's Valuable Lessons." This essay ran in the New Orleans paper in conjunction with the 2003 NCAA men's basketball championship. It expressed the view, based on my research into the rhetoric of coaching, that it is losing, not winning, that is the great teacher. This position is contrary to all of the conventional wisdom about athletics, but true to the experiences of real life.

In all of these op-eds, I take an unconventional stance. These stances are not adopted for their own sake but to express useful alternative points of view and ones that I believe in. The novelty and insight in these essays help to answer the editor's unspoken query: Why should I run this piece? In short, these views are news and newsworthy. They bring together my research to comment on current attitudes and events in the society. In this way, my research is popularized, not primarily for my benefit, but rather to extend scholarly efforts in order to produce practical insight into social issues.

Reference

Davis, M. (1971). That's interesting! *Philosophy of the Social Sciences, 1,* 309–344.

CHAPTER FIFTEEN

A Short Story about Female Characters in Egyptian Soap Operas

Aliaa Dawoud

This chapter will provide an overview of how creative writing was used to expose non-academics to the outcomes of a doctoral dissertation. More specifically, I wrote a short story based on one chapter of my doctoral dissertation, and used four different methods to make it available for non-academics to read. In what follows, I will first provide an overview of how the approach that I used fits in with performance ethnography. This will be followed by an overview of the chapter of my dissertation on which the short story is based. The third section provides a summary of the short story as well as a reflection on how I wrote it. It also explains the methods I used to disseminate the short story to non-academics. Finally, the last section contains some of the feedback I received on the short story from the non-academics who read it.

The idea of using creative writing to present the results of empirical research is not new. It is often used by qualitative researchers in a broad range of disciplines including sociology, anthropology, media studies, women's studies, education, performance studies, and cultural studies. It is referred to as "performance ethnography" (Smith & Gallo, 2007, p. 522). It was therefore an appropriate method to use in this case because my dissertation is a media study that focuses on women and politics.

Like all other performance ethnography texts, my short story "tells a story of the lived experience of others" (Smith & Gallo, 2007, p. 522); my story is based on the focus groups I conducted for my dissertation in which the participants expressed their views on Egyptian women's participation in politics. The purpose of my short story is identical to that of performance ethnography, namely enabling the researcher and the audience to "meet in the liminal (or threshold) space that lies between them" (Smith & Gallo, 2007, p. 522). Yet, I did not read or act the story out to the audience, but they read the short story themselves. Since I disseminated the short story using a website, email, a book, and by providing family with a copy of it, performing it for the audience was simply not necessary or feasible.

Nevertheless, as will be shown towards the end of this chapter, the short story achieved an important objective of performance ethnography, that of conveying some new information to the audience. Furthermore, those who read the short story and provided me with feedback on it expressed a variety of different opinions. This is an observation that many researchers who use performance ethnography make note of, for the audience "tend to understand the text slightly differently based on their gender, ethnicity, social class, or historical or cultural background" (Smith & Gallo, 2007, p. 522). Another factor that seemed to have an impact on how the readers perceived the short story was whether or not they supported women's rights.

A Female Egyptian President: The Study

My doctoral dissertation included an audience study to investigate Egyptian women's views on women's political participation as well as their reception of media treatment of this matter. This section will provide a summary of how I conducted this research. The participants in the audience study consisted of 88 middle-class Egyptian women who are regular viewers of Egyptian drama serials—a genre similar to soap operas. They were all university educated and their ages ranged from 18 to 72. Their occupations included doctors, pharmacists, academics, business professionals, housewives, teachers, TV presenters, undergraduate students, UN employees, engineers, administrators, sociologists, deputy ministers, general managers, engineers, and bankers. They also included people in different relationship statuses.

I chose to interview the participants in groups rather than on an individual basis because previous researchers have noted that people tend to discuss the media products that they consume with others. More specifically, women tend to discuss soap operas with other women, including their mothers, daughters, female co-workers, as well as their female friends. I also ensured that the members of each group consisted of friends and/or relatives in order to come as close as possible to emulating real-life situations.

Since previous researchers have noted that it's preferable to investigate what was on the participants' minds before exposing them to the media content under investigation, I began by asking the participants to describe a female character that they would like to see featured in a drama serial. Depending on the input that they provided me with, I then asked them about other aspects of the character's life. So for example, if they told me about a 40-year-old housewife who is a wonderful mother, I inquired about her relationship to her husband and about her husband's character. After that, I inquired about her siblings, neighbors, friends, and her career. I varied the type and order of questions depending on their input.

After that I screened a clip from a drama serial that directly addresses women's participation in formal politics. The drama serial is called *Mobara Zawgeya* (Marital Match) and one of the main characters in it is a married woman in her mid-40s who is an active member of an opposition political party. Her husband is also a member of the same political party. After screening the clip, I asked the participants to comment on it. Some of them expressed their views on women's political participation straight away. Others commented on other aspects of the clip and so I waited until they expressed all of their views and then started asking them direct questions about women's political participation.

This research revealed that these middle-class university-educated Egyptian women would like women to play an influential role in society. Examples of the types of female characters they would like to see featured in Egyptian drama serials are female rulers, including president and queen, a moderate female Islamic preacher, strong women who are independent and not oppressed by their husbands and women who are capable of striking a balance between their careers and familial duties. Other examples include the president of the body responsible for administering the affairs of the building she lives in, or responsible for its finances, and a woman who heads one of the committees at the club, such as the Cultural or Religious Affairs Committee.

Furthermore, almost all of the participants were willing to vote for a woman who runs for Parliament. In fact, many of them said they are keen on voting for a woman because she would represent them and their issues better in Parliament. Yet they were rather divided when it came to women attaining the post of president. Over 27 percent of the participants were in favour of it; around 20 percent of the participants did not mind it in principle but believed it would be rather problematic in Egypt; 4 percent of the participants were undecided; and around 50 percent of the participants were against it.

Popularizing the Research Results

The short story I produced from my findings is entitled "A Female Egyptian President." It is about three female friends: Sahar, Nadia, and Mona, who gather at Nadia's place to spend some time together and chat. They start off by talking about the latest episode of a drama serial that was aired the night before and they criticize some aspects of it. They then start criticizing drama serials as a whole on the grounds that their plots are repetitive and they tend to be unrealistic. After that they start coming up with creative ideas and plots for drama serials by describing female characters whom they would like to see featured in drama serials. These include women in their 30s who struggle to juggle careers and families, and a woman who plays a significant role in her extended family. Sahar then suggests that a drama serial about a female president should be produced. This leads to a discussion about whether or not women are fit for the presidency and what such a drama serial would be like.

I chose to convey the study's findings in the form of a conversation between three female friends because it is similar to the context in which the research was conducted: focus groups consisting of groups of female acquaintances, family, and/or friends. Another reason behind this decision is that such conversations actually take place in real life in both Egyptian society and elsewhere. Research conducted in various parts of the world has indicated that women tend to discuss soap operas/drama serials with other women.

In order to write the short story, I carefully reread the chapter of my dissertation that included the findings of the focus groups. As I read it, I tried to select which aspects of the results to include in the short story and which ones to leave out. I left out the results that are irrelevant to the theme of this book. My ultimate goal thereafter was trying to ensure that the short story reflected the study's results as much as possible.

Some of the views expressed in the short story are almost direct quotes from the study. For example, in both the chapter and the short story, the characters criticize and mock how servants in drama serials wear full makeup and their hair is dyed, when in reality the attire of Egyptian maids is the complete opposite. Another example is the reference to Hillary Clinton in the short story. When I asked the participants in the study whether or not they supported women attaining the post of president, some of them referred to Clinton. A representative example of the arguments that they put forward was "even Hillary lost the elections in America, where men and women are said to be equal." Thus, I included an almost identical statement in the short story. In addition, all of the ideas for female characters in drama serials that are to be found in the short story were all female characters whom the participants in the study came up with and said they would like to see featured in Egyptian drama serials. These include: a female president; Nefertiti; Shagaret El Dor; a woman who plays a significant role in her extended family; and a woman who is elected to the board of the club and ends up heading one of its committees, such as the Cultural Committee.

In other cases, the thoughts expressed by the characters in the short story are based on inferences from the study. For example, some participants in the study were rather surprised by my question regarding whether or not they supported women attaining the presidential post and some of them actually laughed. That is why in the short story the character Mona is quite alarmed at Sahar's proposition and says "What?! A female president? Here in Egypt? You must be joking!"

I also inserted some phrases in the short story based on my analysis of the study's findings. For example, in the short story, Mona says "I just don't see why they can't be more creative and come up with more interesting plots." I included this phrase in the short story because I believe that the female characters and plots that the participants came up with are far more interesting and creative than the repetitive themes, plots, and characters that are recurrent in drama serials.

Yet I must admit that I failed to include some of the study's findings in the short story. For example, the participants in the study expressed their views on female MPs and some participants were against women attaining the post of president. In addition, some of the participants in the study wanted to watch drama serials about mothers. All of these results are not reflected in the short story.

I used four different strategies to make this short story available to non-academic audiences. I chose a variety of strategies so the short story would be read by as large and diverse a group of people as possible. All of these strategies combined ensured that the short story was read by people from a variety of countries and they also belonged to different age groups.

The first strategy consisted of uploading the short story on a website called Booksie. It's a website that provides aspiring writers with an opportunity to post their work in a platform that is accessed by people from all around the world. Each writer creates an account for free and provides information about themselves on their profile. Writers can then upload short stories, poems, and/or novels. This is an advantage because other websites specialize in just one type of writing, such as poetry, and so writers who write more than one form of writing find it difficult to post all of their work on the same website and build an audience for it. In addition, writers are always required to provide a summary of any piece of writing, which is then made available to potential readers. This provides readers with an insight into the piece of writing without having to click on it and access the full text. Some people have told me this option makes it more interesting.

I have been uploading my short stories and poems on Booksie for some time now and so far a number of people from various parts of the world have read my work. Thus, I have already built an audience on this website and it only made sense that I should upload the short story there.

The second strategy used to disseminate the short story was that I told my students about this book chapter and asked those who were interested in reading the short story to provide me with their email address. I then emailed the story to them and some of them responded with some feedback. I also asked some of my family members to read the story and comment it on it. Finally, I included the story in a book that contains a collection of my short stories and poems. The book will be published shortly.

The Feedback

Some of those who read the short story agreed with the criticism of Egyptian drama serials expressed in it. For example, a 52-year-old married housewife said, "The problems that drama serials address are repetitive and unrealistic and they are always somehow solved at the very end of the drama serial, that's not the way life is." Yet, one reader had some mixed views. A 28-year-old married female physician said, "Drama serials are [indeed] repetitive [but] drama serials about women in their mid-thirties who have kids and are struggling to juggle careers and families are to be found."

The short story led one reader to think about something that had never even crossed her mind. A 28-year-old married female physician said: "I haven't thought about having a female president in Egypt....The president has to control the military and the ministry of interior. He has to be one of them, so we will never have a female President."

Others addressed the idea of producing drama serials about Nefertiti or Shagaret El Dor. For example, a female 17-year-old undergraduate student who intends to major in Integrated Marketing Communication said, "They already produced [a drama serial] about Nefertiti and a movie....about Shagaret El Dor. I don't think they were inspirational."

Finally, the story triggered one reader who has an interest in women's rights into talking about how other types of media treat women. An 18-year-old female undergraduate student who is working toward double majors in Art and Mass Communication said that music videos are a form of regression because they focus on women's bodies; while Mona El Shazli (a prominent female host of an Egyptian talk show) is encouraging women to speak up and play a more significant role in society.

In summary, this chapter has provided an overview of how I used performance ethnography to make some of the findings of a dissertation available to a non-academic audience. I did so by writing a short story based on these results and used four different methods to reach out to potential readers. The readers' comments on the short story demonstrate how rewarding and interesting this process was.

Acknowledgment

I am deeply indebted to my second supervisor, Professor David Gauntlett.

Reference

Smith, C., & Gallo, A. (2007). Applications of performance ethnography in nursing. *Qualitative Health Research, 17*, 521–528.

CHAPTER SIXTEEN

Persuasive Prestidigitation

Exploring the Rhetorical Power of Magical Performance in a Popular Magazine Article

Joseph P. Zompetti

The Metternich Stela, the now-famous inscribed stone slab from ancient Egypt, portrays the magic and persuasion of Isis as, "I am Isis the goddess, the possessor of magic, who performs magic, effective of speech, excellent of words" (Ritner, 2008, p. 34). Seneca the Younger, the controversial Roman philosopher, wrote during the first year of the Common Era that a conjurer's sleight-of-hand was *ipsa delectate*—the deception pleases (Seneca, 1917). He described his fascination with magic in relationship to his fondness for oratorical skill, or persuasion. It should not surprise us, a couple of thousand years later, that there is a connection between persuasion and magic, for both can be pleasing to an audience precisely due to the magic in persuasion, and the persuasion in magic.

Except for Covino (1992), who argues about the magical*ness* in rhetoric, the fields of rhetoric and persuasion have overlooked the art of magic. Scholarly interest in magic has typically occurred in the disciplines of psychology, philosophy, anthropology, and performance studies. Even then, scholars rarely share their research with anyone other than fellow academic colleagues. My interest in magic, however, not only offers a unique perspective regarding persuasion, but it also seeks to bridge different audiences.

Through my research, I explore the scholarship on magic, which is intended for two different audiences: magicians and scholars. While magicians benefit from understanding how to improve their art, non-magician members of the public may find the research interesting (as recent movies and books on magic suggest), and scholars may benefit from additional research in the area of rhetoric and persuasion. This chapter describes how I presented my research to a non-academic public through a magazine article. In what follows, I reflect on the process of publishing in that area and in that medium and genre, and on how some magicians are incorporating my scholarship, as well as on ways in which this particular type of scholarship (i.e., popular culture, entertainment, etc.) is relevant and interesting for non-academics. In so doing, this chapter also seeks to enrich the conversation about how to identify with and ultimately connect with both audiences. On the website for this book, you will find the magazine article, which was published in the periodical *Magic* in May 2010.

Background

Thousands of books, magazine articles, pamphlets, and manuscripts have been written about entertainment magic, most of which focus on different tricks ("effects"), magic history, and theory about the presentation and performance of magic. Very little exploration of magic exists outside the realm of those inside magic, perhaps due to the secretive nature of the magic community. Of course, many magicians have borrowed ideas from the academic community, such as production design, acting, psychology, music, etc. Yet, serious academic study has not directly influenced the magic community as it has other performing arts. Other performance arts have been viewed by academic perspectives throughout history, such as painting, sculpture, music, theatre, dance, and even furniture production and ceramic design. Magic, however, has studied and maintained itself through a system not unlike the master-apprentice model in trade guilds.

So, after centuries of the magic world insulating itself, why would a non-magician scholar want to study magic? How would such a study occur? And, perhaps more importantly, why would the magic community allow the study and why would they think they could benefit from it? These questions are central to my research journey, as I brought my scholarly interests of rhetoric and persuasion to the world of magic.

My research design entailed the use of deep-structured interviews as well as components of participant-observer ethnography (Agar, 1980). In essence, I have become an amateur magician and enthusiast in addition to interviewing more than 70 magicians from around the world to better understand the persuasive techniques used in magical performances. Although I take a highly qualitative methodological approach to this research, the focus of this project is rhetorical. In other words, the purpose of this work is to analyze the rhetorical, albeit persuasive, techniques of magicians that are effective and not effective. By being a participant-observer and through interviews, the rhetorical cues of magicians are ascertained.

According to Aristotle, rhetoric is "the faculty of observing in any given case the available means of persuasion" (1991, p. 1355). The idea that rhetoric focuses on the means of persuasion has guided my view of persuasive acts for many years. Interviewing magicians and examining their performances provides me the opportunity to recognize how persuasion is used in magic. In other words, I look for the techné of rhetorical practices in magical entertainment.

For Aristotle, the techné of rhetoric occurs in three different capacities: *ethos*, *pathos*, and *logos*. These three rhetorical components are used as "proofs" to persuade audiences. *Ethos* is what we commonly refer to as "credibility," which means that a magician's reputation, authority, and credibility can persuade audiences that they are having a magical experience, simply due to the authority and character of the performer. *Pathos* is the use of emotion in a persuasive act, which can include the range of emotions, such as fear, joy, love, pain, ambition, guilt, etc. Thus, in an effort to persuade an audience that the sawing-a-woman-in-half illusion has impact and to make it appear real, a magician might have the woman scream, to appeal to the audience's sense of pain. With *logos*, or logical appeals, a magician might show that handcuffs are real and that a box is actually locked before the magician attempts an escape. The magician can appeal to an audience's reasoning to accentuate the effect. These three rhetorical techniques are extremely useful for a magician to create a moment of wonder, mystery, or awe. A fourth approach, known as "identification," was not elucidated by Aristotle, but rather by a 20th-century scholar named Kenneth Burke. Burke discusses identification as the moment when one person believes they fully share the perspective held by another (Burke, 1969, pp. 20–21).

Houdini, for example, connected—or identified—with his audiences by showing them that their plight from the Great Depression could be overcome, much like he was able to overcome the shackles and straitjackets during his famous escapes.

Popularizing Magic Research

As many magicians have told me during interviews, scholars simply have not paid much attention to the art of magic. Although other arts such as music, dance, theater, etc. have entire scholarly disciplines associated with them, the art of magic does not. Hence, practitioners and experts in magic are very interested in scholars who discuss the importance of magic in various ways, but only if the code of magicians is maintained—keeping the secrets of the effects. Popularizing magic, by means of accessing scholarship to non-academics, is a useful way for many communities (academic and non-academic alike) to appreciate the value of magic in its various ways.

I have always been fascinated by magic, and I am an enthusiast/amateur magician myself. Yet, being an outsider—and an academic at that—poses challenges to entering the magic community. I have been fortunate to meet two individuals who introduced me to magicians and vouched for me in the community—one is an acting professor who also does professional magic, and the other is a professional mentalist who formerly taught communication at the University of Nevada at Las Vegas. Because of them, I began meeting professional magicians. This, in turn, provided an opportunity to meet David Copperfield and visit his secret conjuring-arts museum in Las Vegas, open only to magicians, celebrities, and magic historians. After the honor of experiencing Copperfield's museum, my credibility catapulted as "person of interest" in the magic community, and this gave me the vetting necessary to begin interviewing some of the world's best magicians.

Interviewing magicians was no easy task. Most magicians are easy to contact for booking purposes, but to actually speak or converse via email is quite another situation altogether. Nevertheless, I found that after interviewing a few magicians, it became easier to access others. Additionally, as a newcomer to the magic community, I had no idea what other methods might exist for interviewing magicians, until one of them suggested I attend a magic conference. I attended my first magic conference, which was centered around the theme, "The Theory and Art of Magic," where I also presented on the relationship between rhetoric and magic. As a result of being invited to magic conventions and conferences, I approached the conference host of Magic Live! to request an invitation to that convention so that I could interview some of the world's top magicians. As a result of that relationship, the host, who also edits the periodical *Magic*, asked me to contribute an article that discusses magic from a scholarly perspective. *Magic* is the second-largest magic magazine in the world, and their subscribers are almost entirely magicians and enthusiasts. The result is a direct relationship between my research with the community for which the research is conducted and intended.

Writing for a Popular Magazine

Being invited to write a piece for *Magic* magazine was flattering and exciting. But it was also challenging. As an academic, I am accustomed to write in a scholarly fashion. Scholarly writing is very organized, detailed, and technical. It also tends to emphasize elaboration over succinctness.

Writing for a popular magazine is, in many ways, quite the opposite. It requires a fluid writing style, an everyday vocabulary, and to-the-point explanations. Paragraphs in popular writing tend to be shorter than academic venues, and there is less attention to detail regarding citations and scholarly references. Despite these differences, the magazine's editor was easy to work with, as he offered much constructive criticism and advice on ways to tighten up my new popular-writing style.

One of the things I needed to remember was my audience. Constantly reminding myself that magicians and non-scholars would be reading the article forced me to consider how to frame my discussion. I drew from previous stories from *Magic* magazine to help establish a popular-writing style and perspective. I thought about what I might read in a popular magazine, and then tried to incorporate that style with my own.

In this way, I organized my thoughts in a very linear way, after I used an attention-grabbing device in the beginning—much like a newspaper article—by using a very famous quote known to most magicians. I then explained the topic of my article, introducing the theoretical concept of persuasion (without using academic jargon), and then elaborating on the usefulness of the concepts for my audience.

Finally, I also tried to remember my audience when finding examples to illustrate the concepts of my article. What would my audience relate to? What would they find useful? What examples would best clarify my concepts? Additionally, I tried to conclude the article with practical tips that my audience could use to apply the article concepts to their magic performances. In this way, I attempted to focus on the audience.

Results of Popularizing Magic Research

Some scholars question my purpose to reach non-academics and some magicians question how an academic might offer something useful for them. However, my rationale is to report how magic influences our daily lives, in various ways, especially since magic directly impacts our various persuasive techniques. Non-academics can benefit not only from a deeper understanding of the art of magic, but also because my research can suggest ways of improving various persuasive methods. I can now say with confidence, albeit from anecdotal evidence, that the magicians who have read my article have been very pleased with an academic writing about their community. More importantly (to me), they have also expressed how the article informed them of some ways they can improve their performances.

For example, many magicians whom I interviewed and who read my article are thinking more deeply about the meaning(s) emerging out of their professional repertoires. They are using the concepts of *ethos*, *pathos*, *logos*, and identification as tools to enhance the persuasive power of their performances. One mentalist is now giving lectures on how magicians can incorporate persuasive techniques into performances. The impact of my academic work on the magic community seems to have been very positive.

The overwhelming majority of respondents suggest that magicians enjoy and appreciate how scholars interpret the art of magic. Additionally, magicians have contacted me to help them frame their performances based upon the premise of my research—that is, how can magicians be more persuasive? In fact, my reputation as a scholar and the generous climate of the magic community in general led to my initiative of popularizing my research. And, given the exposure I have received from interviews, attending conferences, and writing the article for *Magic* magazine, I continue to stay involved with the magic community by using academic theories to help magicians expand and enhance their repertoires.

In the process of popularizing and engaging participants in the research on magic, I learned two main lessons. First, magicians, while receptive and generous to a scholar such as myself, are still suspicious of outsiders. As a secretive community, magicians are naturally hesitant to give access to a non-magician. Becoming a participant-observer in the magic community enabled me to overcome this hesitance. Second, attempting to popularize this kind of research is simply not interesting to the majority of the magic community. Many, if not most, magicians are a product of the instant-gratification society, in that they desire immediate knowledge about how effects are done and how to quickly improve their tricks and routines. Nevertheless, a solid core—and incidentally role models—of the magic community are trying to hedge this tendency for a more purposeful and more meaningful pursuit of knowledge generation. In other words, key magicians are trying to persuade the rest of the magic community that they should educate themselves about magic history, drama, and theory to improve the overall status of magic. Thus, research like mine is becoming more popular and more acceptable, even in a secretive society.

The key to reaching audiences like the magic community with academic perspectives is to make scholarly perspectives useful to them. This may seem simple and commonsensical, but this is a consideration often overlooked by academics. I agree with Shavelson (1988), who argues that "our audiences continue to believe that research should provide reliable and relevant rules for action, rules that can be put to immediate use" (p. 11). In other words, if scholars are to cultivate a relationship with non-academics, we must clearly demonstrate how our work has practical utility. The field of rhetoric seems to provide an excellent way to show the practical use of scholarly perspectives to non-academic work. Famous close-up magician Michael Close has argued that "if I want the audience to believe [my magic], then I must *convince* them" (Close, 1993, p. 95, emphasis added). Thus, there is a link between persuasion and magic performance, and this link provides an opportunity to wed scholarly research to a non-academic community.

Conclusion

One thing is for sure: connecting academic studies to non-academic environments can be challenging. Feelings of mistrust, misunderstanding of what different groups do, miscommunication about the utility of what different groups do, the attitude that scholarly work is not useful or unapproachable, and the attitude from academics that their scholarship has "all of the answers," create barriers between the academic and non-academic communities. These barriers also prevent the different camps from learning from each other, and as a result, from improving.

This project has afforded me the chance to connect with a hobby I enjoy while simultaneously connecting with an entertainment community that is often shielded from academic inquiry and influence. I have learned much in the process, including how to gain the trust of non-academics, how to see unique practical utility from my scholarship, and how to show others ways in which they might use my scholarship for their own performance needs. Hopefully my work with magicians will pave the way for future applications of scholarly approaches to the non-academic world of entertainment magic.

References

Agar, M. H. (1980). *The professional stranger: An informal introduction to ethnography.* Orlando, FL: Academic Press.

Aristotle (1991). *On rhetoric: A theory of civic discourse* (George A. Kennedy, Trans.). New York: Oxford University Press.

Burke, K. (1969). *A rhetoric of motives.* Berkeley: University of California Press.

Close, M. (1993). *Workers: Further routines from the professional repertoire of Michael Close* (No. 3). Carmel, IN: Michael Close.

Covino, W. A. (1992). Magic and/as rhetoric: Outlines of a history of phantasy. *JAC, 12.*

Ritner, R. K. (2008). *Ancient Egyptian magical practice* (4th ed.). Chicago, IL: University of Chicago Press.

Seneca (1917). *Ad Lucilium epistulae morales* (Richard M. Gummere, Trans.). On Sophistical Argumentation. Epistle XLV. Cambridge, MA: Harvard University Press.

Shavelson, R. J. (1988). Contributions of educational research to policy and practice: Constructing, challenging, changing cognition. *Educational Researcher, 17,* 4–22.

Part 6

BOOKS AND REPORTS

CHAPTER SEVENTEEN

Narrating Executive Development

Using "Writing as Inquiry" to Enrich the Coaching Dialogue

Daniel Doherty

This chapter differs from others in this book in that it addresses the popularization of a method, or practice, as much as it illustrates the migration of a specific piece of research into the popular domain. The context of the chapter is located in the world of executive coaching, and the practice concerned is that of "writing as inquiry." This practice is of course widely applicable outside of the world of coaching, but this is where the popularization initially occurs in this instance—though a number of those practitioner/researchers who have discovered the practice in this domain have proceeded to apply this practice in other spheres of inquiry in addition, such as leadership development. The "show" piece serves as a research artifact. It is an example of a real-life coaching client's reflective journal in which he commits to record in the style of "writing as inquiry" his reflections on a recent coaching session, by way of retrospective sense-making of the same. This sense-making is then incorporated in the client's portfolio to inform the next face-to-face coaching session. Hopefully the content speaks for itself with regard to the function it performs, illustrating the way in which half-formed reflections crystallize on paper.

The world of executive development has long been characterized by waves of fads and fashions. At some point in the late 1990s, the practice of executive coaching—which has been in existence in many forms since management as a practice was legitimized and has been practiced by management consultants, though not often signified as "coaching"—came to prominence as the practice for managers to be seen to be consuming. The way that coaching practice showed up was in a pattern or regular one-on-one, face-to-face sessions where coach and clients worked in a self-contained environment, often left to determine between them the purpose and direction of their conversation. Contact between coach and coachee during this period would be largely confined to these face-to-face sessions. There was little scope or encouragement for interaction between sessions except in exceptional cases. The major currency of coaching was verbal in nature, occurring in the moment between the coach and coachee, with occasional writing up of achievement of identified goals and objectives, but with little other record or reflection on the nature of the issues under scrutiny being retained or reflected upon.

It was only later in my career, when I entered the world of management education to pursue a doctoral inquiry into consulting and coaching practice following an autoethnographic approach, that it occurred to me that written reflection was almost entirely absent from coaching practice. As I proceeded further into my doctoral studies, I was increasingly taken by the practice of "writing as inquiry" and its power to reveal that which lies beneath the personal surface, often lurking in dark and even forbidden corners. As someone who has kept a journal all my life, I was excited and attracted by what I was discovering through my reading into writing as inquiry. It occurred to me that herein might lay a way of tapping into the hitherto unexplored domain of the spaces between coaching session and the accompanying internal ruminations of a client.

What follows is a description of the process of writing as inquiry, together with some indication as to how it has been applied in this instance to the practical business of capturing reflections between coaching sessions and utilizing those reflections to enrich ensuing coaching encounters.

Writing as Inquiry

Writing as inquiry is best understood as a method of writing in a free way that allows the writer to tap into his/her stream of unconscious ideas, into those thoughts and feelings that flow in all of us, just below the surface. Known also as "free writing," "discovery writing," or "creative writing," the term "writing as inquiry" was first coined by Laurel Richardson, a sociologist who like many of us was taught "not to write until I knew what I wanted to say" (2005, p. 960), and who passionately believed that there was another approach to writing. Writing as inquiry takes the opposite direction of the planned approach, encouraging the writer to write into the text, to break away from the essay plan and to be prepared to be surprised and often delighted by what appears on the page. Writing as inquiry requires that you start writing before you have the slightest idea of what it is that you want to say on any given subject. The product of writing as inquiry, in the form of reflective written accounts, serves as a record of this creative endeavor and can be put to all purposes as the inquirer seeks to broaden their range of reflective practice.

Within the academic world, the support for the use of writing as inquiry is to be found in the work of Richardson (2005), Ellis and Bochner (1996), and other likeminded scholars. Writing as inquiry makes claims to interpretive academic validity, positioned as it is within the broader autoethnographic tradition, where the researcher uses the self as instrument to tap into personal experience and in that way attempts to make sense of the social world. This interpretive academic tradition includes the practice of making public one's research diary, where the account of one's researching is given equal status to that of the research product and is sometimes offered as a parallel interpretative text. In terms of locating this practice within the field of management learning, it nests within the emergent rather than planned learning approach (Megginson, 2004).

The use of writing as inquiry is by no means confined to the world of academic inquiry. Indeed there has been a proliferation of self-help-style publications over the last 15 years or so that actively promote the use of free-style journaling as a tool for personal development. Books such as *Journal Keeping: How to Use Reflective Journals for Effective Teaching and*

Learning, Professional Insight and Positive Change (Stevens & Cooper, 2008), or *Restless Mind, Quiet Thoughts: A Personal Journal* (Eppinger, 1994) are a couple examples of the types of books that abound in bookshops and on internet book sites. The other internet phenomenon that chimes with this upsurge of interest journal-keeping is the explosion of personal web-based journals or blogs that invite readers in for a glimpse of certain aspects of the writer's private world, be it confessional revelations or an account of a personal development endeavor.

Popularizing Writing as Inquiry

My breakthrough in the wider application of writing as inquiry in coaching occurred when working in the management school where I teach in the UK. My work is mainly with practicing managers who are at a variety of stages in their careers, together with in-company management development specialists who show an interest and no little skill in facilitating the development of managers whom they work with. A group of these students had become interested in action-research approaches towards exploring management phenomena, and were also intrigued and at some level somewhat concerned at the unrelieved coaching contagion that seems to be sweeping through the world of management thinking and acting. When I put it to this group that we might take some time over a weekend to experiment with writing as inquiry as a means not only of deepening the coaching experience, but also of allowing qualitative research into the same, the group readily assented and a date was committed to.

To warm up this series of written inquiries into coaching, this group was sent the prompt: "My earliest experiences of coaching were....(finish that sentence.)." This invitation, which was deliberately vague, was subject to a wide range of interpretation of coaching, releasing insights into coaching that we believed would not have occurred if we had asked students to write a purely professional, detached view of the subject. Much of this writing was transgressive of the received managerialist view of the benefits and power of coaching, and was clearly written from the heart. It was my hypothesis that this transgressive writing stimulated a revelatory critical view of coaching that would not have emerged had we pursued a more conventional invitation to comment on the practice of coaching at work.

This spontaneous discovery of a rich critical perspective on coaching gave rise to the exploration of the meta-theme of how professionals become attracted towards and grow to accept without too much question that which is managerially fashionable and faddish. This exploration additionally exposed the related theme of the tendency of professionals towards unthinkingly seeking "how to" solutions, without fundamentally asking the questions "What is going on here?" and "In what way am I being manipulated now?" We noticed that the surfacing of this subtle, unconscious process through reflective writing helped explain how professionals are so often grabbed and then trapped by shiny new management ideas in the first place, seduced by the "how to," by getting it right, rather than asking, at a deep level, the question "Why?" This discovery was not only interesting from an academic and personal viewpoint; it also provided clues as to how the participants might approach the coaching of a client who was deeply in the grip of a management fad—or who had been mandated to be so impassioned by company executives and policymakers.

The insights from this student-based writing experiment were consistent with our own accidental stumbling upon the power of writing as inquiry and also resonate with the theoretical findings of Ellis and Bochner (1996) and Richardson (2005). These insights included the powerful aesthetic of weaving together thoughts and feelings past and present and of discovering a transgressive view of the management practice of coaching through freely writing into it, rather than intellectualizing about it. This experiment did not leave us entirely cynical about this latest management fad. On the contrary, these mature students noticed with interest the emergence of coaching as the successor to packaged management training solutions that in the past were often delivered on a one-size-fits-all-training basis within organizations. Both coaching and reflective practice seem manifestations of a trend towards the personalization of learning and of the recognition and legitimation of the learners' inner worlds in which the learners' reception of experiences is privileged every bit as much as their capacity to absorb technical skills and external competencies.

This discovery excited us, as we believed that writing as inquiry, if used judiciously, can play a vital part in the deeper development of both personal reflection and of coaching practice. One particular benefit that emerged in our various experiments was that writing as inquiry provides a written tangible record of reflection, in a way that conversational coaching does not. This documentation need not be in the public arena for it to be of service to the learner, though there are times when the sharing of the writing with the coach can powerfully accelerate the coaching process.

This discussion of the degree to which this sharing can be demanded by the organization has provoked much reflection on the extent to which it is legitimate to require the coachee to extend the private-public boundary beyond their comfort zone. On the other hand, discovery writing can be of material assistance in finding where that public-private boundary lies in the first place, and puts the coachee in charge of the process of managing those boundaries. At a simple yet profound level, I believe that this process of written inner reflection causes the learner to take themselves and their personal experiences and deeper beliefs seriously, as seriously indeed as they take the predominant discourse of the enterprises that they inhabit.

Early applications of writing as inquiry in coaching among this original inquiry group—including myself—revealed that the method allowed both coach and client to express to each other thoughts and feelings regarding both the coaching process and the substantive content of the dialogue that were not accessible within the boundaries of regular face-to-face sessions. Insights so gained significantly accelerated and deepened the dialogue, while providing a record for future reference.

Practical learning from these experiments were then shared widely and enthusiastically among practitioners via conference presentations and experimental workshops. We felt we were really onto something. One outcome was to ignite the formation in 2006 of a regional Critical Coaching Research Group, centred on Bristol University where I teach, which drew towards us a much wider audience of practitioners and academics who began to experiment with this approach. This growing profile in turn attracted the attention of two practice luminaries, David Megginson and David Clutterbuck, who were editing a volume called *Further Techniques in Coaching and Mentoring* (2009) and who duly commissioned a chapter outlining how this writing as inquiry technique might be applied in practical coaching situations. The heightened profile afforded by inclusion in this popular practitioner publication has meant that a great deal of email and face-to-face traffic has come the way of the author and his co-researchers regarding applications of this approach; to the point where this approach is routinely discussed wherever practitioners and interested researchers meet. These conversations have also attracted practitioners from the areas of narrative inquiry and also those using metaphor extensively in their client-centred practice ("clean" coaching practitioners among them) to add voice and weight to further experiment with this practice. Increasing networking with the Bristol University Narrative

Inquiry network and doctoral group—among whom a number of our student inquirers are enrolled—has also really helped to widen the visibility of this work, in addition to adding more research substance and opening up a wider range of reference points to it.

As I reflect upon the emergence of this popular interest and momentum in writing as inquiry and upon the train of events that gave rise to it, it occurs to me that I could easily style a retrospective rationalization of this popularization phenomenon as an intentional strategy. That would be disingenuous, however, as the viral spreading of this practice occurred as much through organic networking "buzz" as it did through any planful intention or deliberation on my part. If I had a part to play in this popularization process then, this was achieved through opportunistic pursuit of coaching practitioners' interest and energy to the point where critical mass was established and extended beyond a small group of practitioners and researchers to a wider constituency, thus attracting academic interest through that route. The academy was pulled towards an idea in action, rather than playing its more normal role of pushing an intellectualized concept out from the academy in the hope that it will be adopted in the field of practice. If this were a marketing analysis, we would be categorizing it as buzz marketing or viral marketing. Paradoxically though, this practice flies in the face of "buzz," which is typically inspired by waves of excitement and supported by fashion, rather than by privileging reflection.

This increasing momentum has given rise to an appetite for some form of definition of reflective writing in support of coaching, which currently flows as follows. Writing as inquiry in support of coaching relates to the practice of using free writing as an aid to coaches, coachees, and also coaching supervisors in their preparation for and reflection on their coaching practice. This practice can be used to assist in development of the substantive issues and themes that arise during the course of a coaching assignment, where both the coach and the coachee take time out after a coaching session to write into their thoughts and feelings, thereafter to share (within limits of that which the writer feels it safe to disclose) these written impressions with the other party in the coaching conversation. Equally these accounts can be shared outside the coaching dyad—say, with key players in the coachee's world—to assist those involved in the issue under reflection or to understand more of the protagonist's inner reflections.

In addition to shining light on substantive themes, writing as inquiry can also be deployed by those engaged in the coaching process—including the coach's supervisor as well as the coach and the coachee—to address underlying issues relating to the coaching process. We have found that this written form of reflection upon the dynamics of the coaching process has proved to be of considerable value in surfacing the "undiscussables" inevitably attached to coaching practice—issues such as power in the coaching relationship, or the extent to which access to the coachee's private space is volunteered or mandated—and has been valuable in ensuring that both parties to the coaching relationship engage in robust two-way contracting rather than proceeding tentatively along an uncertain coaching ground that is highly likely to exert an inhibiting effect upon open and free expression.

Conclusion

A further recent step on this journey towards legitimation and popularization has been that in recent years I have become increasingly involved in a professional association styled the European Mentoring and Coaching Council (EMCC). This relationship has grown in large part through participation in their various research conferences where this writing-as-inquiry approach has been writ large as an innovative approach to coaching practice and to research. Associated with my growing closeness to the EMCC has been the fact that—under a sustained bombardment of encouragement to become professionally qualified as a coach, wise advice as this has increasingly become a requirement among clients and commissioners of coaching—I undertook last summer to complete the EMCC master- practitioner-level qualification. In my submission I included a large amount of reflective material as well as the more conventional requirements for "competency grid" completion. Among the reflective material I submitted was an extended transcript of a reflective emails conversation that I was engaged in with a client between coaching sessions over a period of two years. (The client in question has recently been appointed to a one of the most senior posts in her profession and was kind enough to cite the importance of this coaching support in helping her gain this recent recognition and advancement). My EMCC accreditation assessors were both intrigued and questioning of the inclusion of such material.

This has led to a conversation within the EMCC as to the virtue of the inclusion of reflective writing as inquiry material in accreditation submissions, particularly for seasoned practitioners going for master-practitioner level, where evidence of a high level of reflexivity might reasonably be expected. There is growing evidence of the EMCC and other professional bodies and development providers being attracted to going beyond the atomization of the competencies approach towards the inclusion of a written reflective element in assessment; that preferably would include client as well as practitioner reflections. This conversation has drawn me progressively closer to the EMCC, where I recently have applied for and been appointed as executive director—Research & Ethics, UK. I have a mandate to utilize this platform to extend and further popularize this writing as inquiry approach not only to practice and to action research, but also increasingly to incorporate it in the education and assessment of those who would seek mastery in this practice.

In conclusion, this journey towards popularization has included an initial element of private experiment and first-person inquiry; extended to second-person inquiry among the group of ready and willing students; from that platform towards the formalization and creation of a research group based in the university that attracted towards it practitioners as well as researchers and academics to form a third-person inquiry group; which in turn widened the invitation to me to occupy high-profile conference platforms where these ideas could be explored and tested; which stimulated incorporation in a populist text; towards widespread experiment and high-level client advocacy; and more recently has led me, as proselytizer of this approach, to secure a professional role and platform from which this approach might not only be further popularized but may become embedded in the assessment of professional practice. This has felt, then, like quite a journey towards popularization. I remain convinced that without some form of action-research component, research in areas such as this is unlikely to break outside of the academy. What is singular in this instance is evidence of the power of networking in the process of popularization.

References

Doherty, D. (2009). The discovery of writing as inquiry in support of coaching practice. In D. Clutterbuck & D. Megginson (Eds.), *Further techniques for coaching and mentoring* (pp. 77–91). New York: Elsevier.

Ellis, C., and Bochner, A. P. (1996). *Composing ethnography: Alternative forms of qualitative writing*. New York: Sage.

Eppinger, P. (1994). *Restless mind, quiet thoughts: A personal journal.* San Francisco, CA: White Clouds Press.

Megginson, D. (2004). Planned and emergent learning: Consequences for development. In C. Grey and E. Antonacopoulou (Eds.), *Essential readings in management learning* (pp. 91–106). London: Sage.

Megginson, D., & Clutterbuck, D. (2009). *Further techniques in coaching and mentoring.* New York: Elsevier Ltd.

Richardson, L. (2005). Writing: A method of inquiry. In N. Denzin & Y. Lincoln (Eds.), *The SAGE handbook of qualitative research* (3rd ed.), (pp. 959–978). Thousand Oaks, CA: Sage.

Schön, D. (1987). *Developing the reflective practitioner.* San Francisco: Jossey Bass.

Stevens, D., & Cooper, J. E. (2008). *Journal keeping: How to use reflective journals for effective teaching and learning, professional insight, and positive change.* Vernon, VA: Stylus Publishing.

CHAPTER EIGHTEEN

It's What You Do with It That Counts

Disseminating Research about Sex and Relationships Using Reports and Leaflets for People with Learning Disabilities

Ruth Garbutt

How do you write up research in a way that is appropriate for an academic audience, for practitioners, for policymakers, for the general public, and also for people with learning disabilities? What kind of language do you use? What medium is appropriate? Do you produce one report or five? These were my dilemmas as an academic researcher working on a collaborative research project with a rights-based grassroots organization in the UK. The research was about the views and experiences of young people with learning disabilities around sex and relationships (hereafter called the Sex and Relationships Project).

This chapter discusses the nature of a shared methodology called "emancipatory research" that was used within the context of the project. It shows some of the ways in which the products of this research were made accessible by and for people with learning disabilities. It explores the rationale for popularizing research in this way. The Sex and Relationships Project (2007–2010) was a collaborative research project that was led by CHANGE, a leading national voluntary organization, based in Leeds (UK), which fights for the rights of people with learning disabilities. It was in partnership with the Centre for Disability Studies at the University of Leeds. The project came about because there had been only small amounts of research undertaken about sex and relationships and people with learning disabilities. The Sex and Relationships Project looked particularly at the views and experiences of young people with learning disabilities.

What Is Emancipatory Research?

Disability research has had a long history of arguing for the active participation of disabled people in the research process. Within the Sex and Relationships Project, disabled people were fully active in all aspects of the research. This methodology can be referred to as emancipatory methodology. One purpose of emancipatory research is to illuminate the experiences of inequality in social groups and to promote change. Within this model, the researcher is situated as (only) one member of a team. Researchers are often conceptualized as providing methodological tools and skills to others involved in the research project. The importance of emancipatory research can be seen in

> establishing a dialogue between research workers and the grass-roots people with whom they work, in order to discover and realize the practical and cultural needs of those people. Research here becomes part of a developmental process including also education and political actions (Reason, 1988, p. 2).

Emancipatory research therefore embodies a model of an inclusive process. However, the products of a great deal of academic research (including emancipatory research) are written up in an academic way without involving other people in the process. Shakespeare (1997) suggests that researchers involved in disability research have a responsibility to support and build the organizations of the disability movement and to document research in a way that can be accessed by "ordinary readers":

> academics have a valuable part to play in the development of our understanding of the world as experienced by disabled people. It is a very privileged position…it would be a pretty poor disability studies researcher who did not repay that privilege by devoting time and energy (and money) to supporting and building the organisations of the disability movement….I would hope that disability studies research retains its accessibility for ordinary readers…(Shakespeare, 1997, p.188)Legislation around disability rights within the UK has given weight to the argument that information should be produced in a way that disabled people can have access to. Part of the requirements of the Disability Discrimination Act (1995), for example, was for "public bodies to promote equality of opportunity for disabled people" (equalityhumanrights.com/uploaded…/ded_code_englandwales.doc). The Disability Discrimination Act also required goods, facilities, and services to make "reasonable adjustments" for disabled people. Among other things, a service provider was required to take reasonable steps to change a practice, policy or procedure which makes it impossible or unreasonably difficult for disabled people to make use of its services (More recent legislation, such as the UN Convention on the Rights of Disabled People (2009) and the Equality Act (2010) state that disabled people have a right to not be discriminated against, including in relation to access to goods and services. It is therefore important to consider, as a rights issue, that any information (particularly information that is important to people with learning disabilities) should be written in an accessible format. That is, we should change the practices we have that make it unreasonably difficult for a disabled person to make use of our services. This, I would argue, should also be applied to the practice of presenting research findings.

Levy suggests that this is even more important for information that is personal: "People may dislike or resent dependence on others to read to them and prefer accessible information to 'read' alone. This is especially the case when the material is confidential" (Levy, 2005, p. 79). It is also important to make sure that people with learning disabilities themselves are consulted on any attempt at making information more accessible, as Ward and Townsley (2005) write:

> producing easy-to-understand information is, perhaps paradoxically, far from straightforward. The key element for success is working in partnership with the target audience—in this case, people with learning disabilities themselves—throughout the process (2005, p. 63).

Ultimately, if the participants of research are denied access to the final product of their research, then, ethically, this brings up questions around power and exploitation from the researcher to the researched, which goes against an emancipatory model of working.

How Did the Sex and Relationships Project Follow an Emancipatory Model?

The Sex and Relationships Project followed an emancipatory methodology in that people with learning disabilities led the research as equal partners. In addition to the academic researcher (myself), the project employed two project coordinators, one with a learning disability and one without; several volunteers with learning disabilities; and an illustrator who was employed to make all documents and reports accessible. Throughout the project, much emphasis was put on the need to develop the products of the research as a shared process, in the same way that other aspects of the emancipatory methodology were shared. As well as academic articles and a plain-language report, the products of the research included a theater production, an accessible summary, and five booklets, all written in simple words and with pictures so that people with learning disabilities could access the findings. All members of the research team contributed to the plain-language report, including the worker with a learning disability and the volunteers.

Within the accessible report and the five booklets, bespoke line drawings were created by the illustrator to illustrate each line of text. The drawings were not merely pictures that added a visual element; they were a communication tool for people with learning disabilities to understand the words. The main purpose of this was that if the text was covered, meaning could be drawn merely from looking at the pictures. This takes into account the low level of literacy within the population of people with learning disabilities in the UK. The drawings were also drawn carefully to reflect a diverse readership. For example, the drawings included pictures of people with physical disabilities and learning disabilities, and people from different minority ethnic communities. The illustrator was also careful not to portray the people in the pictures as stylized, slim, tall models, but as real-life people.

A group of people with learning disabilities at CHANGE advised the research team on the wording and the choice of pictures. The five draft booklets were also taken to other advocacy groups and professionals to ascertain their views and advice. In this way the process was democratic, inclusive, and followed an emancipatory model. There was also an educational element and a process of empowerment for people with learning disabilities themselves, who gained confidence, skills, and respect from professionals.

The purpose of the five booklets was to highlight the topics of concern to young people with learning disabilities. The subjects of the booklets came directly out of the findings of the research. They were an educational tool that developed from the research. This model reflects the academic pressures and economic imperatives to encourage researchers to have a greater impact on wider audiences and to make links with communities and the wider public. It also arose out of a rights-based discourse, emphasising the rights of people with disabilities to have access to research that involves them. By producing the booklets, there was an action-research element to the project and a responsibility to give something back to people with learning disabilities. The five booklets were: Sexual Abuse; Friendships and Relationships; Safe Sex and Contraception; Sex and Masturbation; and Lesbian, Gay, Bisexual, Trans. The booklets gave clear information about these aspects of sex and relationships in easy words and pictures.

The booklets were printed by a local independent printing company. The voluntary-sector organization leading the research (called CHANGE) had undertaken numerous projects previously that had resulted in producing publications in an accessible format, and so they had established an ongoing connection with the local printing company for this kind of work. The budget for the research project had included an amount of money for printing the first run of the booklets. The booklets were then sold, principally on the CHANGE website, and were also advertised to professionals, academics, and people with learning disabilities through contacts made during the research. The aim was that the profit made on selling the first run of booklets would be used to get more booklets printed.

What Were the Difficulties in Popularizing the Research?

There were some difficulties in disseminating the research in this way, in terms of aligning the academic expectations of a university environment with the rights-based, emancipatory model of the research. As an academic researcher, there are inherent contractual expectations to produce academic articles for journals. However, by undertaking the fieldwork of the research within CHANGE, there was an expectation to have the products of the research presented accessibly.

Barnes (1997) recognizes the difficulties that UK academics face in terms of producing publications in formats that are different from those expected by the Higher Education Funding Councils (HEFCE) Research Assessment Exercise (now called Research Excellence Framework). He states, "the two criteria used in the HEFCE grading process are: the number and 'quality' of publications produced by individual academics working in a particular department and the amount of research they do" (1997, p. 241). Barnes goes on to say:

> The "quality" of publications is judged by the level of "scholarship" they exhibit....Articles published in "academic" journals which are edited and refereed by academics, are rated far higher than those which appear in "popular" magazines....Thus, the more sophisticated and, in most cases, the more inaccessible an academic's work is the more highly rated it is by the academic community (1997, p. 241).

In this way, Barnes identifies the need for researchers to write in an academic way and follow expected conventions in order to be "accepted" and to have a research career. However, the scholarship and sophistication required of academia is not always helpful in terms of making research accessible for people with learning disabilities, or in terms of popularizing research.

This dilemma was partly resolved within the Sex and Relationships Project, after much discussion with the key players, by writing different products for different audiences. Articles about the research were written by the researcher for international journals, in an academic format (e.g., Garbutt, 2008a, 2009a, 2009b). Shorter, more accessible, articles were written collaboratively with other members of the research team and the CHANGE volunteers, to go into magazines and onto websites (e.g., Sexuality team & Garbutt, 2008; Tattersall 2008, 2009; Garbutt, 2008b, 2008c, 2009c, 2009d). The magazines were all UK magazines for parents, families, professionals, and people with learning disabilities and included: *The Journal of the Down's Syndrome Association, Community Connecting, Community Living, Learning Disability Today, Ann Craft Trust Bulletin, Interconnections Online Journal,* and *OurSay.* CHANGE had regular subscriptions to many of these magazines. Once the research team had written an article, they sent it to a relevant magazine to try and get it included. Some magazines had heard about the work of the Sex and Relationships Project and approached the team for an article. Some magazines sent a contact person to interview the research team so that they could write their own article. As a result of delivering presentations and workshops at conferences (both academic and non-academic), contacts were made with academic professionals, non-academic professionals, parents, people with learning disabilities, practitioners, voluntary-sector organizations, and policymakers. The research team then wrote short articles to go into the newsletters and onto the websites of these key people and their organizations. In this way, the process and findings of the research reached a wider audience.

The team also challenged the academic community by attempting to get an accessible article (in easy words and pictures) into an academic journal. This they did successfully (see Garbutt, Boycott-Garnett, Tattersall, & Dunn, 2009). To further popularize the research, presentations and workshops involving drama and visual methods were also carried out by the research team and by the volunteers. These were at both academic and practice-based conferences and at smaller meetings and seminars. The five booklets mentioned earlier were sold on the CHANGE website. By working in this way, the project had an impact on mainstream sexual health clinics, teachers, advocacy groups, academics, people with learning disabilities, and other practitioners. Thus many audiences outside of academia were reached.

The purpose of popularizing research in this way was to uphold a rights-based, emancipatory paradigm; to follow Reason's (1988) suggestion that emancipatory research should become part of a developmental process including education and political actions; to promote the dissemination of disability research as a joint enterprise between disabled people and researchers; to establish a dialogue between research workers and grassroots disability organizations; to support and build the organizations of the disability movement; and to make research findings accessible to those to whom they affect (e.g., people with learning disabilities and "ordinary readers").

What Lessons Were Learned?

The following lessons were learned from this process of popularization:

- It is important to recognize that there can be different research products for different audiences;

- It is important to consult with the different audiences to make sure that the products reflect their needs and interests;

- It is important for the products to be in a format that is relevant to the audience. It is helpful to think laterally and creatively about this;

- The products of research can be more than just an account of the findings—they can include educational material that can help to build up relationships with practitioners and the public and therefore influence social action.

The Sex and Relationships final report (which includes the accessible summary) is included on the website for this chapter, at www.popularizingresearch.net.

References

Barnes, C. (1997). Disability and the myth of the independent researcher. In L. Barton & M. Oliver (Eds.), *Disability studies: Past, present, and future*. Leeds: Disability Press.

Disability Discrimination Act (1995). London: HMSO. Available at http://www.legislation.gov.uk /ukpga/1995/50/contents.

Equality Act (2010). Available at http://www.legislation.gov.uk/ukpga/2010/15/contents.

Garbutt, R. (2008a). Sex and relationships for people with learning disabilities: A challenge for parents and professionals. *Mental Health and Learning Disabilities Research and Practice, 5*(2), 266–277.

Garbutt, R. (2008b). People with learning disabilities and sex education. *The Journal, Downs Syndrome Association*, Middlesex. Issue No. 116.

Garbutt, R. (2008c, Jan./Feb.). The forbidden fruit: A sexually fulfilling life. *Community Connecting Magazine*, 9–10.

Garbutt, R. (2009a). Let's talk about sex: Using drama as a research tool to find out the views and experiences of young people with learning disabilities. *Creative Approaches to Research, 2*(1), 8–21.

Garbutt, R. (2009b). Is there a place within academic journals for articles presented in an accessible format? *Disability & Society, 24*(3), 357–371.

Garbutt, R. (2009c, Sept.). Barriers to relationships and sexuality for young people with learning disabilities. *Community Living*.

Garbutt, R. (2009d, June). The project: Sex and relationships. *Learning Disability Today*.

Garbutt, R., Boycott-Garnett, R., Tattersall, J. & Dunn, J. (2009). Accessible article: Involving people with learning disabilities in research. *British Journal of Learning Disabilities, 38* (1), 21–34.

Levy, G. (2005). Seeing for ourselves: Producing accessible information for people with learning difficulties and visual impairments. *British Journal of Learning Disabilities, 33*, (2) 77–82.

Reason, P. (1988). *Human enquiry in action: Developments in new paradigm research.* London: Sage.

Sexuality Team, & Garbutt, R. (2008, July). Sex and relationships for people with learning   disabilities: Young people, parents and professionals have their say. *Ann Craft Trust Bulletin*.

Shakespeare, T. (1997). Researching disabled sexuality. In C. Barnes & G. Mercer (Eds.), *Doing Disability Research*. Leeds: Disability Press.

Tattersall, J. (2008). People with learning disabilities can be professionals too. *Interconnections Online Journal, 1*(3), 30–33.

Tattersall, J. (2009, May/June). Let's talk about sex. *OurSay Magazine*.

UN Convention on the Rights of Disabled People (2009). Available at: http://odi.dwp.gov.uk/disabled-people-and-legislation/un-convention-on-the-rights-of-disabled-people.php.

Ward, L., & Townsley, R. (2005). "It's about a dialogue . . ." Working with people with learning difficulties to develop accessible information. *British Journal of Learning Disibilities, 33*, 59–64.

(*A screenplay*) ?

CHAPTER NINETEEN

Public Ethnography and Multimodality

Research from the Book to the Web

Phillip Vannini

Good ethnographic research is known to *show* first and then *tell*. By way of showing, ethnography paints a vivid portrait of places, people, and their actions and interactions. By way of showing, ethnography engages in thick description—in the kind of reporting that animates, evokes, ruptures, and renders the lifeworld in colorful and vibrant ways (Stoller, 1997). This is what most obviously sets ethnography apart from other research strategies. Whereas for the most part other research strategies focus on "telling"—for example, displaying statistics, contextualizing interview excerpts, summarizing laboratory findings, or deconstructing the meanings of texts—ethnography, or at least good ethnography, focuses on enlivening multiple realities and on bringing the reader "there." And to do this effectively there is only one way: good writing. Or, well, at least that is what most ethnographers have been taught.

When ethnography became an accepted research strategy in anthropology and sociology early in the 20th century, no mode of representation other than writing was available to ethnographers. While sonic recordings (see Neumann, this volume) and photographs became more common as the years went by, it wasn't until the latter part of the century that ethnographers began to employ media other than the written word. Visual ethnography, however, still remained uncommon for a while—limited by high costs of image collection and reproduction, lack of training opportunities, and relatively low acceptance. So, while film and photography seemed an obviously efficient way to show the details of a lifeworld, ethnographers for the most part continued to rely on the monograph—in book and article form—as the dominant way of sharing knowledge and advancing their careers. Methodological debates and advances, therefore, mostly concentrated on writing and very little on other modes and media.

However, as various cultural turns and the qualitative-inquiry movement in the social sciences continued to blur genres and to lead to experimentation with alternative strategies of representation in the 1980s, 1990s, and early 2000s (Denzin & Lincoln, 2005), new options to collect, organize, and disseminate ethnographic knowledge became more available and accepted. Thus, ethnographers began to exploit more meaningfully the full range of visual options, as well as newer approaches including performance, narrative, and arts-based forms of ethnographic inquiry (Denzin, 1997). By now, audiences of ethnographic research have not only become fully accustomed to a way of showing that de-centers the role of the written word, but in some cases audiences that include young students seem to even prefer descriptive representation that is fully multimodal.

Recent developments in the process of communicating research multimodally—that is, through a diverse range of modes of communication such as combinations of sonic and visual elements—are bound to change drastically the way in which ethnographic knowledge is generated and shared. These effects are compounded by the potential of digital technologies to make these productions easier, cheaper, and more aesthetically compelling. This chapter focuses on these developments, concentrating in particular on the multimodal ethnographic book series *Innovative Ethnographies*, published by Routledge. I begin by introducing the series and highlighting my own contribution to it as an example, and then reflect on its potential to change the way audiences learn from ethnographic research. I conclude by examining a few lessons learned in the process of producing this series.

Innovative Ethnographies

In the fall of 2009, I decided to pitch to Routledge a new book series, to be titled *Innovative Ethnographies*, which would combine the book with the web. The idea was simple: every book published in this series would come with material to be uploaded on the book series' website. Such material was not intended to be ancillary educational material (such as test banks, PowerPoint lectures, appendix-style writings, etc.) or what I called "incidental postcards from the field" (such as amateurish photographs). Rather, inspired by ethnographers' calls such as Behar's (1999), I launched a call for contributions that stated the following:

> Recent methodological innovations have opened the door for a new kind of ethnography. No longer insecure about their aesthetic sensibilities, contemporary ethnographers have expanded upon the established tradition of impressionistic and confessional fieldwork to produce works that not only stimulate the intellect, but that also *delight the senses*. From visual to reflexive ethnography, from narrative to arts-based ethnography, from hypertext to multimodal ethnography, and from autoethnography to performance ethnography, fieldwork has undergone a revolution in data collection practice and strategies of representation and dissemination. Contemporary ethnography is no longer a matter of taking good notes and writing them up with abstract theory in mind; it is now a catalytic field of experimentation and reflection, innovation and revelation, transformation and call to action.
>
> The Routledge *Innovative Ethnographies* series is meant to be at the forefront of this movement. It will publish innovative ethnographic studies that appeal to new audiences of scholarly research through the use of new media and new genres. It will interest both informed general publics and scholarly audiences, as well as students in the classrooms. It will challenge the boundaries between ethnography and documentary journalism, between the scholarly essay and the novel, between academia and drama. It will not invite authors to abandon analysis or methodological sophistication, but by eschewing theoretical excesses it will strive to be more popular than the traditional scholarly monograph. From the use of narrative and drama to the use of reflexivity and pathos, from the contextualization of ethnographic documentation in felt textures of place to the employment of artistic conventions for the sake of good writing, this series would invite ethnographers to produce works that aren't afraid to entertain while being enlightening.

Well-written books—the call for proposals continued—would no longer be sufficient on their own. What I wanted (and still want, as the series is ongoing) was ethnographic work ready to exploit the full potential of multimodal communication and electronic distribution. High-resolution photographs, professionally produced HD documentary films, digital audio documentaries, electronic art exhibits, graphic design, and painting were some of the multimodal opportunities the book series' website was intended to make available to ethnography audiences. While the books would continue to be printed and sold by Routledge, the material posted on each book's microsite would be entirely free of charge to the public.

The purpose of this series was to rejuvenate ethnographic book publishing. To do so, the proposed series was designed to be characterized by the following three features. First, it would publish ethnographies that move beyond the old writing canon as an exclusive genre of representation. Drawing inspiration from various popular culture formats, it would include writings that are highly appealing to readers because of both their content and their style. Ethnographies—as opposed to other scholarly monographs—can be moving, can be passionate, and can be fun and popular. Borrowing from the conventions of popular-culture formats would mean actualizing the aesthetic potential of ethnography. This would mean that books in the series would feel more like film, or art, or music, or literature, or performance than like the same old scholarship of the past.

Second, it would publish ethnographies that transcend the limitation of the book as a medium of dissemination. As more and more students, scholars, and other audiences of research become familiar and comfortable with contemporary media of communication, the traditional written page runs the risk of falling out of grace, especially with younger publics like undergraduate students. Publications in this series would address this trend. Books reporting ethnographic studies would be accompanied by other media material produced by the books' authors and hosted on the web. This material could then be easily integrated into the classroom and into the electronic (i.e., distance-learning) classroom.

Third, it would publish ethnographies that appeal to new audiences. In virtue of their high aesthetic appeal and their popular media-readiness (and usability in the classroom), the books in the proposed series would be easily marketed to multiple audiences. First, they could be marketed to the general public—since every book's substantive topic and research approach would be lively and of great contemporary relevance or popular interest. Second, they could be marketed to forward-thinking scholars and students, since more and more researchers are seeking novel examples of research crafting and distribution, and also sources of inspiration for reaching out to new audiences.

In sum, books and multimodal web material in the series would lead the way toward a popular and humanistic approach to ethnography and qualitative social-scientific research; an approach marked by the flavors and tones of the art and popular culture that so powerfully draws us to movie theaters, galleries, performance venues, and concert halls. Rejecting anonymous experiences, faceless informants, storyless field practice, uncommitted analysis, un-interactive interaction, and the instrumental logic of making "data" subservient to theory, this series of books would inspire audiences just like the great documentaries and films of our time do and make ethnography more fully public. A lofty goal indeed.

How It All Happened

When the publisher agreed to run the series, the difficult task of finding contributors began. It is hard enough to find well-written ethnographies that show first, and only tell in the second instance, let alone to find ethnographers who are also prepared to produce high-quality multimodal material. Another problem compounded this challenge: the ethnographers who are the most likely to produce innovative multimodal material are generally young. From junior faculty with limited time to produce artistic material that some tenure committees still struggle to recognize, to fresh PhD researchers with limited name recognition (and therefore limited chances of convincing editorial boards to issue a contract), the editorial struggle to find contributors was obvious from the get-go. With time, patience, and extensive distribution of the call for proposals, however, the first solid examples of this new approach started flowing in. While still in its infancy, today the *Innovative Ethnographies* site has begun to showcase some of these works. Because I was fortunate enough to be given the opportunity to share my own fieldwork this way, I now proceed to reflect on this process.

Between 2006 and 2010, I worked on an ethnographic project funded by the Social Sciences and Humanities Research Council of Canada. This project aimed to understand the multiple roles played by ferry transportation in the everyday life of residents of British Columbia's islands and coastal towns. The research required a lot of travel, since about three dozen different routes serve multiple destinations throughout this vast region. Some 250 trips and about 400 interviews later, I began to assemble the material with an eye to making it fully public. Thanks to the assistance of Phil Saunders—my university's media-relations manager (see his chapter in this book)—and due in large part to the profound local relevance of the topic, my ongoing research had been regularly featured on the pages of local newspapers and magazines, and on local and regional radio and TV stations. Throughout this time, it had become apparent that the local public wanted to access the final outcome of my fieldwork. My pool of interviewees alone had enthusiastically asked to read what conditions other ferry-dependent community residents experienced.

Therefore, I decided early on to produce the outcome of my fieldwork through three different media to maximize outreach. The first medium was the book. Scholarship often demands written reflection and storytelling, and this case was no exception. Writing a book that captured the attention of both specialist audiences and the general public, however, was no easy task. Hence, aiming the writing "in the middle" seemed the only solution. While specialist audiences were "targeted" through a series of peer-reviewed journal articles, and simultaneously local audiences were "targeted" through a series of radio appearances and newspaper op-eds and interviews, the book—I felt—could appeal to both audiences by losing its pesky edges. I shaved off a lot of high-level terminology from my writing, as well as a lot of local politics and parochial references, and I aimed to write for the typical undergraduate university student. If a freshman who has never been to British Columbia can fully understand and enjoy mostly every page of my book—so would (mostly) anyone else.

Writing a book that way entailed thinking outside the box a little bit. Chapters became shorter and shorter—to keep the writing fluid and the attention alive. Some three dozen chapters, each consisting of 2,000–3,000 words, made up the book. The book was also organized to mix up the pace of showing and telling evenly. For the most part, organization demanded that a chapter of evocative and narrative showing of the "data" would be followed by a chapter filled with interpretations and contextualizations. That way the stories could stand on their own—without much theoretical interference. The main title of the book, *Ferry Tales*, was designed to denote its storytelling value. Along the same lines, ethnographic representation featured dialogues, events, and descriptions similar to those you might find in a paperback novel. While I make no claim to being a novelist or a particularly good writer, for that matter,

I tried to emulate some of the good travel writers whose tales I like to read in my spare time. I did not shy away from including humor, colorful characters, and oddball details to make the ethnography, as much as possible, a fun read. Finally, to allow the writing to flow better, I did not employ in-text citations, using footnotes instead.

The book's chapters were assembled in seven different parts: an introduction followed by six parts built around the ethnography's main focus. Each of the seven parts of the book came with a seven-minute audio documentary, uploaded on the book's website. The audio documentaries were produced in collaboration with Lindsay Vogan, a student of mine with a technical background in radio. Lindsay's talent caught my attention one day in class, when during a presentation on a small fieldwork project she played a clip from an audio documentary she had been working on. Her voice was that of a professional, and her skills—it later turned out—were award winning. The decision to hire her was a no-brainer. I had set aside some funds in my grant for this type of work, so soon enough Lindsay was following me around boats and taking part in interviews—digitally recording informants' words and ambient sounds. Lindsay and I co-scripted the seven documentaries, she edited everything with her software, and quickly after that the work was done. Lindsay's work was of such high quality—and the research topic so easy to sell—that regional CBC Radio 1 stations played segments of the documentaries, followed by interviews with me.

At that point, the work of assembling everything for the web remained. Because most people living outside of the region (e.g,. anonymous reviewers of journal articles, colleagues at conferences, etc.) complained that it was rather difficult to visualize the area and how it feels, my research assistant for this project—April Warn—suggested we create an artistic map-like rendition of the area. That is, not quite a map drawn to scale—which would have been somewhat dry and unimaginative—but rather an artistic map. All the ferry-dependent communities on the map were drawn larger than normal to facilitate the insertion of hyperlinks. Clicking on any of these destinations opens up a slideshow of images and other material (poems, letters, songs, newspaper articles, etc.) collected through fieldwork in that community. The website, of course, also serves as a navigation point for downloading and playing the seven audio documentaries. Some written material excerpted from the book was also made available on the site.

To spread the word about the book, I generated a media release and sent it to local and regional media outlets. Because news media outlets are generally interested in following up on a story or a project after they first cover it, the media release yielded a very good amount of attention—free publicity, as it were. I also notified all my informants who had expressed a desire to see the final outcomes of the research. While it's early to determine popular response to this communication plan by book-sale volumes, it seemed rather clear to me that the response was very positive. As an informant-turned-reader/listener told me, "It's nice to see academic research that you can easily relate too—as a matter of fact, this doesn't even really feel like academic research." And to me, that sounded like a compliment.

While it is early to gauge the success of the *Innovative Ethnographies* series, or of *Ferry Tales*, it is obvious that it's necessary to rethink the book as a sole medium for the dissemination of academic research to the public. But of course, we should not do away with books. Books are fun to read as much as they are fun to write, but if we are keen on exploiting the potential of the written word, we need to think carefully about the material we select for our research, about the way we tell research stories, and about the way we organize them, and market them—as well as to the way they lend themselves to multimodal rendition. My intent in creating the *Innovative Ethnographies* book series is an attempt not only to make ethnographic books more pleasurable to read, but also to exploit the potential of other media to show ethnographic tales.

References

Behar, R. (1999). Ethnography: Cherishing our second-fiddle genre. *Journal of Contemporary Ethnography*, *28*(5), 472–484.

Denzin, N. (1997). *Interpretive ethnography: Ethnographic practices for the 21st century*. Thousand Oaks, CA: Sage.

Denzin, N., & Lincoln, Y. (Eds.). (2005). *The SAGE handbook of qualitative research* (3rd ed.). Thousand Oaks, CA: Sage.

Stoller, P. (1997). *Sensuous scholarship*. Philadelphia: University of Pennsylvania Press.

CHAPTER TWENTY

Mobilizing Research Publications to (Re)Frame Neoliberal Welfare Reform

Shannon Daub

Soon after its election in 2001, British Columbia's new Liberal (read: neo-liberal) government embarked on an ambitious program of tax cuts, deep spending cuts, deregulation, and privatization. Employment standards and labor rights were dramatically rolled back; environmental protection was slashed; one-third of all government regulation was earmarked for elimination; family services and child protection were gutted; and a host of other changes were introduced. A centerpiece of the government's agenda was a package of welfare reforms that reduced monthly benefit rates; restricted access to welfare; imposed an arbitrary time limit on benefits; and set out a 30 percent budget cut for the Ministry of Human Resources (then responsible for welfare) (Klein et al., 2008a, pp. 20–21). At the same time, the government cut or eliminated funding for a host of advocacy and support services, such as women's centres, housing offices, and legal aid (among others) (Reitsma-Street & Wallace, 2004).

The reforms sparked opposition that coalesced initially around the new arbitrary time limit. This rule—unprecedented in Canadian social policy (Klein & Long, 2003)—limited single welfare recipients deemed "employable" by the Ministry to two years of benefits within a five-year period. Characterized as a "ticking time bomb" (Klein, 2003), the time limits meant that in just over 24 months, as many as 29,000 people would be cut off and left with no source of income (Mickleburgh, 2003).

Reitsma-Street and Wallace (2004) chronicle the fight against the two-year limit, noting that a diverse and informal alliance of anti-poverty groups, lawyers, academics, social policy organizations, labor unions, faith groups, professional associations, and others worked at different levels, using "diverse tactics and relevant arguments" in their efforts to abolish the rule (Reitsma-Street & Wallace, 2004, p. 173). Among these groups was the Canadian Centre for Policy Alternatives (CCPA), a national public-policy research institute, and my employer. Together we succeeded in raising widespread concern, in particular about the likelihood of a sudden spike in homelessness, with some journalists and a number of municipal governments calling on the government to rescind the time limits (Wallace & Richards, 2009). And while we did not succeed in abolishing the rule, the provincial government rendered it virtually meaningless by introducing myriad exemptions before any welfare recipients were impacted. This chapter tells the story of how collaborative research played a central role in challenging the time limits and other reforms, using primary research studies; opinion research regarding public knowledge and attitudes about welfare; plain-language educational materials; mainstream media stories; and, multimedia tools.

The Project

Against the backdrop of the fight against the time limit, the CCPA convened a group of progressive researchers and community groups to address the need for research that would document and raise public awareness about a government agenda with especially severe consequences for vulnerable populations. The group created the Economic Security Project (ESP)—a multi-year research and public-engagement effort focused in three areas: welfare and social policy reform; community healthcare restructuring; and employment standards and labor market policy.

In 2002/03, the network applied for and received a $1 million grant through the Social Sciences and Humanities Research Council of Canada's (SSHRC) Community-University Research Alliance program. Jointly led by the CCPA and Simon Fraser University, the ESP brought 20 academic collaborators from four universities together with two dozen community partners. Many of the organizations and researchers fighting the two-year time limit also helped to create the ESP.[1] We worked together on a large series of policy briefs and major studies, two of which played an especially important role in public debate about welfare and poverty.

Between 2001 and 2004, B.C., total welfare caseload shrank by 42 percent, and the number of people in the "expected to work" category (meaning people deemed employable) shrank by 78 percent (Wallace, Klein, & Reitsma-Street, 2006). The provincial government argued this was good news and a result of its reforms, which were designed "to break the cycle of welfare dependency" (Hagen, 2004, p. 8707), and "divert people to employment" (Government of British Columbia, 2002, p. 6). Our research, *Denied Assistance: Closing the Front Door on Welfare in B.C.*, tested these claims. The mixed-methods study paired qualitative, in-depth interviews (with people who unsuccessfully sought access to welfare, front-line community workers, and Ministry staff) with quantitative analysis of detailed welfare caseload figures (accessed through Freedom of Information requests) and economic data (using regression analysis to isolate variables that determine caseload trends) (Wallace, Klein, & Reitsma-Street, 2006).

The study found that only half the caseload drop could be explained by economic factors; the other half was the direct result of restrictions on access to benefits. In other words, the caseload reduction was not about moving people from welfare to work; rather, it was very much a "front door" story of people being denied assistance when in need (Wallace et al., 2006). The study also found that, while some people were being "diverted to employment" (as the Ministry liked to say), many others were being "'diverted' to homelessness, charities, survival sex and other forms of hardship" (Canadian Centre for Policy Alternatives, 2006).

A second study focused on the other side of the welfare reform coin—the policies and practices that affect people who are able to access benefits. *Living on Welfare in B.C.: Experiences of Longer-Term "Expected to Work" Recipients* documented the experiences of people who had been receiving welfare for more than a year but were deemed employable by the Ministry (Klein et al., 2008a). The two-year qualitative study recruited 62 people who participated in in-depth interviews every six months, plus monthly check-ins.

The findings painted a stark picture of the often harsh, and sometimes brutal, conditions the recipients faced, with little support from a welfare system that is supposed to prevent hardship and misery, not institutionalize it. The study found that welfare forces people into a daily fight for survival, providing benefits that are far too low, and creating "a public welfare system that is structurally dependent on food banks and other charities in order for people to make ends meet" (Klein et al., 2008a, p. 10). One in five of the female participants engaged in prostitution/survival sex during the two-year study; one in three in a relationship experienced abuse, with all but one staying in or returning to the relationship for financial survival reasons. Nearly one-third of participants were homeless at some point during the last six months of the study alone. Seven were arbitrarily cut off welfare during the study; all seven had a history of addiction; four had hepatitis C.

Together, *Denied Assistance* and *Living on Welfare* established a clear link between the government's welfare reforms and the rapid increases in homelessness that began in 2002—a problem that not only affected large urban centres like Vancouver, where homelessness more than doubled between 2002 and 2005 (City of Vancouver, 2005), but also smaller cities and towns across the province. These studies also helped explain how B.C., among the wealthiest provinces in Canada, could experience record-low unemployment and strong economic growth, and simultaneously have the highest poverty rate in the country (Klein et al., 2008a). In doing so, the studies helped reframe the government's welfare reforms as punitive, arbitrary, and counterproductive.

Popularizing the Research

Of course, this research did not have an impact on public debate simply by virtue of being published. It also had an impact because it was embedded in the collaborative research processes of the Economic Security Project. And the researchers and ESP partners were themselves embedded in the broader, loose coalition of groups fighting the welfare reforms. The initial idea and broad research questions for the *Denied Assistance* and *Living on Welfare* studies were born during "full-team meetings," where the full ESP network of academic collaborators and community partners gathered to discuss needs and priorities. The individual research projects were refined and carried out in teams that included community partners, academics, and non-academic researchers.

These collaborative arrangements not only shaped the research itself, but also how the findings were made available. While individual members of the ESP network published academic papers, the bulk of the findings were published in monographs made freely available on the CCPA's website, where they have been heavily accessed (*Living on Welfare* has been downloaded more than 70,000 times at latest count, and *Denied Assistance* more than 24,000 times). Rather than forcing people to choose between a brief abstract and a 60-page document, we created summaries that presented the key findings in some detail, in relatively plain language, with definitions of key terms, and with vivid (anonymous) profiles and stories from the research participants. These summaries were turned into mini-versions of the full report (designed and printed as booklets) and actively made available online and off.

The studies were also co-published with community partners. Co-publishing formally recognized the central contribution of community partners, and enhanced the impact of the research, with organizations other than the CCPA taking ownership of the material. Co-publishers, researchers, the ESP network, and the broader loose coalition of groups fighting the reforms provided mutual support and reinforcement to one another. People working on the ground—advocates, social-service providers, representatives from low-income neighborhoods—brought their knowledge of the concrete ways the cuts and policy changes affected vulnerable people to the news conferences, radio interviews, and meetings with government officials where the research findings were discussed. And in turn the research became a source of ammunition for groups that already knew firsthand how the government's policies were unfolding, but whose voices were amplified when supported by peer-reviewed research findings.

Another reason these studies had an impact on public debate is that we used the research to systematically challenge the provincial government's discourse on welfare reform. The authors of *Denied Assistance* noted in 2006,

> For many people working the front lines against poverty in this province, the Minister responsible for welfare seemed to speak as if he despised the very public service he was responsible for....Welfare was described as a service that "encourages dependency and represents a waste of people's potential." Standing the in Legislature, the Minister described how welfare will "drain the human spirit, kill self-esteem and bring a sense of hopelessness" and "can lead to other problems like alcohol and drug abuse, family neglect and physical abuse" (Wallace et al., 2006, p. 13).

But while we found the government's discourse to be an offensive assault on the poor, we wondered how the public might see it.

Anti-poverty advocacy presents some difficult communication challenges. It is one thing to talk about child poverty—an approach often understandably favored by advocates (though one that downplays the reality that for every poor child, there is a poor family). Similarly, it is relatively straightforward to talk about homelessness—a problem so visible and threatening to people's sense of social cohesion that it prompts strong concern. It is quite another thing to talk about welfare—a program that has been vilified by right-wing columnists and talk-show hosts, undermined by overblown stories of welfare fraud, and immortalized in the stereotype of the "welfare queen" (courtesy of the pioneer of welfare reform himself, Ronald Reagan). As we prepared for the release of *Denied Assistance*, we worried about how it would play in the mainstream media, and whether we could overcome the stereotypes that seemed always to plague discussions about welfare.

We decided to test the waters by undertaking a very modest, but extremely useful, set of polling questions and focus groups, which aimed to help us talk about the government's welfare reforms in a way that would resonate with the public. Of all the interesting things we learned from this exercise, two stood out. First, we had a tendency to talk about the welfare system and the government's policies as though most people had at least a basic knowledge of both. We quickly learned this was not the case—which is not to suggest the people who took part in the focus groups were ignorant or disinterested in current events, but simply that busy people who have no direct experience with the welfare system know very little about it.

Lack of knowledge about the welfare system did not, however, stop the participants from having ideas about how it worked, which leads to the second and related valuable lesson. The knowledge gap about welfare was filled by all kinds of assumptions and beliefs about what the system must be like. These assumptions and beliefs seemed to flow largely from the participants' sense that in Canada we take care of one another and that while welfare should not be generous, neither should it be arbitrary or punitive. And so, many of the participants believed that welfare was reasonably accessible, that benefit rates were sufficient to meet basic needs, and that the system should fundamentally be geared towards helping people "get back on their feet."

When confronted with descriptions of the actual eligibility requirements and benefit rates, the participants' conversation changed. Questions of basic human dignity, fairness, and what it means to be Canadian were suddenly on the table. One woman responded to a description of the welfare application process by insisting, "Whoever wrote this must be lying." She simply could not believe that a program that ought to help people in need would put them through such a complicated and arbitrary application process. Similarly, our poll results indicated that when British Columbians were told what welfare actually pays in monthly benefits (at the time $510 per month to a single person), then asked if they would support an increase, 74 percent said yes, 44 percent strongly so.

Armed with these lessons, we set out to intervene in public discussions as often and effectively as possible. We briefed the ESP network, and other allies, and suggested effective communication approaches. We wrote newspaper opinion pieces. We met with influential journalists. We held news conferences. We went on radio talk shows. We spoke at public events, in college and university classrooms, and at rallies. We created multimedia tools featuring the voices of welfare recipients and advocates. In all cases, we made sure to take the time to explain how the welfare system works, and to describe the government's new rules and policies. And we made the link between these policies and the growing problem of homelessness that, by the time *Denied Assistance* was published in 2006, was a source of widespread alarm.

Conclusion

I wish I could conclude this story with a clear victory, that the provincial government had been forced, at minimum, to rescind its welfare reforms. That didn't happen. Most of the policies introduced in 2002 remain on the books. But the link between these policies and the growing problem of homelessness became the new conventional wisdom among journalists. The related idea that the government's policies were not only punitive, but also counterproductive, was reflected in the tenor of the media's coverage of poverty issues more broadly. And the provincial government itself was forced to acknowledge the failure of its own policies, if unofficially.

In 2006, the government began funding "homeless outreach workers" to actively find homeless people, bring them to local welfare offices, and see to it that the government's own eligibility and application rules were bent or broken in order to get them on welfare. No doubt this shift was also prompted by the prospect of negative international attention during the 2010 Winter Olympics. In 2007, the government was shamed into raising welfare rates by 20 percent (for single "employable" recipients), after a large number of municipal governments joined the call for increased rates and an end to arbitrary barriers to access. And in the last four years the government has, albeit belatedly and insufficiently, invested in new homeless shelters and social housing.

In the meantime, the terms of the debate have shifted. Anti-poverty advocates have gone on the offensive, joined by a growing number of "mainstream" organizations that are making links between the government's social policies (including, but not limited to, welfare reform) and their societal costs (to social services, healthcare, policing and courts, and community cohesion). In 2009, these groups formed the B.C. Poverty Reduction Coalition. The coalition's call for a legislated poverty-reduction plan—based on one of the Economic Security Project's final publications (Klein et al., 2008b)—is gaining momentum. With leadership races underway in both of the province's major political parties, and a provincial election on the horizon in 2013, further victories in a long-term battle for dignity and equality seem possible.

Note

1. The ESP was co-directed by Seth Klein, director of the Canadian Centre for Policy Alternatives' B.C. Office, and Marjorie Griffin Cohen, professor of Political Science and Women's Studies at Simon Fraser University. See http://www.policyalternatives.ca/projects/economic-security-project for more information.

References

Benford, R. D., & Snow, D. A. (2000). Framing processes and social movements: An overview and assessment. *Annual Review of Sociology, 26*, 611–639.

Canadian Centre for Policy Alternatives. (2006, March 27). Study finds B.C.'s welfare system denying assistance to people in need, "diverting" many to homelessness and hardship (press release). Available at http://www.policyalternatives.ca/publications/reports/denied-assistance.

City of Vancouver. (2005). *Homelessness action plan.* Available at http://vancouver.ca/commsvcs/housing/pdf/hap05jun.pdf.

Government of British Columbia. (2002). *2004/05–2006/07 service plan—Ministry of Human Resources.* Available at http://www.bcbudget.gov.bc.ca/Annual_Reports/2003_2004/hr/hr_performance_link2.htm.

Hagen, S. (2004, February 23). *Hansard. Official report of debates of the Legislative Assembly of British Columbia.* Available at http://www.leg.bc.ca/hansard/37th5th/h40223a.htm.

Jeppesen, S. (2009). From the "War on Poverty" to the "War on the Poor": Knowledge, power, and subject positions in anti-poverty discourses. *Canadian Journal of Communication, 34*(3), 487–508.

Klein, S. (2003, October 1). The ticking time bomb of B.C.'s welfare time limits (opinion piece). *Canadian Centre for Policy Alternatives.* Available at http://www.policyalternatives.ca/publications/commentary/ticking-time-bomb-bcs-welfare-time-limits.

Klein, S., Pulkingham, J., Parusel, S., Plancke, K., Smith, J., Sookraj, D., Vu, T., et al. (2008a). *Living on welfare in B.C.: Experiences of longer-term "Expected to Work" recipients.* Canadian Centre for Policy Alternatives; Raise the Rates Coalition. Available at http://www.policyalternatives.ca/sites/default/files/uploads/publications/b.c._Office_Pubs/bc_2008/bc_LoW_full_web.pdf.

Klein, S., Griffin Cohen, M., Garner, T., Ivanova, I., Lee, M., Wallace, B., & Young, M. (2008b). *A poverty reduction plan for B.C..* Canadian Centre for Policy Alternatives. Available at http://www.policyalternatives.ca/sites/default/files/uploads/publications/b.c._Office_Pubs/bc_2008/ccpa_bc_poverty_reduction_full.pdf.

Klein, S., & Long, A. (2003). *A bad time to be poor: An analysis of British Columbia's new welfare policies.* Canadian Centre for Policy Alternatives; Social Planning and Research Council of B.C.. Available at http://www.policyalternatives.ca/sites/default/files/uploads/publications/b.c._Office_Pubs/welfare.pdf.

Mickleburgh, R. (2003, October 21). B.C. document details welfare cuts; New regulations will force up to 29,000 people off rolls as of next April, NDP says. *The Globe and Mail*, A8.

Reitsma-Street, M., & Wallace, B. (2004). Resisting two-year limits on welfare in British Columbia. *Canadian Review of Social Policy, 53* (Spring 2004), 169.

Wallace, B., Klein, S., & Reitsma-Street, M. (2006). *Denied assistance: Closing the front door on welfare in B.C..* Canadian Centre for Policy Alternatives; Vancouver Island Public Interest Research Group. Available at http://www.policyalternatives.ca/sites/default/files/uploads/publications/b.c._Office_Pubs/bc_2006/denied_assistance.pdf.

Wallace, B., & Richards, T. (2009). Policy resistance: The rise and fall of welfare time limits in British Columbia. In B. Wharf & B. Mckenzie (Eds.), *Connecting Policy to Practice in the Human Services* (3rd ed.), (pp. 81–201). Don Mills, ON: Oxford University Press.

Part 7

DIALOGUE

e-Dialogues

Real-Time Online Conversations

Ann Dale, Jason Luckerhoff, & François Guillemette

This chapter describes an e-research agenda and project that the first author developed in order to bridge some of the asymmetries of place, space, and scale that researchers at smaller universities face. In particular it explains the genesis and rationale for e-Dialogues, synchronous online conversations that bring together diverse experts and eminent personalities to talk about critical public-policy issues of the day, in particular sustainable development and ecological literacy. It then goes on to detail research collaboration between the authors of this chapter to evaluate what works and doesn't work with these online critical conversations. It also describes, on a more practical level, how to use electronic platforms for transdisciplinary qualitative research teams.

Three specific questions informed this research project. Can the internet be used to re-enlarge the public space for substantive dialogue; can it be used to increase public literacy about critical public-policy questions, specifically ecological literacy; and can the internet be used to inform public policy development?

e-Dialogues

e-Dialogues were created to investigate why and how the internet can be applied to substantive online conversation around three critical issues: first, to explore its application for increasing citizen literacy around complex social issues, in particular, sustainable development; second, to see if it has the capacity to develop shared meanings, in individual communities, communities of interest, and among Canadians as a whole around these complex issues; and third, to examine its applications for e-democracy in the information age, where all sectors of society need to be increasingly engaged in public policy discussions leading to new models for governance—a somewhat ambitious goal, but without dreams what really fundamentally changes?

e-Dialogues are deliberately designed synchronous online spaces that bring together leading-edge researchers, practitioners, decision makers, and civil society leaders who bring diverse perspectives and expertise to bear on public policy issues (www.e-dialogues.ca). Normally, a well-recognized researcher or civil society leader, who ensures that underlying tensions and differing perspectives are revealed through the dialogue, expertly moderates them. They occur in real time and the online expert panel dynamically converses with each other, and online e-audiences are invited to "listen in." e-Dialogue expert panelists can directly include any references, PowerPoint presentations, and so forth into their conversation, to reinforce any points they wish to highlight. This also augments greater access by the public to critical information highly germane to the public policy under discussion.

The public audience or the e-audiences were invited to "listen in" through advertising to the researchers' networks across the country, and in cases where the dialogues were led in partnership, with their networks as well, augmenting the outreach. The e-audience can both "listen" to the expert panel dialogue, and at the same time converse among themselves, and questions can be posed to the expert panel. Audience numbers in the beginning averaged about 100 people per dialogue, and now vary far more, we believe due to the increasing noise on the internet. For example, in the years 2001 to 2005, the e-audience varied from 97 to 260, and appeared very dependent upon how aggressive the marketing was for each dialogue. In terms of outreach, for example, the dialogue on used nuclear fuel in Canada attracted more than 10,000 Canadians, who either visited the website or listened in to the online dialogues over a six-month period.

e-Dialogues help to overcome the costs of transdisciplinary research in seven ways: (1) the transaction costs of bringing together experts are much lower; (2) travel costs and personal time are minimized; (3) e-Dialogues appear to force more integrated thinking about broader, complex social issues resulting from the linearity of the medium; (4) they can reach a diverse cross-section of Canadians; (5) they create new e-communities of practice; (6) they increase the speed of connectivity and dissemination of knowledge and research between policymakers, researchers, and community decision makers; (7) they offer a unique window for government decision makers into the points of convergence and more critically divergence in emerging and existing public policy issues (Dale, 2005).

What We Learned from Our Project

A transdisciplinary team was built for this one-year research project, composed of researchers, policy experts, and practitioners who participated in four online dialogues, each of which was observed by Luckerhoff and Guillemette. These e-Dialogues tested the online collaboration effectiveness of three outcomes: peer review of an academic journal article, an international meeting of online researchers, and the co-authored writing of a book manuscript chapter. The fourth conversation, moderated by Luckerhoff and Guillemette, brought together all of the participants from the first three dialogues to evaluate the functionality of the e-platform. Another research outcome was to link sustainable development research and grounded theory, by asking "how do researchers use electronic platforms to do qualitative research?" A series of interviews, observations, and references to literature allowed for analysis to be conducted in an iterative and inductive way.

The satisfaction of panelists with the e-Dialogue process was very positive. Of the 34 panelists who took part in e-Dialogues completed to date during the study period, 69 percent (20) completed our survey questionnaire. All panelists except one of those surveyed felt they were able to contribute to the discussion sufficiently, and the individual who did not believe he or she had sufficient opportunity was neutral on that point. More crucially, the survey data revealed that all but one participant agreed completely (5) or at a scale of (4) that the technique was "professionally significant," all but two agreed that it "contributed to their understanding of the subject matter," and all but three thought the process was "effective in bringing people together with diverse experiences from different sectors." In all these cases, those who did not agree were neutral on these questions. Fifty-five percent of panelists also agreed that the real-time nature of the dialogue was a more satisfactory way to collaborate than the more traditional online forum that operated asynchronously (30 percent did not answer the question, and one panelist preferred the asynchronous environment). In addition, the majority of respondents stated that the economic/ecological benefits of using the e-Dialogue tool more than offset any technical difficulty as compared to face-to-face meetings.

In terms of practical use for panelists, there is no apparent correlation between computer proficiency and satisfaction with the system. In fact, the individual with the least experience (completely and somewhat disagreeing with statements on computer, typing, and technical skills) was one of the most satisfied with the platform (consistently agreeing with statements concerned with participation). This may be in part due to the provision of panelist training in advance. Expert moderation was evaluated as critical to both the quality and facilitation of meaningful dialogue. All panelists apart from one considered moderation necessary (the dissenter being neutral on the question) and all except one appreciated the moderation process (with one being neutral on the question and one who did not appreciate the moderation, although agreed it was necessary, which is a somewhat contradictory position). The dissenters did, however, agree strongly or completely to other statements relating to their satisfaction with the flow and opportunity to meaningfully contribute.

The most dissent concerned the flow of the conversation. The statement the panelists were asked to agree or disagree with was "the time delay between responses inherent in the online dialogue medium inhibited the conversation." Ten percent completely disagreed, 20% somewhat disagreed, 35% were neutral, 25% somewhat agreed, and 10% completely agreed. This cannot be explained by technology as the responses to this statement do not match operating system use or browser use and all panelists were connected through high-speed connections. Nor can it be explained by gender or age characteristics of the panelists. In any event, the slight dissatisfaction with the flow was not mirrored by dissatisfaction with the process as a whole.

Our most interesting finding was that 65 percent of the e-panelists found that their sense of connection with other panelists changed during the dialogue in spite of the anonymity of the medium. Those who didn't agree most were neutral on the question or did not answer it. There were only two panelists who disagreed, both of whom were consistently less positive about the conversation and its impacts than the others surveyed, although generally positive in their assessment. In addition, both these panelists were higher than average in age, and lower than average in reported technical ability, which may explain the lack of connection felt during the process.

With respect to content, grounded theory analysis revealed the importance of leadership and expert moderation, and specific techniques used by the moderator. We observed that in a leadership role, the moderator specifically invited individuals to make specific comments and to build on another's comments. Another technique we observed was summing up preceding points, searching for points of convergence, in order to reinvigorate the conversation. For example, right at the start, she invited her colleagues to: "Let's start quickly with…" The platform allows, therefore, for active moderation of meetings and discussions in the same way as would be possible in a face-to-face meeting.

With respect to moderation, it demands critical literacy skills, especially being able to read very fast in order to link (thread) people's ideas together, to compensate for the "flatness" of the medium. As the moderator observes,

> in order to compensate for this flatness and to improve the flow of dialogue, I often ask what appear to be "dumb" questions to facilitate, to enhance the dialogue, but it is a very unforgiving medium, you are so much in the public sphere, the communication and publication is immediate. Interesting observation, many older academics, although I am older, my experiences are still novel in the academy, are loathe to participate as the written word is seen as so sacred. But I love the anarchy, the dance, the play of it all, and the novelty.

The moderator's influence on the group phenomena is important because it is proactive and diversified (different types of questions and different types of answers) in her actions and in her leadership, thereby compensating for the limitations of the medium.

The specific use of the e-Dialogue platform was the topic of the last e-Dialogue moderated by the second and third authors of this chapter, and it served as a research focus group for both the research team and some of the participants in the previous dialogues. More critically, it also allowed the three authors to make explicit much of their implicit learning in their use of the e-platform. A key distinction was made between e-Dialogues and forums. As one of the participants stated: "Forums are normally held over a period of time, a week. I led a year-long forum on climate change (archived). They are asynchronous, people post when they feel like it. You know what e-Dialogues are, my team no longer holds e-forums, the participation rate is far too low, given the 'noise' of the internet." Many participants see an advantage in the synchronous aspect of e-Dialogues. For example, one participant considers that:

> Regarding preparation I think Jim gets to the root of the problem—people in general will not read preparatory material as to them the dialogue is probably not a priority. But I think the lack of preparation and analysis time is an advantage in transdisciplinary work. Preparation and analysis tends to reinforce conventional bias and a retreat into comfortable paradigms. By contrast the reactive pace of an e-Dialogue forces people to introduce a bit of instinct and engage more with the subconscious. This is often lost in western methodologies—to the detriment of debate I think. One can be over analytical.

The fact that all responses are written and are an immediate public record, as well as archived, imposes some constraints on spontaneity, especially for academic researchers who place a high value on written literacy. There is anecdotal evidence that the platform allows researchers to be more reflexive because of the slight delay time in posting responses, as well as the ability to also include journal articles, PowerPoint presentations, or website links that back up the points they wish to make.

The e-platform gives the moderator, as well as the expert panel, the ability to refer back to previous threads of the conversation, while simultaneously "listening" to the ongoing dialogue, to probe further, to ask supplemental questions, demand clarifications, or provoke a reflection on an aspect that might have been overlooked. In an ordinary meeting, it wouldn't be possible for the moderator to animate so dynamically, think about how to reinforce key points, think about some interventions, and think of what clarifications might be necessary all at once. As well, the e-Dialogues allow the moderator to excerpt from one of the panelists and formulate a question directly to that participant.

The moderator has more time for reflection than in an ordinary meeting, but the fact that the online conversation is synchronous is critical for motivating the participants to become involved, many of whom are some of the best minds in Canada around public policy, and on the basis of our research, who feel they are actively involved in an actual conversation.

Another technique we observed in the moderation was attempts by the moderator to encourage and valorize the panelists in diverse ways. By ensuring inclusion, people are directly quoted and supplementary questions are then asked, which is a very good way to valorize. The moderator manifests this by saying certain points are interesting and that the panelist is considered as an important resource: "Diane has touched on a key point . . ." Specific appreciations are given to each panelist, and the moderator thanks many after significant interventions. These are not general (polite, which would already be positive in a leadership perspective) but specific thanks: "Thanks for broadening the discourse, we had not thought of this, by affordability, we were restricting ourselves to reasonable access to housing, but of course, density and walkability are also key components."

Deterministic approaches to studying the use of online communication tools would probably consider the influence of the medium itself. We analyzed social interactions happening in a virtual meeting place and found that the medium itself allows for much interaction, but the medium never replaces the role of a moderator and the participants. The synchronous dialogue exacerbates possibilities in a meeting room but doesn't replace the need for understanding how good dialogues are moderated and how leaders attain goals by asking experts to get together. Active moderation, as is the case for productive face-to-face meetings, is key to ensuring the dynamic interaction of both the expert panels and the e-audience.

In face-to-face interviews or focus groups, individuals don't have much time to think about what has just been said. The interactions are rapid and there is no time for reading documents during the encounter. To the contrary, synchronous dialogues allow for slow interactions that are made of listening and thought before speaking. In other words, the participants can take the time to understand one another and to think before writing. The interactions don't happen only with the moderator. Compared to the face-to-face focus groups, there are more interactions among the participants than in more traditional meetings.

There is an "emotional" feel in the conversational exchange, and we think that the synchronous character of the e-Dialogue facilitates this. A more personal relationship is established compared to using email, asynchronous forums, or other such tools. Not only is the "intellectual" dimension present, but we also found a very emotional quality in the online conversation. Working with Google Docs, for example, would not allow for such discussions that include more than an exchange of information on proposed modifications to a text. The participants are not speaking to a virtual receiver who will be known to them later on, as on a forum for example, but to actual participants who are present in a real-time conversation. The conversation starts and ends by introductions from the moderator in the same way as in a physical meeting.

Conclusion

Our research demonstrates that online internet communication technologies can make a significant contribution to initiating and augmenting inter- and transdisciplinary research and, specifically, collaboration. In addition, they contribute to enhanced qualitative research methodology by the direct expert voice immediately recorded in the public domain, as well as the archived conversations for future access by scholars from across the country and internationally. In this way, perceived biases from traditional subject/object research methods are made transparent and are mediated by the interactive dialogue directly in the public record, without interpretation or thematic coding by researchers, thus working ultimately as a transformative methodology. Their efficacy as a tool for leading online focus groups was also very clearly demonstrated by the data collected from the fourth e-Dialogue.

We invented this tool to re-enlarge the public space for meaningful dialogue with continual enhancements, improving its ability to facilitate meaningful conversations about what is important to us as a society, and its capacity is limitless (Dale, 2005). e-Dialogues are one tool that can be used to enlarge the public space (Dale & Naylor, 2005) to re-engage the publics and in the long term, the space online, real-time dialogues create to address questions of power and equity may be its most valuable contribution.

References

Dale, A. (2005). A perspective on the evolution of e-Dialogues concerning interdisciplinary research on sustainable development in Canada. *Ecology and Society, 10*(1), 37.

Dale, A., & Naylor, T. (2005). Dialogue and public space: An exploration of radio and information communications technologies. *Canadian Journal of Political Science, 38*(1), 203–225.

Jantsch, E. (1972). Toward interdisciplinarity and transdisciplinarity. *Education and Innovation in Center for Education Research & Innovation (CERI) OECD, Problems of Teaching and Research in Universities.*

Jervis, R. (1997). System effects: Complexity in political and social life. Princeton, New Jersey: Princeton University Press.

Koo, M., & Skinner, H. (2005). Challenges of internet recruitment: A case study with disappointing results. *Journal of Medical Internet Research, 7*(1). Available at http://www.jmir. .org/2005/1/e6.

CHAPTER TWENTY-TWO

Using Social Media to Empower Parents in the Digital Age

Ask the Mediatrician

Brandy King & Michael Rich

In the 1950s, when television became the center of American households, psychologists and politicians raised concern for its effects, calling researchers to testify to Congress about the influence of television on juvenile delinquency. Television executives did not challenge the research, instead suggesting that worries about negative influences were driven by values that were not universally shared. Framing television effects as a values-based issue drove the debate headlong into the First Amendment of the Constitution of the United States, effectively diverting politicians and the public from concerns for the well-being of individuals and society and uniting them around freedom of expression. The discourse over media effects on the health and development of children has been dominated and decided by First Amendment considerations to this day, stalemating serious public discourse and limiting funding for research.

Concerns about negative effects on children gave rise to increasing attention from pediatricians starting in the 1970s (Rich, 2007), but the public was reassured by educational television and relieved that freedom of expression allowed them to embrace rapidly expanding media technologies and diversifying content. The evidence was growing, but it was fragmented and isolated by the rigid silos of individual academic disciplines. Parents, teachers, and others working with children became increasingly worried about distraction, aggression, isolation, and obesity as media technologies proliferated, became cheaper and more accessible to children of all ages. Today, 8- to 18-year-olds use media for an average of seven hours and 38 minutes each day (Henry J. Kaiser Family Foundation, 2010), and more than one-fourth of children under age two have televisions in their bedrooms, watching for an average of nearly one and a half hours a day (Rideout & Hamel, 2006).

The Center on Media and Child Health (CMCH) was established in 2002 to take an evidence-based approach to the issue. The goal of CMCH is to be a values-neutral, unbiased resource for all stakeholders, from media consumers to producers, who seek to understand and respond to the positive and negative influences of media on children. Approaching media use through scientific fact, much as we approach children's nutrition or automobile safety, CMCH can respond most effectively to what may be the most ubiquitous environmental influence on children's physical, mental, and social well-being. By reframing what has been values-based and contentious discourse to a quantifiable measure of public health, CMCH allows all stakeholders to come together around a common interest in children's well-being, understand the facts, and work together to improve the environment in which children develop.

The foundation of CMCH's evidence base is a comprehensive, up-to-date library of the "state of the knowledge" on media and their effects on children drawn from more than a dozen academic disciplines. Citations for the research papers in the CMCH Database of Research (www.cmch.tv) have been standardized into a format that includes both scientific abstracts and plain-language summaries. Yet even the most user-friendly database is not how parents typically learn parenting. So how do we translate this research into useful information to inform parents about the benefits and risks of media use?

Ask the Mediatrician®

One way to engage parents in dialogue with each other and experts is to hold workshops where they can learn the current research and best-practice recommendations. When CMCH staff give these workshops, parents typically arrive feeling a vague sense of unease about how much TV their preschooler watches or the kinds of video games their teen plays. Most don't endorse their children's media use but feel helpless to intervene.

We started noticing that in each presentation we gave on the scientific research about media effects on children's health, the Q&A session became the richest part of the workshop. Parents became energized by an immediate need to know how to change their family's media habits. What was evident from all of this question asking and answering was that people need an expert who can answer these questions when they arise in their lives. Because the media landscape, and research about it, is constantly evolving, parents need to be able to find an expert when they run into a new or developing situation surrounding media. Much parenting information is static. This is not the case with media-related questions and answers. As media and media-related research evolves, new but also widely shared sets of questions arise, as do best practices for dealing with these situations.

Since a more responsive format than print is required for this topic, we created a blog in order to formalize common media questions and their answers into a flexible online resource. We named the blog "Ask the Mediatrician®," a nickname that CMCH director Michael Rich earned due to his current occupation in pediatrics and former career as a filmmaker. With this combination of experiences, along with the vast amount of knowledge he gained as a parent of four, and the credibility of being based at Children's Hospital Boston, Harvard Medical School, and Harvard School of public health, Rich is a reliable source from whom parents can learn about the effects of media on children's health.

We were attracted to the idea of using a blogging platform because blogs are designed to accommodate constant publication of new content. With all the permutations of the three factors in media-effects research (age groups, health outcomes, media platforms), we knew we would have a lot of questions coming. We also knew that we would need to respond to users' questions quickly or we would lose their attention. With no dedicated funding for this project, the goal was to create the website, bring an audience to it, and then have a functional resource in pilot form available to show to possible funders. Our hope was that once funders could see for themselves there were enough questions to keep it going, that our answers were balanced, actionable, and research-based, and that there was an audience responding to it, we could easily demonstrate why it should be supported.

In June 2009, we launched www.askthemediatrician.org. When we launched, we had already answered some of the most common questions about media and health including:

- My daughter got scared by a movie, what should I do?

- How much TV is too much TV?

- Should I worry about the violent video games my son plays?

- Will baby videos help an infant learn?

Earning an Audience

Our first marketing attempt was to create a postcard to send to 5,000 people along with their registrations for an upcoming walk-a-thon for our homebase organization, Children's Hospital Boston. We also worked with the hospital's Public Affairs department to create a press release. In our first month, the website logged 1,000 visits and we started to receive questions from users. Another promotional opportunity was to showcase Ask the Mediatrician® to our existing audience. Since they were already aware of our website, newsletter, and Facebook page, we took advantage of these outlets to highlight new questions being answered and encourage people to submit their own questions. Facebook has proven to be our best avenue for promoting this content. Not only was there an upsurge in middle-aged users of Facebook (parents of elementary school children) when we started using it, but the younger users who had been using Facebook all along were starting to become parents of infants and preschoolers.

Conversations about parenting were happening on Facebook and we wanted children's media use to become part of those conversations. Every question we answer on Ask the Mediatrician® is posted on Facebook, along with encouragement for users to tell us how they would have answered the question. Not only do we want our information to be passed virally along to parents, we want to hear back from parents about what worked in their own families as they face media-related decisions. Their discussions and comments provide essential functions that improve the likelihood that our message will go viral while strengthening our content:

- *New questions for Ask the Mediatrician®.* By asking questions in response to the information we post, our Facebook members are constantly providing us with new topics.

- *Parent-to-parent recommendations.* When Facebook members read our answers, they often respond with solutions of their own providing a variety of peer-to-peer suggestions based on in-home use.

- *New research opportunities:* Parental, home-based solutions provide fodder for new research.

- *Word-of-mouth.* Facebook newsfeeds are an important source of promotion: when members post comments about our work, it appears on their newsfeeds. This sparks conversations about families and media among their friends, which in turn attracts a new audience to Ask the Mediatrician®.

- *Increased engagement.* As Aaker and Smith (2010, p.100) point out "engagement and empowerment are best achieved when information flows in both directions." This process of "collective creation" allows for users to act as the experts they are, and allows CMCH to draw from the wisdom of the crowd.

We recently had a perfect example of this collective wisdom. A mother wrote to Ask the Mediatrician® about how to handle a homework assignment for her 12-year-old son.

> Q: My 12-year-old son's history assignment last night was to think about the news he watches (it said watches, not reads) and write an essay relating a news story to something in his history book. I don't let him watch the news because I think it is often more scary than the movies or video games he sees. What would you recommend we do?

Our answer confirmed that the mom was valid in her concerns about her son watching the news, since research shows that watching the news increases our perception of the presence of violence in the world (Smith & Wilson, 2002) and that the impact of exposure to frightening media can affect kids for a long time (Harrison & Cantor, 1999). We went on to recommend that the child "write the essay comparing what he read in his textbook to a news story he encountered from a different source, like a newspaper or website, and then explain to his teacher why he made that shift" (Rich, 2010).

When we posted this Q&A on Facebook, three of the comments we received included other useful suggestions that accomplished the same goal of avoiding scary and sensationalized media: watching PBS Newshour, listening to podcasts from NPR, or watching specific news stories online rather than an entire news program. These additional suggestions empowered users and demonstrated the power of collective approaches to common problems.

Aaker and Smith point out that "collective creation...take[s] practice. Those of us accustomed to traditional media tend to think of our efforts as individual art, not as a community mural. We tend to be defensive in the face of feedback, and that just doesn't work in new media" (2010, p.100). When CMCH asks for recommendations from our Facebook members, we have to give up a certain amount of authority. Rather than insisting we know the absolute correct answer, we open ourselves up to the possibility that others have useful solutions. While many researchers and academics may consider this a poor move, in the world of social media, it allows for our users to become more engaged in working toward the common goal of healthy media use for children.

Another positive aspect of using social media to speak to parents about media and child health is that it gives us an opportunity to "walk the talk." Much of our messaging at CMCH revolves around using media and technology appropriately as the powerful tools they are, rather than condemning them all together. Social media give CMCH a chance for us to demonstrate directly to our audience that we embrace these tools for their ability to spread important messages and to communicate directly with our audience (both talking and listening).

One year after the launch of the page, we won a Top 40 Facebook Pages award from Likeable Media (a Facebook marketing firm). We were the only research center listed, named alongside national corporations with big pockets like TJ Maxx, Whole Foods, and Best Buy. This award also helped to promote our work and we now have over 3,000 users connected to our page. The demographics of the members of our page reflect that we are reaching our target audience. Fifty-seven percent of our members are between the ages of 25 and 44, the years when most people are actively involved in parenting young children.

Ask the Mediatrician® is now also distributed through two additional outlets: Education.com's Just Ask forum and Thrive, the Children's Hospital Boston blog. The Just Ask forum allows parents to post questions on any topic. These questions are answered by parents, teachers, and other members of the Education.com community, as well as by experts whom Education.com has partnered with, such as Michael Rich. Thrive, the Children's Hospital Boston blog, posts one Ask the Mediatrician® question per week on their blog. This helps bring the message to those interested in pediatrics that media consumption is an important area to consider as part of a child's overall health experience. Occasionally, these *Thrive* posts are also featured on the Facebook page of Children's Hospital Boston, which has almost half a million fans. These posts always link to the CMCH Facebook page, generate a lot of discussion, and lead to more hits on the Ask the Mediatrician® website. Through a combination of all of these outlets and types of promotion, the Ask the Mediatrician® blog has averaged 2,100 visits per month over the past year.

What Lessons Were Learned?

Lesson 1: It's easy to get people to seek advice on an existing health problem; it's difficult to get people to talk about preventive care. When people have had a personal experience with an illness or injury, they often want to talk about it, finding comfort in both venting their suffering and achieving solidarity with fellow sufferers. Our medical system is built on disease interventions; thus it, and we as consumers, have largely failed with preventive medicine. Even the few who recognize that media consumption may contribute to violence, obesity, sexual-risk behaviors, and substance abuse, rarely believe that it can happen to them or their family. This self-protective "third-person syndrome" allows them to worry about how media influence other people's children, while enjoying their own media use. Popularizing research on the health effects of media is a process of helping us all to see our own daily media use with new eyes. Once families are able to reflect on their own risk, we provide information and strategies with which to address their issues in pro-active, preventive ways.

Lesson 2. Find organizations similar to yours in mission or audience, then cross-promote your work. Pairing up with Education.com allowed us to reach parents, teachers, and others who care about the well-being of children and are accustomed to turning to online resources for help in raising children. Working with Thrive, the Children's Hospital Boston blog, allowed us to reach those involved in clinical pediatric work and those who research pediatric health issues. We provide content for these organizations, and in turn, they provide an audience for the content we want to spread. We have taken this tactic with Facebook as well, teaming up with organizations such as the Media Education Foundation and Parents for Ethical Marketing who each have audiences who are attuned to hearing and talking about the effects of media on children. By linking to the work of similar groups and tagging their Facebook pages, and having them do the same for us, all of us broaden our audiences and spread our messages.

Lesson 3. When change is the goal of popularizing research, one must provide opportunities for people to take action. In preparation for writing this chapter, we read two books that opened our eyes to the real power of social media to affect change, and we highly recommend them both: *The Dragonfly Effect: Quick, Effective, and Powerful Ways to Use Social Media to Drive*

Social Change (Aaker & Smith, 2010), and *The Networked Nonprofit: Connecting with Social Media to Drive Change* (Kanter & Fine, 2010). Though we make suggestions for action in each of our Ask the Mediatrician® answers, these actions are very situation specific. The books just mentioned have made us realize the tremendous potential we hold to harness the power of social media for larger-scale change toward healthy media use. As Aaker and Smith so boldly state in *The Dragonfly Effect*, "The final goal is not just to get 100,000 people into your group; rather, now that you have the attention of 100,000 members, your goal is to inspire and enable your group to take action. In moving forward, you must be cognizant of where the true power of social technology lies: not in the technology itself but in the people who use it" (2010, p.158).

References

Aaker, J., & Smith, A. (2010). *The dragonfly effect: Quick, effective, and powerful ways to use social media to drive social change*. San Francisco, CA: Jossey-Bass.

Harrison, K., & Cantor, J. (1999). Tales from the screen: Enduring fright reactions to scary media. *Media Psychology, 1*(2), 97–116.

Henry J. Kaiser Family Foundation. (2010). *Generation M2: Media in the lives of 8- to 18-year-olds*. Washington, DC: Henry J. Kaiser Family Foundation.

Kanter, B., & Fine, A. (2010). *The networked nonprofit: Connecting with social media to drive change*. San Francisco, CA: Jossey-Bass.

Rich, M. (2007). Is television healthy? The medical perspective. In N. Pecora, J. P. Murray, & E. A. Wartella (Eds.), *Children and television: 50 years of research* (pp. 109–148). Mahwah, NJ: Erlbaum.

Rich, M. (2010). My son's school assignment is to watch the news, but I don't usually let him; what do I do? *Ask the Mediatrician* Available at http://cmch.typepad.com/mediatrician/2010/10/my-sons-school-assignment-is-to-watch-the-news-but-i-dont-usually-let-him-what-do-i-do.html

Rideout, V., & Hamel, E. (2006). *The media family: Electronic media in the lives of infants, toddlers, preschoolers and their parents*. Menlo Park, CA: Henry J. Kaiser Family Foundation.

Smith, S. L., & Wilson, B. J. (2002). Children's comprehension of and fear reactions to television news. *Media Psychology, 4*(1), 1–26.

CHAPTER TWENTY-THREE

New Media, Participatory Methodologies, and the Poularization of Mètis History

Mike Evans & Jon Corbett

For a growing number of academics, the relevance of our research is directly linked to how we popularize it. We do not mean this in the sense that the value of our work needs to be measured against whether and how our research results appear on the pages of local or national news outlets, though this matters to an extent. A more immediate concern, especially for those of us whose practice is participatory in nature, is whether and how our research can be understood and used by the communities with whom we work.

For work with marginalized communities, participatory or participatory action research methodologies are the standard against which other research paradigms are now read and critiqued. After scholars like Paulo Freire (1970), participatory researchers embrace the notion that communities have an active role to play in all elements of the research process. Stringer (2007) identifies that a fundamental premise of participatory action research is that it assists community members in deepening the understanding of their situation and collectively highlighting the skills and tools available to them, with the intent to resolve the problems they confront. Indigenous communities, in particular, expect that researchers will shape research to meet community priorities and goals. Further, there is a growing body of literature that insists that research methodologies be framed by Indigenous values (Smith, 1999) and that research methods themselves be drawn from Indigenous practices (Armstrong, 2000; 2005). Indeed, there are a number of common elements between participatory and Indigenous research methodologies (Evans et al., 2009d).

Associated with this participatory impulse is a growing concern about how we can shape new communication strategies that are consistent with the underlying values of this type of research. That is, how do we make the research products match the research process? Here the intent is to popularize the work in very specific ways because the target of the communication and the target of the research are the same. New media technologies have been particularly helpful in this regard. In the case study described in this chapter, digitized historical documents and a Google Map's enabled interface have been central to both the research and its popularization.

Google Maps is one of a growing body of geospatial web technologies increasingly referred to as the Geoweb. Elwood (2008) defines these new applications as "not-quite-GIS." The Geoweb's principle strengths are its ability to support the contribution, access, and the sharing of location-based information. This functionality fits well with the participatory intent of the project described in this chapter.

Métis Nation British Columbia

The Métis are an Indigenous people born of the interaction of European fur traders and First Nations communities throughout the northern and northwestern North American continent beginning in the 17th century (see Brown, 1980; Van Kirk, 1980). Towards the end of the 19th century, family-based alliances and relationships within the fur trade began to coalesce (Brown, 1983; Foster, 1994; Peterson, 1985). In the period from 1793 to 1821, a series of dramatic events led to the genesis of a self-conscious and separate Aboriginal people. The Métis of this period dominated the plains and parklands of northcentral North America, becoming the major military and economic power in the decades of the mid-19th century. It was not until direct military intervention by the newly emerging Canadian state that they were defeated and dispersed. Over the course of two armed resistance movements (that is, the Riel and Northwest Rebellions of 1869–1870 and 1885), the Canadians established their own dominance in the region, and subsequent settlement by Europeans pushed the Métis and their First Nations cousins to the socioeconomic and political margins.

In spite of systematic attempts to extinguish Métis rights and absorb Métis people into the mainstream of Euro-Canadian settlement, many Métis remained distinct and somewhat hostile to the Canadian state. There was a protracted period of political struggle to seek formal state recognition that has, of late, borne some fruit. The Métis were recognized as one of the three Aboriginal peoples (along with "Indians" and Inuit) of Canada in Section 35 of the Constitution Act of 1982; and in R. v. Powley (2003), the Aboriginal right of Métis to hunt was affirmed by the Supreme Court of Canada.[1] R v. Powley was a landmark case that spurred the Canadian state into action. Indeed, much of the research agenda described below has been generated by so-called post-Powley funding; these were resources earmarked by the government of Canada to assist in the identification of Métis people and communities.[2]

Today, the Métis National Council—a political body made up of representatives appointed by Métis provincial bodies from Ontario, Manitoba, Saskatchewan, Alberta, and British Columbia—is the national voice of the Métis. Provincial organizations represent Métis communities within their provinces (Weinstein, 2007), and via a number of bilateral agreements with the federal government, provide a limited range of services to those communities. In their role as the provincial body representing Métis in B.C., the Métis Nation of British Columbia (MNBC) initiated a research relationship with a team of researchers at the University of British Columbia in order to develop research and research tools that pertain to the historical and contemporary B.C. Métis communities. In the first instance, this led to historical research designed to identify and collect materials relevant to understanding Métis history in B.C. . Consistent with a participatory approach, a core value informing the research design was the facilitation of community involvement in the collection and database archiving of materials. For the most part, the historical research proceeded as historical research commonly does, but very quickly we realized that there were significant ways that popularizing the research in the community could enhance the quality of the research in an iterative way.

The R. v. Powley decision discussed above establishes two things: (1) that Métis communities have rights, hunting rights in particular, and; (2) a series of criteria by which a rights-bearing Métis community may be known in law (see Teillet, 2009). Such communities must be established in both historical and contemporary terms, and their members defined. Organizations like the MNBC must therefore engage in a two-sided process through which the history of the community as a whole, and its members individually, are drawn together. The MNBC uses the national MNC definition of Métis citizenship: "Métis means a person who self-identifies as Métis, is of historic Métis Nation Ancestry, is distinct from other Aboriginal Peoples and is accepted by the Métis Nation" (MNC, 2010). Here, "Historic Métis Nation" refers to "the Aboriginal people then known as Métis or Half-Breeds who resided in Historic Métis Nation Homeland" and, "Historic Métis Nation Homeland" is defined as "the area of land in west central North America used and occupied as the traditional territory of the Métis or Half-Breeds as they were then known" (MNC, 2010).

This was a vast area complicated by the presence of other Aboriginal Nations with whom the Métis interacted regularly, and to whom many Métis are variously related. The MNC further clarifies that "Métis Nation" means "the Aboriginal people descended from the Historic Métis Nation, which is now comprised of all Métis Nation citizens and is one of the 'Aboriginal peoples of Canada' within s.35 of the Constitution Act of 1982," and that its citizens are "distinct from other Aboriginal Peoples." The Métis have always been a dispersed community linked by family ties; therefore, genealogy and history share common ground, and a great deal of time has been spent systematically collecting and using both historical and genealogical information. This allows individuals to establish their citizenship as Métis, and at the same time helps define the collective political entity—the Historic Métis Nation. The central tool for achieving this for Métis in B.C. is the MNBC Historical Document Database.

Historical Document Database (HDD)

The HDD is an indexed database that contains a variety of primary and secondary historical documents pertaining to Métis. It is mounted on proprietary software called KnowledgeTree, a document management package, and accessed through custom-designed web pages. Each document is indexed (by subject and patronym[3]) as well as geo-located (using a latitude-longitude coordinate system), and there is a custom search engine that allows users to search using keywords and/or a map interface, and download relevant documents as needed. Users also have the ability to browse the entire database using patronym and category classifications, as well as browse the entire database through the Google Maps interface. Access to the database is open, though certain functions are limited to particular user groups. For example, there is a different level of access for Métis citizens than there is for the general public.

The database is used by MNBC staff and potential MNBC citizens to undertake the genealogical research required for MNBC citizenship; indeed it is used daily by MNBC citizenship registry staff to verify citizenship application. It can also be used for more general family-related or historical research. As of October 1, 2010, it consisted of nearly 16,000 documents, just less than half of which were indexed and accessible. The database has been populated by MNBC staff,

University of British Columbia (UBC) Okanagan researchers, Métis citizens, and members of the general public, and it is in this regard that the structure is truly innovative. The database is designed to promote a two-way flow of information; the MNBC and its citizens use what the researchers provide, but then in turn can contribute their own documents to the common pool contained within the database. There are two avenues for this. First, an individual citizen can agree to release the documents they submit to the MNBC in order to establish their citizenship; a release form is built in to the citizenship approval process (see application package at http://mnbc.ca/citizenship/adult_citizenship.asp). Secondly, there is a page where anyone can contribute documents for indexing and inclusion in the database (see upload link at http://document.bcmetiscitizen.ca/sendfile.php). People have used these routes to contribute everything from baptismal certificates to family photos.

The HDD was developed at UBC Okanagan in conjunction with the staff and citizens of MNBC. However, consistent with the principals of participatory research, control of the database and responsibility for maintaining and adding to it have been incrementally shifted to the MNBC. In March 2010, the database was physically moved to the MNBC head office, and in October 2010, full control and responsibility passed to MNBC. Training materials for staff have been developed, and outreach materials for community members were developed and piloted in early 2010 (see Figure 1: Map of Boucher-related documents).

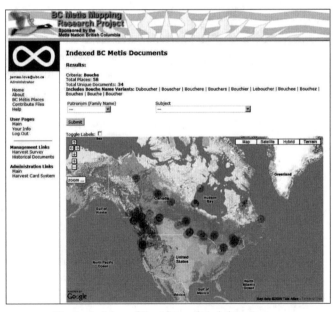

Figure 1: Map of Boucher-related documents

The outreach process was part of the participatory process. Workshops were held with Métis citizens in two communities. In both cases, members arrived with handwritten family trees, photographs, and in one case, a book. Using online forms, workshop participants input their family information from the paper format directly into the HDD. In subsequent workshops designed specifically to upload existing digital documents onto the database, community members brought digital material on USB thumb drives. This material included historical photographs of family members, a photograph of a marriage certificate from an important ances-tor of one family, as well as entire family genealogies stored in word-processing files. Surveys conducted during these workshops suggested that the document submission and retrieval process was usable by community members with only rudimentary computer skills. These sur-veys also supported the notion that from a practical perspective, the HDD was a highly rele-vant tool in supporting community-driven participatory research.

It should be noted that the HDD is most effective for engaging community members who already have access to and use the web regularly; this is partially because they are not intimidat-ed by the user interface. However, here as elsewhere, we find a digital divide as well as a skills divide. Nonetheless, the interface between the HDD research and the public is the web. Overcoming infrastructural and usability challenges has been a significant focus of our outreach activity. In the two outreach pilots described above, the local Métis community already had limited access to the web via their local organization; in both cases, the project provided a computer and scanner to facilitate the skills transfer at the workshop, and to enhance the existing infrastructure.

Beginning at the introductory page (at http://document.bcmetiscitizen.ca), users can move through the site searching by patronym or category; or by location keywords, they can also search directly through a map interface; and download the documents they need. The Google Maps Geoweb interface is particularly helpful as it provides both a graphic representation of the number of documents bearing on a particular search set, as well as an interface to access those documents. For example, the image in Figure 2 (Search of Metis Families in the Central Interior) was generated by a search of the patronym "Boucher"—a prominent Métis family of the central interior of B.C.. This family has figured centrally in our recent research (Barman & Evans, 2009). Figure 2 is a search of patronyms from a wider network of related families. From the map interface, by simply zooming and moving the cursor over the heat mark, a pop-up describes the material at that point. In two clicks, the material can be downloaded by the user (see Figure 3: Download Interface in the HDD). More often than not, the user is a member of the community from which and with whom the research itself derives.

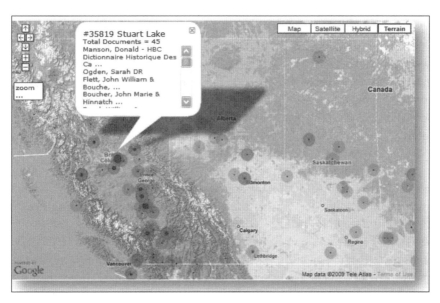

Figure 2: Search of Metis Families in the Central Interior

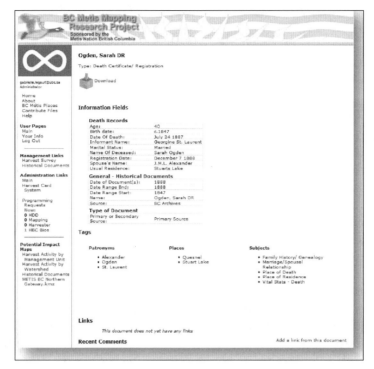

Figure 3: Download Interface in the HDD

Conclusion

The HDD is just one element of a research relationship that has spanned close to a decade now. We have also completed a set of digital videos (*The Métis of British Columbia: Culture, Tradition, and the Contemporary Community* [Evans et al., 2009b] and *The Métis of British Columbia: Music and Dance* [Evans et al., 2009c]), and these too are aimed at popularizing work that is, at root, participatory (see Evans et al., 2009a). These video materials were developed in direct consultation with key experts at MNBC and reviewed by a group of elders and experts at a two-day workshop before final edits were made. We have recently moved these digital-video materials to the web, again in order to facilitate access for members of the community (see http://ubc.bcmetis.ca/dvd/). Although at present there is no way for community members to contribute to the digital-video materials in ways that parallel their ability to contribute to the HDD, this too may simply be a matter of time.

Recent political developments, especially in the area of Aboriginal–Settler society relations, have pushed participatory research methodologies to the forefront. Parallel to this participatory impulse is an emerging concern that the research and matters emerging from it be accessible to the communities at the centre of the research relationship. While this is one particular take on the issue of popularizing research, there is a growing consensus that social-science research needs to be both engaged and engaging. The revolution in new media technologies, serendipitously, provides many avenues to match process, product, and audience in research today.

Acknowledgments

This paper describes research that has occurred over several years and has engaged dozens of people in various ways. Those who have had the greatest impact in the growth and development of the database central to the discussion below are: Geoff Appleby (computer programmer), Jon Corbett (co-investigator), Erin Dolmage (research associate), Gary Ducommun (MNBC staff), Mike Evans (principal investigator), Gabrielle Legault (research associate), Laurel Katernick (MNBC registrar), Stephanie Krause (computer programmer), James Love (computer programmer), Rob Lauriston (computer programmer), Zach Romano (research associate), Dean Trumbley (MNBC staff), and Kasondra White (research associate).

Notes

1. Although the Constitution Act of 1982 acknowledges that Métis may have some Aboriginal rights, these rights are in no way defined or delineated by that Act.
2. Note the exact definition of the term Métis—or more correctly, the understandings about who may claim the term as an identity—is contested and complex. For the sake of brevity, we refer the interested reader to Boisvert and Trimble (1992) for a good general discussion, and Barman and Evans (2009) for a detailed look at the situation as it pertains to B.C. .
3. The Métis social universe is complex, but one of the key organizing mechanisms that people use to place each other within that universe is their last name or patronym. Learning what family someone is from, combined with what area they come from, is the first step in establishing connections in two senses. First, people can connect each other by tracing family lines into actual kinship connection. Second, people can know of each other by connecting the names to Métis history more generally. Thus, a knowledgeable Métis person will associate someone who is related to the Arcand families from northwestern Saskatchewan with the noted Métis author Maria Campbell, or the famous fiddler John Arcand, or perhaps the Battle of Batoche, where the Métis met their defeat at the hands of the Canadians (at which several Arcands were present). Such a knowledgeable person might also be able to trace contemporary and historical kinship relationships using the patronym as a starting point.

References

Armstrong, J. C. (2000). Let us begin with courage. In Z. Barlow, & M. Crabtree (Eds.), *Ecoliteracy: Mapping the terrain* (pp. 8–12). Berkeley, CA: Center for Ecoliteracy.

Armstrong, J. C. (2005). En'owkin: Decision-making as if sustainability mattered. In M. Stone, & Z. Barlow (Eds.), *Ecological literacy* (pp. 11–17). San Francisco: Sierra Club Books.

Barman, J., & Evans, M. (2009). Reflections on being, and becoming, Métis in British Columbia. *B.C. Studies, 161*, 59–91.

Boisvert, D., & Trimbal, K. (1992). Who are the Métis? In J. Sawchuk (Ed.), *Readings in Aboriginal studies. Vol.2: Identities and state structures* (pp. 108–141). Brandon: Bearpaw Publishing.

Brown, J. (1980). *Strangers in the blood: Fur trade company families in Indian company.* Vancouver: University of British Columbia Press.

Brown, J. (1983). Women as centre and symbol in the emergence of Métis communities. *The Canadian Journal of Native Studies, 3*(1), 39–46.

Elwood, S. (2008). Volunteered geographic information: Key questions, concepts and methods to guide emerging research and practice. *GeoJournal, 72*, 133–135.

Evans, M., Foster, S., Corbett, J., Dolmage, E., Gervais, J., Mann, R., & Romano, Z. (2009a). Representation in participatory video: Some considerations from research with Métis. *Journal of Canadian Studies, 43*(1), 87–108.

Evans, M., & Foster, S. (Producers), Corbett, J. (Associate Producer), Foster, S., Gervais, J., & Mann, R. (Directors), Gervais, J., & Mann, R. (Editors). (2009b). *The Métis of British Columbia: Culture, tradition, and the contemporary community* (video).

Evans, M., & Foster, S. (Producers), Foster, S., & Mann, R. (Directors), Mann, R. (Editor). (2009c). *The Métis of British Columbia: Music and dance* (video).

Evans, M., Hole, R., Berg, L., Hutchinson, P. Sookraj, D., & the Okanagan Urban Aboriginal Research Health Collective. (2009d). Common insights, differing methodologies: Towards a fusion of Indigenous methodologies, participatory action research, and white studies in an urban Aboriginal research agenda. *Qualitative Inquiry, 15*(5), 893–910.

Foster, J. E., (1994). Wintering, the outsider adult male and the ethnogenesis of the western plains Métis. *Prairie Forum, 19*(1), 1–14.

Freire, P. (1970). *Pedagogy of the oppressed*. New York: Continuum International. Métis National Council (MNC). (2010). Who are the Métis?: National definition of Métis. Available at http://www.metisnation.ca/who/definition.html.

Peterson, J. (1985). Many roads to the Red River: Métis genesis in the Great Lakes Region, 1680–1815. In J. Peterson, & J. S. H. Brown (Eds.), *The new peoples: Being and becoming Métis in North America* (pp. 37–73). Winnipeg: University of Manitoba Press.

R. v. Powley. (2003). SCC 43, 2 S.C.R. 207. Available at http://csc.lexum.umontreal.ca/en/2003/2003scc44/2003scc44.html.

Smith, L. (1999). *Decolonizing methodologies: Research and Indigenous peoples*. London: Zed Books.

Stringer, E. T. (2007). *Action Research* (3rd ed.). Thousand Oaks, CA: Sage.

Teillet, J. (2009). Métis Law Summary 2009. Available at http://www.pstlaw.ca/resources/MLS-2009%20FINAL.pdf.

Van Kirk, S. (1980). *Many tender ties: Women in fur-trade society*. Norman: University of Oklahoma Press.

Weinstein, J. (2007). *Quiet revolution west: The rebirth of Métis nationalism*. Calgary: Fifth House Publishers.

Part 8

PERFORMANCE

CHAPTER TWENTY-FOUR

A Performance of Special Education Meetings

Theatre of the Absurd

Jessica Lester & Rachael Gabriel

With this quote, "What do I know of man's destiny? I could tell you more about radishes," Samuel Beckett evokes the spirit of the theatre of the absurd (Esslin, 1961); a dramatic tradition focused on that which is constructed as absurd, specifically in terms of language use and the ways in which plot is constructed and theatrical conventions challenged. After World War II, a group of playwrights including Samuel Beckett, Eugene Ionesco, Tom Stoppard, and Harold Pinter, among others, wrote plays in a particular absurdist style called the Theatre of the Absurd (Esslin, 1961). This style of theatre took up the philosophy of existentialism and the notion that human existence has no meaning or purpose; thus, communication inevitably breaks down. Plots in absurdist plays often take an illogical, circular, or repetitive structure, as do the lines of the individual characters. For example, Beckett's *Waiting for Godot*, a well-known example that follows the tradition of the theatre of the absurd, has a series of repeated phrases, characters who talk to each other without having a clearly cohesive conversation, and a plot that ends where it begins. Further, one of the features commonly associated with this style is that of experimentalism. Pirandello, for example, famously challenged the dramatic convention of the "fourth wall"—the suspension of disbelief involved in imagining an invisible wall separating the audience from the world of the stage, as though the audience is behind a fourth wall.

Though Pirandello wrote in the earlier part of the 1900s, his work is considered a precursor to the Theatre of the Absurd style, as it pioneered many of the techniques playwrights used to challenge theatrical conventions. Characters in his work were often created as stereotypical, archetypal, or composites; language was repetitious or nonsensical; and plots had nontraditional structures. In Pirandello's 1921 play, *Six Characters in Search of an Author*, character names invoke archetypes (Father, Manager, Mother, Stepdaughter, Son, etc.), and the characters themselves take over the play from the director, arguing with him about the story that should and will (eventually) be told. With a hope to transgress convention in our own production and representation of research findings, we were drawn to all the theatre of the absurd offered, as it eschewed the theatrical conventions of actor versus director, "real" life versus play, and the notion of stock or archetypal characters. Ultimately, Pirandello's play served as a mentor text for us as we constructed a performative text around what we oriented to as absurd and nonsensical in our research—where we noted problematized boundaries between archetypes, official versions of ability and dis/ability, and unexamined assumptions.

More particularly, we came to this work as educators and qualitative researchers engaged in an ongoing project focused on the experiences of individuals who participate in the special education meetings that ultimately result in the naming of a child as dis/abled (Office of Special Education and Rehabilitative Services, 2000). Situating our understanding of dis/ability within a social-relational model of disability (Thomas, 2004), we view dis/ability as a social construct, which often functions as a "form of oppression involving the social imposition of restrictions of activity on people with impairments and the socially engendered undermining of their psycho-emotional wellbeing" (Thomas, 1999, p. 60). While not denying the reality of bodily impairments, for us the notion of "disability" comes into play when a restriction is placed on one's activities or way of being. As such, for the purposes of this project, we aimed to problematize the very practice of labeling one's way of being dis/abled, particularly learning disabled (LD). We named such technical practices a "theatre of the absurd" in hopes of conveying, at least partially, the inexplicable universes that exist in many special education meetings and in much of what we as qualitative researchers examined.

The Project

Our research included interviews with various stakeholders who had participated in US-based special education meetings. At these meetings, the "experts" presented findings to children and parents as if their findings were rationale, taken-for-granted, and unquestioned knowledge. We came to view the experts' findings as absurdities, which led us to begin to play with the notion of these "special" meetings as performative moments—moments that might be exposed, relived, re-presented. So, we "played" with the language of those involved in these meetings, interrogating, whenever possible, all that counted as valid knowledge, pointing out the discursive limitations and messed-up-ness across the multiple meanings of the names, titles, and labels. Little research attends to the ways in which the *official* (i.e., privileged) and culturally familiar ways of talking about LDs are worked up in the context of the *official* special education meetings—the space in which naming, placing, and tracking are often unquestionably constructed as "beneficial" to the recipient. Orienting to a LD as that which is always already embedded in a network of histories, discourses, and normalized practices, we attended to the ways in which the available regimes of talking about and re-presenting LDs were taken up by the participants.

We situated this work within a performance studies framework (Conquergood, 1998), as we aimed to construct our research findings as the staged retelling, re-remembering, and re-enacting of "ethnographically derived notes" and/or other data sets (Alexander, 2005, p. 411); and as a critical performance (Madison, 2008), attending to the varied discourses that act to position, manage, and at times contest labeled identities framed within normative and deficit models of human development. As we re-presented the discursive practices of our participants, we problematized the very practice of labeling one's way of being dis/abled, orienting to the very practice as a theatre of the absurd (Esslin, 1961).

As an alternative format for disseminating research, performance texts create a space for stories to be told and retold, while providing readers and audiences a chance to participate in the retelling. According to Denzin, "performance approaches to knowing insist on immediacy and involvement" (2003, p. 8), rather than analytic distance or detachment on the part of the researcher or the audience/readership of that research. Thus, we drew upon performance studies and assumed that the participants' lived experiences (de Certeau, 1984) could and perhaps even should, be retold through a performative lens.

Throughout this project, we worked to practice recursive reflexivity (Pillow, 2003), recognizing that our biases and presuppositions shaped how we chose to re-present the data. As such, we aimed to position ourselves "as no longer transparent," but as "classed, gendered, raced, and sexual" beings who engage in constructing and negotiating our social locations (Fine, 1994, p. 76). Since our positions on the process of labeling/naming another's identity affected the ways we constructed this performative text, we explicitly named ourselves directors in the script and acknowledged the power we have as researchers in selecting participants, conducting interviews, interpreting data, and presenting findings. We reflected on the ways in which we exercised power as researchers to determine which voices are potentially heard, how long they're heard, and in what order; as well as which excerpts of the transcripts were made present and relevant and which we left out of the script. Instead of attempting to minimize our positionalities, we sought to increase transparency of the analytical process by highlighting the ways in which we literally and figuratively directed this project, showing the ways in which we used our power to ask participants to stop, continue, repeat, or be quiet.

We interviewed teachers, parents, school psychologists, and students. We learned throughout these interviews that many participants had experiences within special education in which they embodied a variety of roles. Throughout the interviews, the intersectionality of identities (e.g., professors having been teachers and parents, parents having taught, teachers having been parents, etc.) added layers of complexity to our understandings, blurring the distinctions between the stakeholder categories. So, as we constructed the performative text and selected key players, we created composite characters in order to demonstrate the themes and contrasts within and between the individuals and groups with which the participants self-identified.

As an expression of our positionalities, we chose to allow the student character to be "present" in the play and to lead the discussion of the meeting in which students are often the literal and figurative "off-stage characters." We began by allowing the student character to pose each of the questions she wanted to ask, along with some we asked as researchers. Ultimately, we organized our participants' responses to her questions. We worked to stay close to the words of the participants, and whenever possible we used the participants' responses to questions in their entirety, adding only transition words to introduce or conclude the excerpt where necessary. We attempted to preserve as much context as possible around each excerpt—letting the director say the researchers' words and the characters say the participants' words.

In order to provide a framework for the questions and answers to become a story, we studied and learned from Pirandello's 1924 comedy, *Six Characters in Search of an Author*—a controversial work in which the six characters invade the stage and demand to be included. Like Pirandello, we constructed this text in a polemical spirit, working to present the characters as shifting and complex beings, regardless of how the script casts them. We asked our readers/audience to imagine each character as complex, contradictory, and layered. As we envisioned a space in which a student could speak to and query the people present at her initial IEP meeting, we envisioned a somewhat stark rehearsal space with minimal setting or props. Pirandello's play is performed in one act on a minimalist set consisting of an empty rehearsal space with some chairs. We used the mentor text to provide a theatrical frame—borrowing the opening stage directions and opening lines from the play, and using it as a model for a structure as we ordered the questions and responses and constructed a finished text. Although we stayed close to the "actual" words of the participants, we recognized that getting the story "right" is impossible. We did not seek to do so. Instead, we retold a partial version (Noblit, Flores, & Murillo, 2004), recognizing that for every story told, there is a story untold (Krog, 1998).

Throughout the process of writing the play, we returned to several participants and asked who they wished would be in the audience of a performance created from their input. They most often identified people like themselves. For example, the student wished other students and teachers would attend, learning from her experiences. We wanted pre-service teachers, counselors, psychologists, and future parents to engage in the reading in order to provide a glimpse behind the closed door of such meetings and to provide a counter-story (Solórzano & Yosso, 2002) to the stories told about special education in formal graduate-school classroom settings. In an effort to reach both sets of people, we began generating a list of friends and colleagues who had an interest in education, research, or performance art. We asked those who taught courses to educational researchers and/or pre-service teachers to invite their students, and those with family nearby to invite relatives.

The Performances

We spread the word about the show by first creating an electronic invitation welcoming people to participate in a critical performance reading at a local art space. This invitation described our project, thus popularizing both the theme and the notion of performative readings of research findings, as well as the contested nature of LD. We circulated the invitation using an "evite" (www.evite.com), an electronic invitation service, as well as a public Facebook event page. As a social networking site, Facebook allowed us to network with a large group of people quickly and without cost, including people we were not acquainted with and who would not otherwise have had access via fliers or local advertisements. The evite served as a resource for those outside the Facebook network, or those who wanted to invite people (e.g., students in their university classes, parents, colleagues) with whom they preferred not to connect via Facebook. We sent the original evite to ten friends and colleagues. Within a week, our Facebook event page had responses from twelve people, and 92 people had been notified of the event. Further, the event descriptions had been posted on personal sites by several individuals for viewing by anyone connected to them.

After polling the early responders about their weeknight commitments, we offered the performance on two evenings. In an effort to provide more access to the play, we enlisted the help of student interpreters studying sign language at the local university. Some were allowed to earn credit for attending and/or interpreting as they were in classes that reward attempts to seek out a variety of language experiences. In the end, so many volunteered that we had a separate interpreter for each character. Thus everyone had the opportunity to experience speaking their lines and having their words relayed through someone else in a language that was often unfamiliar to them.

In total, 16 audience members attended the first performance and 20 attended the second. From these audience members, eight volunteers each night took on the role of a character and performed the text. Though we cast ourselves as directors in the play, we did not perform those roles, but rather let our words be reinterpreted, reproduced, and embodied by audience members. After a brief welcome and introduction, audience members were encouraged to make themselves comfortable in a rough semi-circle in front of the other audience members to make it easier for everyone to see each other. Most sat, some laid on the floor, others leaned up against the wall. Those reading a role were asked to begin reading when they felt comfortable, and were encouraged to embody the lived experiences and words of the characters in whatever way they desired. At the end of the reading, we took a short break for refreshments and then invited people to share their responses to the reading in a variety of forms. For example, we mounted butcher's paper along the walls and provided markers for people to write or draw with. Others chose to type a response in a blank MS Word document set up on a computer nearby. Others responded using movement or silence. Some requested recorders that they could speak into without having to speak out loud to others. After leaving time for the audience members to explore alternative forms of response, we invited them to join us in an open-ended discussion.

Rather than passively receiving research findings as readers, our audience members actively engaged with them both during and after the performed reading. Though the reading itself lasted only about 30 minutes, each evening lasted for more than two hours, as audience members and "actors" shared how the discourses moved them, troubled their understandings, and left them wondering. Even after the formal discussion ended, many individuals engaged in further discussion with two or three peers, at times retelling a part from the play, situated within their own experiences. Participants suggested we bring the performance to future audiences as varied as YouTube viewers, school assemblies, teacher education classes, and parent organizations. Others asked to meet with us to discuss revisions, memories, and other potential audiences and media for the text. We asked the participants to take and retell these stories in their own work and social spaces.

As we continue to share our research findings in texts and performances, we aim to work against simplistic notions of "helping" the "failing" child and continue to ask: Who benefits? Who loses? Who holds the power? We hope that each retelling leaves audience members wondering, pondering, pushing against static and normalized definitions of "disability," and perhaps even embracing the poetics of resistance (Ayers, 2009).

References

Alexander, B. K. (2005). *Performance ethnography: The reenacting and inciting of culture.* In N. K. Denzin & Y. S., Lincoln (Eds.), *The SAGE handbook of qualitative research* (3rd ed., pp. 411–441). Thousand Oaks, CA: Sage.

Ayers, W. (2009). Barack Obama and the fight for public education. *Harvard Educational Review, 79*(2), 385–395.

Conquergood, D. (1998). Beyond the text: Toward a performative cultural politics. In S. J. Dailey (Ed.), *The future of performance studies: Visions and revisions* (pp. 25–36). Washington, DC: National Communication Association.

de Certeau, M. (1984). *The practice of everyday life.* London, England: University of California Press.

Denzin, N. (2003). *Performance ethnography: Critical pedagogy and the politics of culture.* Thousand Oaks, CA: Sage.

Esslin, M. (1961). *The theatre of the absurd.* Garden City, NY: Anchor Books.

Fine, M. (1994). Working the hyphens: Reinventing self and other in qualitative research. In N. Denzin & Y. Lincoln (Eds.), *The SAGE handbook of qualitative research* (1st ed., pp. 70–82). London, UK: Sage.

Krog, A. (1998). *Country of my skull: Guilt, sorrow, and the limits of forgiveness in the new South Africa*. New York: Three Rivers.

Madison, D. S. (2008). Narrative poetics and performative interventions. In N. K. Denzin, Y. S. Lincoln, & L. T. Smith (Eds.), *Handbook of critical and indigenous methodologies* (pp. 391–405). Los Angeles, CA: Sage.

Noblit, G. W., Flores, S. Y., & Murillo, E. G. (Eds.). (2004). *Postcritical ethnography: Reinscribing critique*. Cresskill, NJ: Hampton Press.

Office of Special Education and Rehabilitative Services. (2000). A guide to the individualized education program. Jessup, MD: US Department of Education.

Pillow, W. S. (2003). Confession, catharsis, or cure? Rethinking the uses of reflexivity as methodological power in qualitative research. *Qualitative Studies in Education*, *16*(2), 175–196.

Solórzano, D. G., & Yosso, T. J. (2002). Critical race methodology: Counter-storytelling as an analytical framework for education. *Qualitative Inquiry*, *8*(1), 23–44.

Thomas, C. (1999) *Female forms: Experiencing and understanding disability*. Buckingham, UK: Open University Press.

Thomas, C. (2004). How is disability understood? An examination of sociological approaches. *Disability & Society*, *19*(6), 569–583.

CHAPTER TWENTY-FIVE

Learn Dis!

A Community Does Research on Itself through Playback Theatre

David Jan Jurasek

Approximately one person in 20 has a disability that profoundly affects how he or she learns or does things. While to the untrained eye it's not clear why people have disabilities, people with learning disabilities (LDs) have historically been labeled as "stupid," "slow," "defiant," and "lazy."

In 2009, working as a therapist with families affected by LDs, I was struck by three staggering realities. First, almost everyone felt alone and unique in his or her situation. Hearing the common themes of isolation, shame, confusion, frustration, and loneliness often made me wonder about how much more solidarity people may feel if they only met others who shared their experiences. Second, some of my clients were gifted creatively and wanted to find ways to express what they were experiencing. Some would write poems, which they shared with loved ones, while others found ways to speak directly in front of their schools about living with their learning disabilities. Third, everyone who engaged in the confidential cocoon of therapy had some form of wisdom that I judged to be worthy of sharing with others. Every client I had eventually came to offer me tips about parenting, friendship, dealing with limitations and bullies, and other important life lessons. It continues to be an incredible honor for me to behold such hard-earned gems of insight and universal common sense on a daily basis. Thus, I wanted to share with others—in an ethical and respectful way—the wisdom I've been privy to.

There was also a personal motivation at play. I am someone who has used various forms of art since early childhood to work through all sorts of painful emotions and complex situations, including having been a child refugee. I am also professionally trained to use art and theatre in communities as a form of research, communal ritual, and also group therapy. I believe that people become more powerful and better equipped to heal when they are given the tools and support to express themselves. I also did not like the fact that much of what is said about learning disabilities comes from those who study it and try to help, rather than from those who actually live it. Therefore, I wanted to be more creative with my clients and to engage the greater community with what they themselves had to share.

Playback Theatre as an Integrated Research Methodology

In selecting the methodologies that would best fit the deeply personal content and our intentions of honoring and empowering people with LDs and their supporters, I came to realize that I was not only treading in a territory where multiple forms of qualitative research overlapped (heuristic inquiry, arts-based, and participatory), I was also drawing upon the form of Playback Theatre as the primary tool of research itself.

Playback Theatre is a form of theatre that is spontaneous—while there is no script, the stories told in the moment by audience members supply the content. It is a "poor-man's theatre" (Fox, 1994) since it can be done anywhere without props and external resources. It's done by members of the community who are trained in the art of theatre as well as that of listening deeply with their hearts and intuitive faculties. Because of its simple yet dynamic and sensitive nature and how quickly it can build a sense of community and interconnectedness, I felt it was the right frame for this study. In the process of creating it, I also discovered that a Playback performance perfectly integrates all of the research modalities mentioned above.

As a way to honor the subjective experiences of clients, parents, teachers, and clinical staff alike, we began together from a phenomenological approach by asking: "What is it like to live with a learning disability and/or support someone who does?" To be authentic in our receiving of answers and to be transparent as research investigators, we adopted a heuristic form of inquiry so as to "enter into a dialogue with the phenomenon, allowing the phenomenon to speak directly to one's own experience, to be questioned by it" (Moustakas, 1990, p.16). This meant that while my clients, their parents, teachers, and my colleagues responded to this question, the Playback company and I explored our own responses to the stories we collected and heard from them. We investigated our own gut reactions, professional and aesthetic judgments, as well as the memories and stories from our own lives that emotionally resonated with the "subjects" of our inquiry. When it came time to perform, we would "draw upon the perceptual powers afforded by...direct experience" (Douglass & Moustakas, 1985, p. 44).

In obvious and not so obvious ways, a Playback performance can also become a form of arts-based research, which is an "integrated inquiry involv[ing] thorough and systematic study while the artistic component offers ways of communicating information and methods of investigation" (McNiff, 1998, p. 51). McNiff (1998) purports that such a creative methodology springs from the unique interplay between the researcher's talents and needs, the nature of the research question, and the field of inquiry. In this case, it was obvious and clear to use Playback Theatre—given my talents and the natural call of some my clients, hungry to tell their stories and be seen and heard by their community. Using such an improvisational and live form of art gave us a way to distill, synthesize, and represent the data almost immediately back to our audience: the "subjects of study." Such is the joy and directness possible with arts-based research (Bagley & Cancienne, 2001) and inherent in Playback. As well, the art of storytelling gave us a framework with enough depth and breadth to hold and reflect the true complexity of human experience with compelling accuracy and accessibility (Campbell & Moyers, 1988; McAdams, 1993; Rubbin, 1996).

How Did We Prepare?

If we, the actors, musicians, and me as conductor (live show director), were to serve the intended community as the instruments of synthesis and reflection, we needed to be as highly trained and prepared as possible.

We began by gathering stories and themes directly and indirectly from the community through questionnaires and interviews. It seemed also necessary for me as the director to sensitize my artistic crew more personally to the issues I saw raised by my clients daily. Though they were already trained or in process of training in the art of Playback Theatre, I also wanted our creative team to have plenty of time walking in the shoes of my clients. In rehearsals, they would take the data I collected and "play" them back. A beautiful thing happened to these people when they started working through their minds and their hearts: a lot of power and wisdom began to emerge. By the fourth week of rehearsal, many of my actors began to share stories of personal difficulty, disability, as well as what it is like to be parents and teachers of children and teens with resonating challenges.

The content was synthesized into short scenes, developed by our professional and nonprofessional actors, dancers, choreographers, and musicians—a few of whom also have a LD. All of this was simply to provide an opening act and as a warm up for when the spontaneous and unpredictable nature of Playback Theatre would take over.

The Performances

After six months of immersion and creative preparation, two separate feature-length performances were planned to take place on October 16 and 18, 2009, in the downtown core of Toronto. The support of many leaders and agencies invested in the service of children, teens, and families with LDs was enlisted to help make the show a success. The LDAO (Learning Disabilities Association of Ontario), YMCA Academy (alternative school), INTEGRA Foundation, and key players from Disabilities Services and the Social Work Department at the University of Toronto stepped up to help us promote and host the shows.

Tickets were presold, with discounts offered to low-income families and people coming in groups. Partners in the project and audience members who couldn't afford tickets were also enlisted as volunteers in managing the door, being ushers, or as part of our back-stage team. The two performances attracted a total of 204 people—surpassing our expectations and selling out both venues. The website of this book visually outlines one of the performances.

The audience members were both the "subjects" and "objects" of our phenomenological study, as they told their own stories, live before one another. As part of the research team, we were watching during and after the shows for signs of congruence or dissonance, especially in regards to whether we were understanding them well enough and re-presenting (through the art of Playback Theatre) their stories with accuracy.

A positive indication of this was the level of trust and willingness of our audience members to tell very personal stories openly to one another. The majority of audience members raised their hands when asked whether they could relate to what was spoken or seen enacted. And many volunteered to tell their stories firsthand.

It was important to us to encourage and evoke a range and diversity of shared experiences. Without it, the result would lack a sense of depth and breadth of insight and understanding. Senior clinicians, academics, parents, children, and teens all told from their own perspectives what it is like to engage with LDs as a big part of their lives. The power of Playback Theatre was in evoking a plurality of experiences, valuing each subjective truth fully, while also allowing a natural sobriety and ambiguity, casting away any hopes of simplistic reductionism (Salas, 2009).

Prior to these performances, my own professional peers expressed some skepticism (regarding the efficacy) and worry (regarding the emotional safety of our common clients). In the course of the shows, some of these colleagues ended up sharing their own stories and gave many accolades, which showed their changed perspectives (see below). Following are a few selected quotes from a broad range of our audience members:

Aweso-mazing! (Boy in the audience).

Like watching ten people stand on the edge of a cliff—exciting and scary. You don't know what to expect. Then they jump—then they soar. It's exhilarating to watch—the courage, the risk, the art. Wow! BRAVO! Kudos! I'm still thinking about your show hours later (Ann T.).

I was amazed by David's ability to zero in on the themes, get people involved at their comfort level, and keep things rolling for two solid hours. And the skills of the actors and actresses were great. Congrats to you and the players for a fun and important evening and to all those who shared their stories (Mike Faye, Executive Director, INTEGRA).

I just wanted to let you all know that this event was absolutely fabulous!…Completely helpful, therapeutic, and really creative and energizing. (Ellen, teacher and parent).

Ethical Considerations and Lessons Learned

Originally, I wanted to invite my own mental-health clients on stage, performing not only parts of their stories but perhaps also playing active parts in someone else's story. Such a framework would have fit into a style of ethnodramatic research (Foley & Valenzuela, 2005) that I admired for its complete participation of "research subjects" along with the level of accountability and empowerment. When I first proposed doing so, my clinical supervisor was somewhat nervous about this idea. Even though she supported a play being staged with client stories, has a passion for empowering our clients and for working collaboratively with community settings, she raised the boundary of what is "safe" for mental-health clients and what trespasses over the domain of clinical confidence.

I share that concern, and as a drama therapist—a field that has at times beautifully blended therapy and community development (Emunah, 1993), I contend that, with proper time for training, preparation, and mindful design, mental-health clients can be supported therapeutically, as well as aesthetically to represent themselves in community with much success and full consent and awareness (Emunah, 1993; Snow, 2009).

Rea Dennis (2008), a Playback practitioner, also raises further ethical points of accountability and aesthetic representation. The concern I see in our use of Playback as research is that in playing back stories, we may over-identify and/or assume too much of our tellers. They may not feel safe in a public context to challenge our representations of them. They may be left misinterpreted and misunderstood. Some people are prone to be too polite in correcting even glaring and vital errors of the troupe. As the Playback team, we are keenly aware that we are still interpreting our tellers, rather than having them show us directly and in their full bodies what they mean, by hopping on stage to do so, for example. However, it is to be noted that every teller does get to tell their story first. And it was vital to our work as ethical Playbackers and respectful researchers that during the performance, we offered space to our tellers (after they were played back), to respond vocally whether we were accurate in portraying their perspective or not.

There are two potent lessons I have reaffirmed while engaging in this research and that only deepen within me as I look back now a year later. First, I believe that it is important to be as open and collaborative as possible. There is much more possibility and wisdom in the work co-created by many than there is in a work created by any one of us. This was clearly evident for me in the rehearsal process as well as the outcome of the shows. Our 204 audience members offered rich and textured stories with far more compelling truths and immediate saliency than what we in the creative team of 20 were able to predict or foresee from reading their words on the questionnaires or imagining ourselves in their shoes.

My second lesson was to trust the spontaneous ability of people, when they have agreed to work together, to be able to take care of themselves beautifully and to be willing to contribute what's necessary for the greater good. This was exactly what happened behind the scenes in staging our shows: many people who were inactive prior to it came out of the woodwork to lend help, offer resources, and put support behind the endeavour. Also, people who were vulnerable, living with disabilities and various forms of hardship, found ways to bow in to contribute and bow out to take care of their own families first.

Acknowledgment

My gratitude to Julia Gotz for allowing me to utilize the images contained on the book website.

References

Bagley, C., & Cancienne, M. B. (2001). Educational research and intertextual forms of (re)presentation: The case for dancing the data. *Qualitative Inquiry, 7*(2), 221–237.

Campbell, J. & Moyers, B. (1988). *The power of myth*. Edited by B. S. Flowers. New York: Doubleday.

Combs, G., & Freedman, J. (1990). *Symbol, story, and ceremony: Using metaphor in individual and family therapy*. New York: W.W. Norton.

Dennis, R. (2008). Refugee performance: Aesthetic representation and accountability in playback theatre. *Research in Drama Education: The Journal of Applied Theatre and Performance, 13*(2), 211–215.

Douglass, B., & Moustakas, C. (1985). Heuristic inquiry: The internal search to know. *Journal of Humanistic Psychology, 25*(3), 39–55.

Emunah, Renee. (1993). *Acting for real: Drama therapy process, technique, and performance*. New York: Brunner-Routledge.

Emunah, R., & Johnson, D. R. (1983). The impact of theatrical performance on the self-images of psychiatric patients. *The Arts in Psychotherapy, 10*(4), 233–239.

Foley, D., & Valenzuela, A. (2005). Critical ethnography: The politics of collaboration. In N. K. Denzin, & Y. S. Lincoln, (Eds.), *The SAGE handbook of qualitative research* (3rd ed., pp. 217–234). Thousand Oaks, CA: Sage.

Fox, J. (1994). *Acts of service: Spontaneity, commitment, tradition, in the unscripted theatre.* New Paltz, NY: Tusitala.

McAdams, D. (1993). *The stories we live by: Personal myths and the making of the self.* New York: William Morrow.

McNiff, S. (1998). *Arts-based research.* London, UK: Jessica Kingsley.

Moustakas, C. (1990). *Heuristic research: Design, methodology, and applications.* Detroit, MI: Sage.

Rubbin, S. (1996). *The role of the storyteller in self-revelatory performance.* (Unpublished master's thesis). California Institute of Integral Studies, San Francisco, CA.

Salas, J. (2009). Playback theatre: A frame for healing. In R. Emunah & D. R. Johnson (Eds.), *Current approaches* (pp. 445–460). Springfield, IL: C. C. Thomas.

Snow, S. (2009). Ritual/theatre/therapy. In R. Emunah & D. R. Johnson (Eds.), *Current Approaches* (pp. 117–144). Springfield, IL: C. C. Thomas.

CHAPTER TWENTY-SIX

Moving Poetic Inquiry beyond the Academy

How Two Poets Popularize Their Research

John Guiney Yallop & Sean Wiebe

In this chapter, written in three parts, we present two separate journeys that detail the use of poetic inquiry in conducting research. We describe the processes and the products, and we offer possibilities for how others might conduct this form of inquiry. Poetic inquiry has many forms (Prendergast, 2009), but essentially it is about using poetry to investigate and come to deeper understandings of the topic or subject of our research (Guiney Yallop, 2008; Wiebe, 2008; Prendergast, Leggo, & Sameshima, 2009; *Educational Insights*, 2010).

In part one of this chapter, John writes about how he, as principal investigator, with co-investigator Kathleen Naylor and two graduate-student participants, Shamimara Sharif and Nancy Taylor, explored graduate-student identities using poetic inquiry; all four considered themselves participants in the project. They met at four locations and wrote poetry about their identities. They then performed their poetry for a public audience where they launched a chapbook that contained selected poems from the research. The poetry has also been performed in the authors' homes and home communities.

As a researcher in poetic inquiry, Sean has been researching the ways that poetry enlivens or enchants what we know. Part of his search has included participation in poetry slams hosted by the Prince Edward Island Diversity Office. In part two of this chapter, Sean discusses his participation in the poetry slams and the usefulness of this type of participation in the dissemination of his research.

We conclude this chapter with a third part in which we reflect on our work as poetic researchers, writing and performing individually and collaboratively. We offer no conclusions, but we do open up, we hope, spaces for further conversations about what might be possible when researchers turn to poetry to explore and represent what they are studying and what they are learning. As our "show" component to this piece, available on the book's website, we offer readings by three of the graduate students from John's research and readings by Sean of two of his poems that have brought him deeper understandings of what it means to do research. The texts of the poems are also available on the book website.

Part One (John): Gathering as a Way to Popularize Research

If we are to tell our stories to each other, if we are to share our lives, then we need to gather together in community to tell, to share, to listen to each other, to hear each other, to live in each other's presence, and to allow the stories of others to change how we understand and live our own stories. We began by gathering together to tell our stories, to share parts of our life journeys. This sharing is documented in two earlier pieces of writing, the chapbook we created from our work together (Guiney Yallop, Naylor, Sharif, & Taylor, 2008), and the article we co-wrote (Guiney Yallop, Naylor, Sharif, & Taylor, 2010). It was also documented in a presentation I gave with the co-investigator, Kathleen Naylor (Guiney Yallop & Naylor, 2009).

The project was conducted at Acadia University and in the surrounding community. The four participants met in four locations to write poetry and to share the writing we did between the sessions. We wrote poems on themes in response to the work of other poets; excerpts from my own doctoral dissertation (Guiney Yallop, 2008) were used, as well as collections of poetry by Cornelia Hoogland (2005), Carl Leggo (2006), and Lorri Neilsen Glenn (2007). The themes were: What is poetic inquiry?; Who am I?; Relationships; Longing; Possibilities. I selected the themes from the writings of the authors whose work we studied. We also wrote and talked about how those works connected with our lived experiences as graduate students; in my case, that experience came from the recent past, but for Kathleen Naylor, Shamimara Sharif, and Nancy Taylor, it was an experience they were living as they were writing.

In sharing our journeys, we came to know other journeys, others' journeys. In sharing our journeys, we also created new journeys, individually and together. We also created a poetry chapbook from our writing (Guiney Yallop, Naylor, Sharif, & Taylor, 2008), selecting pieces that we felt best expressed the journeys we shared and created. Each poet selected some poems from the writing over the time of the project; the poems selected were ones the poet felt best conveyed her journey. I decided to write the foreword to the chapbook (Guiney Yallop, 2008), but not include my own poetry; I wanted the poems of the three women who were living the experience of being graduate students to ring out those experiences through the pages, and I believe they did. We had the chapbook printed at the Copy Centre of the Acadia Student Union, using funds from the grant provided by the Acadia University Research Fund to pay for the printing; the 100 copies of the chapbook were distributed free of charge at the performance described below and at other events. Copies were also sent to the Acadia University Library and to the authors whose work we studied. Because of the interest in the project, and the poetry produced, and because of our desire to distribute the chapbook as widely as possible, a reprint of the chapbook was necessary.

We then performed our poetry at an advertised poetry performance. Advertising was done mostly through email attachments, using a flyer announcing the event. The performance was held in the University Club at Acadia University. We used some of the funds mentioned above to rent the space for the performance and to provide snacks for the audience. A cash bar was available and door prizes, copies of the books by Hoogland (2005), Leggo (2006), and Neilsen Glenn (2007), were distributed at the end of the performance; audience members also received a copy of the chapbook. Family, friends, and colleagues gathered to hear our work. Since that event, the poems have also been performed at other locations, including readings at the homes and in the home communities of some of the participants.

By putting their work in our chapbook, giving me permission to include their poetry in other publications, performing their work in public locations, inviting family members and friends to attend their readings, and making their work available here for many other readers and listeners, Kathleen Naylor, Shamimara Sharif, and Nancy Taylor are contributing to a circle of giving. They are, first of all, giving back to the very individuals, families, and communities who nourished them—who made it possible for them to step into the academic community. They are also giving to the academic community, and they are giving to other communities beyond the academic community and beyond their immediate circles of family, friends, local or personal and professional communities, to broader communities—to communities they may not even know exist. I believe that giving is part of how we create and sustain community. I believe that giving our gifts is a moral responsibility as members of communities.

Reading poetry or hearing poetry read is an opportunity to receive the gifts offered. While I hesitate to summarize the responses of our audiences, both listeners and readers, I would say that the responses have been encouraging. We are, first and foremost, our own audience. Kathleen, Shamim, and Nancy all commented on how the process gave them new understandings of their own identities and how the process itself was transformative for them in that they noted shifts in their identities over the time of the project. The process was also transformative for me. As my first funded poetic-inquiry research project, I felt that the project was a solid example of what is possible using poetry as a way to do research; the responses to the performances and the publications affirmed that feeling.

And it is that audience response that has been particularly significant. At the public performance, it was stated that the poetry created new understanding both of the identities of graduate students and of the individual authors themselves. One audience member in the session where Kathleen and I performed (Guiney Yallop & Naylor, 2009) said that we had created a space for her to pause and reflect, a space she had not been aware she needed until she had been given it. Another audience member in the same session, a graduate student, said that the performance had valued his experiences. Carl Leggo, in an email communication after receiving a copy of our chapbook, described our work as "heartfelt journeys into tangled places of complicated truths and desires." We were so moved by Carl's words that we used them in the subtitle of our article (Guiney Yallop, Naylor, Sharif, & Taylor, 2010). We invite our audiences, our listeners and readers, into those heartfelt journeys, which are also conversations; and those journeys, those conversations, are tangled places filled with truths and desires that are indeed complicated. They are also spaces for connection, for community. And they are spaces for understanding our identities, the relationships that are so much a part of our identities, our longings, and what is possible for us. They are also spaces for experiencing, and even better understanding, poetic inquiry.

Part Two (Sean): Poetry Slams

My research includes poetry as a means to make my research more accessible to a broader audience, but also to deepen my research and to bring coherence to what I do as a social-science researcher, and what I do as a poet. Poetry prompts great conversation, and in so doing the hard edge of research is tapered for an audience more inclined to interact with ideas. I find that my poetry humanizes my research, giving it a blended quality of reason and emotion, prompting readers to consider the values and assumptions of their world.

When I write poetry, the phenomenon of my experience is subject to textual plays, each acting to translate, transform, and transgress what might normally be too readily seen and understood. As I construct the poem, I keep in mind the tension between the textual play and the spoken-word performance. The texts are not oppositional in nature, but complementary. For example, knowing that my poems will be performed at a poetry slam, I often write actively, on my feet, rehearsing as I write new lines. This gives my text a more rhythmic and narrative appeal, which is an expectation for an audience that will only hear my poems. At the same time, readers who experience my poems as text on the page often demand concision. Being able to come to a poem many times, being able to analyze a poem in detail, these readers enjoy ambiguity, line breaks, allusions, and so forth. Both the slam performance and the fixed-on-the-page poem are texts; both are ways into knowing; both are translations of the phenomenon of our lives. Taken together, I find that it is in this back-and-forth writing of poetry that I learn to think critically, to imagine alternate possibilities. Foucault (1988) writes that one's scholarly task is to "question over and over again what is postulated as self-evident" (p. 265).

Poetry provokes. In my poem "Wittgenstein on Tap," for example, the imaginary circumstances of branding scholars as beer labels considers the implications of what it means to be a scholar and promote one's work. That is, what does a professor profess in the process of popularizing an idea? As I set down in prose this research question for the "tell" portion of this chapter, I am happily aware that the poems included with this chapter do not articulate the question so directly, so precisely, as to transmit a message in the same way a research question might. What poems do not say, what they leave open, is one of the reasons why I continue to write poetry and to include poems as part of my research.

Pragmatically, important to my practice has been ongoing attendance to a writers' group, where in workshop format we share and edit each other's work. As I make suggested revisions, I often begin to see which of my poems can be selected and brought together for a manuscript to be submitted to a literary press. Acorn Press, a medium-sized press in Atlantic Canada, recently published my collection titled *How Boys Grow Up* (Wiebe, 2010). It was the ongoing process of writers' workshop and work with my editor that helped shape this collection.

Also important to my slam performances is the regular gathering for readings. Having recently moved to Prince Edward Island, I was a complete newcomer and needed to find out where and when I could perform. I attended a book launch and bought a book from a local author. She pointed me to the open mics at the public library, and soon I was also connected to the regular open-mic sessions at UPEI. I was also on the lookout for events, sometimes as simple as seeing a poster at a coffee shop, which is how I found out that the local Fringe Festival was vetting submissions. Two months later, I was onstage performing a 35-minute one-act show, which was billed as a spoken-word performance.

Once a month on PEI, there are opportunities to perform my poems on the UPEI campus. Sometimes the format is open mic; sometimes it is a slam competition. I like the cross pollination of my work. Before a reading, I'll promote my book; to popularize my social-science research, I do readings; and in my research, I write poems. Each activity is an opening, as these poetic openings can authenticate experience for audiences and readers who often feel that what emerges in a poem, whether performed or preformed on the page, are the subtle motivations and causes that test the limits of knowledge and emotion.

I also promote the political quality of what poetry provokes. In the last few centuries, the materialist explanation of everything, from the behaviour of atoms to the libidinal desires of the unconscious, has seemed to fail to adequately convey the broad range of human experience.

Even in the social sciences, there is a growing consensus that qualitative research must become more exploratory in its ways to represent lived experience in all its rich diversity. Politically, this means being ever aware that the neo-liberal penchant for technocratic and instrumental solutions has a tendency toward generalization. Poetry is political when it remembers the particularity, when it promotes diversity, when it professes freedoms for alternative ways of thinking and being. Unlike a law, poetry cannot guarantee freedom. What is beautiful about poetry, as it relates to freedom, is the need for another poem. Poetry underscores the point that freedom is an ongoing process, that freedoms are pursued, and that word play is part of that process. In my poem "Another Parable About Neighbours," the notion of freedom is juxtaposed with a glass of lemonade on a hot day.

While not always readily apparent, I look for the transformative possibilities in poetry. What matters for me is not the accuracy or truth of the events as they unfold in the poetic narrative, but the writing of a new line of existence. Writing and rewriting create new relations, as new interpretations arise from the present selves looking backwards. What matters for me are the political questions a poem can provoke: What would we need to believe about the world in order for this to be true? What would we need to believe about the world in order for this action to make sense? How have we constructed the world so that what I'm doing, thinking, and seeing is socially acceptable?

Part Three (John and Sean):
Being and Collaborating as Poet Researchers

As noted above by Sean, when we write, we are writing a new line of existence. We have found, as John notes, that we need a community for that writing. In many ways, we have found parts of that community in each other. We have also found that, with and through each other, we are brought into, or we step into, new realities. In our collaborative work, whether in writing (Wiebe & Guiney Yallop, 2010a) or in performance (Wiebe & Guiney Yallop, 2010b), we have found a deepening understanding of ourselves, each other, and the many others who surround us and receive our work, who remind us of what is important and refresh us in our individual and shared journeys.

Our writing and our performances, as with the writing and performances of Kathleen, Shamim, and Nancy, are expressions of gratitude. They are also offerings of possibility. They are invitations into new lines of existence, new ways of being, and being with, each other. We often begin our writing together, side by side or across from each other, with an articulation of our difference. By articulating and exploring our difference, we discover connection. We stay in, and further explore, our connection in order to come to better understandings of what our difference offers us—individually and together. Our collaborative work becomes an opportunity not only for us to explore our difference, and connection, but for others to bring their own deep and varied experiences to our conversations, making connections with us and with others, thus enriching their own lives, the lives of others, and the writing and performing we do as poet researchers.

For us, whether we are writing poetry at home with our children, with our colleagues at an academic conference, or with students in a language-arts classroom, our hope is that we will have an opportunity to explore the world differently. As we write poetry together, we look for ways to disrupt the normalizing processes of social institutions. We are careful to create the space in such a way that we are never the only poets in the room. Together, we embrace the permission of our senses, desires, and illusions to explain the lived realities of our lives, of what it means to be human.

Acknowledgments

We gratefully acknowledge the Acadia University Research Fund for financial support of John's project, and the Prince Edward Island Diversity Office for hosting poetry slams where Sean performed his poetry. We also acknowledge the contributions of Kahleen Naylor, Shamimara Sharif, and Nancy Taylor.

References

Educational Insights, (2010). (Online journal for the Centre for Cross Faculty Inquiry in Education, University of British Columbia. Volume 13, Number 3. Available at http://www.educationalinsights.ca/.

Foucault, M. (1988). The concern for truth. In L. D. Kritzman (ed.), *Michel Foucault: Politics, philosophy, culture, interviews and other writings 1977–1984* (pp. 255–267). New York: Routledge.

Guiney Yallop, J. J. (2008). *OUT of place: A poetic journey through the emotional landscape of a gay person's identities within/without communities*. (Unpublished doctoral thesis). University of Western Ontario, London.

Guiney Yallop, J. J. (2009). Foreword. In J. J. Guiney Yallop, K. Naylor, S. Sharif, & N. Taylor. *Exploring identities through poetic inquiry*. Unpublished Poetry Chapbook: Authors.

Guiney Yallop, J. J., & Naylor, K. (2009). Exploring identities through poetic inquiry. Performance at Society for Teaching and Learning in Higher Education "Between The Tides" Conference, University of New Brunswick, Fredericton, NB.

Guiney Yallop, J. J., Naylor, K., Sharif, S., & Taylor, N. (2008). *Exploring identities through poetic inquiry*. Self-published poetry chapbook: Authors.

Guiney Yallop, J. J., Naylor, K., Sharif, S., & Taylor, N. (2010). Exploring identities through poetic inquiry: Heartfelt journeys into tangled places of complicated truths and desires. *Collected Essays on Learning and Teaching, 3.*

Hoogland, C. (2005). *Second marriage*. London, ON: Canadian Poetry Association.

Leggo, C. (2006). *Come-by-chance: A collection of poems*. St. John's, NL: Breakwater Books.

Neilsen Glenn, L. (2007). *Combustion*. London, ON: Brick Books.

Prendergast, M. (2009). Introduction: The phenomena of poetry in research. In M. Prendergast, C. Leggo, & P. Sameshima (Eds.). *Poetic inquiry: Vibrant voices in the social sciences* (xix–xlii). Rotterdam, Netherlands: Sense Publishers.

Prendergast, M., Leggo, C., & Sameshima, P. (2009). *Poetic inquiry: Vibrant voices in the social sciences*. Rotterdam, Netherlands: Sense Publishers.

Wiebe, S. (2008). Poetic tactics: Teaching writing for critical literacy. Paper presented at Canadian Association of Curriculum Studies (CACS), University of British Columbia.

Wiebe, S. (2010). *How boys grow up*. Charlottetown, PEI: Acorn Press.

Wiebe, S., & Guiney Yallop, J. J. (2010a). Ways of being in teaching: Conversing paths to meaning. *Canadian Journal of Education, 33*(1), 177–198.

Wiebe, S. & Guiney Yallop, J. J. (2010b). Ways of being in teaching: Conversing paths to meaning. Presentation at Canadian Society for the Study of Education Conference, Concordia University, Montreal, QC.

CHAPTER TWENTY-SEVEN

Popularizing Research as a Career

Personal, Powerful, Political

Kimberly Dark

"We are creating the world, even as it creates us." I communicate this idea continuously in my work. It's simple and memorable, and sets the stage for a performance of sociology. My contributions in writing and performance are concerned with everyday life, how we create and nurture the systems that either support or thwart our best efforts at fairness and creativity. My creative work is about nurturing conscious culture-makers. I use humor and stories and poetry to remind the audience that we already are culture makers, constrained as we may feel by social circumstances. Our lives are our own: we have agency. I've found that this is not widely known. It's helpful to see culture-creation modeled, to see it in one's family or community, to see it normalized on stage.

In my case, I work to reveal the intersections of individual agency and social privilege. My interest as a sociological practitioner is to encourage considered everyday speech and action in the service of creating better systems; to make it easier for oppression to seem merely like a bad idea, unsatisfying and unrewarding. I advocate for systems of thinking and creating culture that will make it easier for individuals to behave with kindness and respect toward one another, rather than limiting kindness and respect to certain recipients, or enshrining those activities as noble ideals toward which the common person can only inspire. In my writing and performances, power is not an evil to be controlled; it is generated internally and externally and can be manipulated to greater or lesser good (see Moore Lappe, 2010). Understanding how our individual lives are constrained by our culture and the meaning our culture gives the circumstances of our birth (gender, race, class) and attributes will lead to greater agency in creating systems that benefit all who participate in them.

This chapter about a career in autoethnographic research and public presentations of sociological thought follows in two parts: part one is a personal story about how this type of career emerged from training and life experience, and part two describes methodology and dissemination. The performance clips available on the website provide two experiences of the work:

one performance poem, "Public Woman" (from my audio CD *Location Is Everything*), and excerpts from a theatre show, *Complicated Courtesies*.

Part One: The Personal—How Did This Happen?

One thing I've learned as a sociologist is that the hidden architecture of social systems affects how people think and feel about their everyday lives. We are all learners, all creators, though many do not feel entitled to act upon their surroundings. The tools of research, scholarship, and creativity could be public tools. We could be better at sharing them, for everyday use.

One thing I've learned as an artist is that in order to inspire, my work must bring pleasure and evoke emotion. Performative work is a way to show "what is" in various ways, and a way to show the possible. Creative expression can call up feelings that aren't yet acceptable in the everyday world and let us try on more powerful selves.

And one thing I've learned as a person who makes a life and a living teaching sociology, doing research about the social world, and making art for public consumption is that the human ability to constantly create culture is always personal, powerful, and political.

She needed me to do more: 1993

As the teacher introduced me, the young men in the back of the high-school classroom were already shuffling their chairs. Then he left the room, knowing full well what my reception might be. I can't be sure of that, of course, but I felt his disrespect from the moment he met me in the school office. Happy enough at his departure, I introduced myself and explained that I came from an organization called GenderPeace and that today's discussion would focus on violence against women in the media. As I began showing a video clip featuring Anne Simonton and the "Myth California" beauty pageant protests, the chant began as a murmuring in the back of the room. It rose to coordinated protest: "Femi-nazi! Femi-nazi! Femi-nazi!"

Despite the volume of the chant, the teacher didn't return. As the boys chanted and rattled their chairs like weapons, the other students clucked and rolled their eyes, looking from me to the boys—waiting to see what I would do. One young woman in the front row slumped down in her chair, looking frightened. Her gaze was locked on me and her brow was furrowed as she wept silently. Occasionally, she used the sleeve of her sweatshirt to wipe her streaming nose. I put the film on pause and I stood silent in front of the room until those boys lost interest in their disruption. I held a calm, steady, external demeanor. Then I released those boys to the library and continued my discussion with the remaining students (a dozen girls and one boy). During the three to four minutes of chanting, the feeling of rage those boys projected was palpable in the room. The remaining students seemed relieved when those seven or eight boys left—despite the chanters' air of triumph.

I felt powerless to reach or engage those boys. All I could do was wait them out—then send them out. Though my offerings were well researched and interesting enough for an audience who wanted to hear them, my material and delivery fell short of reaching half the students in the room. Some of my other offerings as an anti-violence educator were a bit more personal, more engaging. On themes such as rape or child sexual abuse, I was able to engage most students. But my offerings on media representations of women and sexual harassment were assailable—perhaps because they most indicted everyday actions. I'm a good teacher. And that wasn't enough.

That young woman crying in the front row at Carlsbad High School affected me profoundly. She was no older than 16 or 17, weeping openly, looking so threatened in her classroom with no one to comfort her. Her eyes pleaded for me to do something. Do something. Do something that will change this. Anything. Do more than you're doing.

Within a year of that presentation, I attended a poetry slam for the first time. It was fun, and a little ridiculous. What I found most compelling was the audience response. While audience members may or may not have liked the content of a certain poem, the passion and immediacy of the performances were unassailable. One couldn't argue the effects of a person, speaking from the "I," alone-on-the-stage vulnerable, using rhythm, presence, audible breath, and emotion.

That frightened, weeping teenage girl stays with me. She takes so many forms I can't even begin to name them. So, this is my unique contribution in the world—my work as a sociologist and an engaged citizen. I tell stories. I do it on stage because embodied presence matters. And I do it in print and with the help of research in the social sciences because clarity and precision matter. I make my own research by mining my experience for the veins that intersect both my life and the cultural landscape, traversing the borders of social systems. Every story is about me, but I am not the subject. I am not the subject; I am the conduit, breath and voice for scholarly thinking that makes the world more fertile for diverse lives and respectful interactions. I'm not trying to change the academy—I'm trying to change the world around it through pleasure and emotion and engagement.

Part Two: Methodology and Dissemination

My process continues to change and has become less defensive of "social science as art" than when I began this endeavor. For my first and second performance pieces, I used a process of informal interviews on my chosen themes, systematic introspection, and meditative free-writing (Dark, 1998). And then, I re-created those dialogues and introspections on stage, in poetic vignettes. The scripts included my inner-landscape related to my themes. They also included my uncertainties and allowed me to ask the audience for help with those uncertainties. Though I constructed a methodology that was reasonably sound, I was not yet skilled in handling the artistic process of using my presence and revealment to move an audience. The question "what if I do *this*—how will it affect the audience?" began emerging again and again in my work.

My first show: *The Butch/Femme Chronicles: Discussions With Women Who Are Not Like Me (and Some Who Are)* debuted in 1997. And here's what the Kimberly Dark of the time would have said: "I am not a playwright. I am not an actor. I am a sociologist and this is simply the most engaging way to render this particular research (damnit!)." The show toured modestly for nearly seven years. My efforts were a novelty and I was asked to explain "sociology-as-performance" and do the show at a handful of universities. I also created press kits and booked the show at a few theatres. After that, it was word of mouth—someone saw the show and requested it for another venue. My performance work was fascinating to me and well received, but not yet a career (I still spent the majority of my time as principal of a community engagement and research consulting firm). I also gave occasional lectures about the methods that created the show for students and social-science audiences at colleges and universities, but I felt more like a visiting curiosity than a visiting scholar. Interestingly, it wasn't until later—when I more fully embraced my role as an artist—that I began to truly feel my scholarly role as well.

A literature professor at University of Colorado said to me, after one such lecture on "why this is sociology (damnit!)" pulled me aside and said: "You know, you're a good writer. The text is strong. You don't need to keep claiming this is social science. The writing can stand on its own. Some might need that kind of posturing, but you don't."

Whether or not my performance work "needed" to be legitimized as social science, to me it was—and it was important that social science be useful. My ways of explaining the work, and the methods, have evolved over time. I feel far less defensive of the work because it simply matters less to me to be acceptable within big tent of sociology. I'm happy enough doing good work in the academic circus sideshow. I love the circus, but my primary audiences don't even buy a ticket to that show; that's my fun, not theirs. Scholarly community enriches me, but I've never wanted to work full-time in the academy. Audience response (including the response of interdisciplinary scholars) has become my litmus. I no longer work, as I did in my master's thesis, to place a creative work alongside a sociological analysis guarded by academic language, precedent, and methodological justifications. Theory and methodology are still important, but in a more organic way. I do scholarly work just as I suggest other non-academics do it—as a set of processes and focused investigations that serve a purpose, as a way to investigate how to live a better life, make a better world.

Where's the sociological research component now? Some of it is auto-ethnographic and some of it is teaching—in that way that teaching can also be a method of inquiry. Teaching, whether from the stage or in the classroom, is a generative practice. It prompts me to keep seeing anew, not just the specific material I'm teaching, but myself, within the discipline, with the audience—anew and anew. I don't present the phenomenological and ethnomethodological theory and research that says we can invent culture through our everyday lives; I enact them. Through writing and contact, the greater purpose is not to deliver content, but to inspire.

These days, I write almost daily, about what I see in the social world, about specific stories that compel me. I love how the specifics of everyday life can illustrate a sociological concept, or a piece of research with greater clarity. For example, "Public Woman" is a story that appears in my educational performance *Becoming the Subject of Your Own Story (Rather Than the Object of Another's Gaze)* and on my 2008 audio CD, *Location Is Everything*. I was conscious of using concepts from Carol Brooks Gardner (1980) along with other scholarly articles and discussions I've read and digested on these themes. I used a series of personal accounts to construct a narrative that is once a story, and a set of suggestions to the audience on how to take responsibility for their everyday lives in gendered interactions. This example uses autoethnographic storytelling, though I don't see it as research in the strictest sense. It is a way to use sociology, via an understanding of the audience's need for pleasure, a way to prompt recognition of human agency, the possibility to change the social world through everyday interactions.

In addition to writing as a daily practice, I let the theorists have at it in my mind, in order to make something new of their work. Perhaps this is a common scholarly practice, but then I proceed to creative writing directly. For my current show, *Complicated Courtesies*, Erving Goffman and Audre Lorde had long discussions in my dreams and musings as I reread some of their work. I look for ways to engage these authors as more than just sources of information. The scholar-me is always present. Do I cherry-pick and decontextualize the work for my performances? Absolutely. I am a social scientist, but I am also an artist. I take responsibility for both, but my pact with the audience is that they will be entertained. I start out as the social scientist—laying out everything I would want to "tell" the audience, and I end as the performance artist—the one who cares about the gestalt of the experience, the way an audience is moved, not just what the audience thinks.

Learning the Rules of the Artistic Marketplace

Arts marketing is a business. My agent represents a full range of "campus offerings" from hypnotists to nutritionists, comedians to lecturers and performers. Some are scholars whose work is judged academically—some are "novelties" (No, really, that's what they're called in the brochure: www.kirklandproductions.com). I'm also represented on a speakers' bureau that specializes in social-justice activism (www.speakoutnow.org). I didn't readily embrace the business of making a living as an artist, and maybe this is in part traceable to academic norms. We learn that peer reviews and small audiences are our business—putting the right spin on a press release or poster is somehow beneath us. On the contrary, I've learned that it's an integral part of my work. Since 2005, this representation has cemented a career path that had been pulling me away from "other research" for years. And I'm still learning how to market the complex offerings I proffer. My agent finds me to be a challenge because my messages are complex. "Simple" just isn't what I'm selling.

I've learned that performing my work at universities most often has little to do with being recognized as a sociologist. I arrive as campus programming toward student development goals: diversity, women's issues, healthy sexuality, body image, and personal responsibility. Visiting a few dozen college campuses each year to do performance work is a beautiful irony. Sometimes I get to stay a few days and explain the sociology behind the work, but often I'm the edu-tainment. At theatres and festivals, the "sociologist" piece of my bio is nothing but a curiosity—hopefully not a detriment (because I don't know if you've heard, but social scientists have a public reputation of being a giant snooze). Entertainment value is my currency now and it matters how the product is framed. I'm still learning. My web presence is an ever-evolving exercise in identity management as an artist and scholar.

I've learned that the combination of presence, vocal rhythm, and humility—being in the fix of social life with the audience—prompts audiences to take in and extend my thinking with greater ease and verve than lecture alone (Dark, 2009). I look for the balance between show and tell—and ways to make the "tell" more entertaining. The one truly negative review I ever received from a daily newspaper's arts reviewer compared me to a "motherly women's studies professor" (I'm not sure what this conjures for you, but the reviewer did not mean this kindly). That performance, I think, veered too close to the tone or content of "telling." And so I learn; I modify and enhance my content, style, and clarity.

My performance projects take different forms, as is appropriate to my (partially) market-driven work. Most of my research is auto-ethnographic. Sometimes I do an interview-based project, and sometimes my performance texts are based on others' sociological research. In all cases, writing is a method of inquiry (Richardson, 2000). Performance is also a method of inquiry. I collect audience views and input in various ways, and process them according to my training and to the internal logic of my projects. The arguable questions include: Are we still true to our disciplines when we innovate? And without the academic constraints, can I do good scholarly work? It's important to keep answering these questions—and in the meantime, I'll keep creating sociology, even as it creates me.

References

Brooks Gardner, C. (1980). Passing by: Street remarks, address rights, and the urban female. *Sociological Inquiry*, *50*, 328–356.

Dark, K. (1998). *Nested identities: Stories of symbiotic social construction in a community-based collaborative.* (Unpublished master's thesis). California State University, San Marcos.

Dark. K. (Speaker). (2008). *Location is everything* (CD). San Diego, CA: Durga Sound Studio.

Dark, K. (2009). Examining praise from the audience: What does it mean to be a "successful" poet-researcher? In C. Leggo, M. Prendergast, & P. Sameshima (Eds.), *Poetic inquiry: Vibrant voices in the social sciences* (pp. 171–186). Rotterdam, Netherlands: Sense Publications.

Moore Lappé, F. (2010). *Getting a grip 2: Clarity, creativity and courage for the world we really want.* Cambridge, MA: Small Planet Media.

Richardson, L. (2000). Writing: A method of inquiry. In N. K. Denzin, & Y. S. Lincoln (Eds.), *The handbook of qualitative research*, 923–948. Thousand Oaks, CA: Sage.

Part 9

PUBLICITY

CHAPTER TWENTY-EIGHT

Tips for Generating a Media Release and Media Coverage

How the Media Ate Up My Research on Aussie Horror Movies

Mark David Ryan

The focus of this paper is preparing research for dissemination by mainstream print, broadcast, and online media. While the rise of the blogosphere and social media is proving an effective way of reaching niche audiences, my own research reached such an audience through traditional media. The first major study of Australian horror cinema, my PhD thesis *A Dark New World: Anatomy of Australian Horror Films* generated strong interest from horror-movie fans, film scholars, and filmmakers. I worked closely with the Queensland University of Technology's (QUT) public-relations unit to write two separate media releases circulated on October 13, 2008, and October 14, 2009.

A key lesson from this experience is that redeveloping research for the media is an acquired skill. It requires a sharp writing style, letting go of academic justification, catchy quotes, and an ability to distil complex details into easy-to-understand concepts. Although my study received strong media coverage, and I have since become a media commentator, my experiences also revealed a number of pitfalls that are likely to arise for other researchers keen on targeting media coverage. This chapter reflects upon the process of working with the media and provides tips for reaching audiences, particularly in terms of strategically planning outcomes. It delves into the background of my study, which would later influence my approach to the media, the process of drafting media releases, and key outcomes and benefits from popularizing research. The website contains the two original media releases.

The Media Release Process and the Coverage That Followed

Before the release of *Wolf Creek* (2005), *Daybreakers* (2010), and the documentary *Not Quite Hollywood* (2008), which rekindled local interest in Australia's genre-movie heritage in the 1970s and 1980s, Australian horror movies were rarely associated with Australian cinema. While Australian fright flicks have been a relatively successful export industry since the 1970s, Australian cinema has long prided itself on cultural films depicting notions of Australianness from *Crocodile Dundee* (1986) to *The Man from Snowy River* (1982). As a result, Australian horror movies had largely been written out of film history. Yet in 2005, Australian horror movies were on the verge of growing popularity and strong commercial success. *Wolf Creek* would go on to make A$50 million in gross revenue from a production budget of $1.4 million. *Saw* (2004), created by Melbourne filmmakers, became the most successful horror movie franchise of all time, and *Daybreakers,* earned over US$50 million at the global box-office. Between 2000 and 2009, the production of Aussie horror films surged—the number of horror flicks produced tripled during this period. Beginning my PhD at the peak of this resurgence, my doctoral research focussed on the history of Aussie horror movies, and the market forces driving production.

Nearing the end of my research in late 2008, I began thinking about promoting my study. It was apparent early in my candidature that my project had potential to reach a much broader audience than my PhD supervisors and examiners. A common adage is that a PhD student spends at least three exhausting years of his/her life writing a monograph for it to be read by around seven people. By the final year of my research, I had a mailing list of more than 60 filmmakers, policymakers, and horror aficionados who had requested a copy of the study following its release. After continual requests during my fieldwork, I quite simply collected people's email addresses and promised to send them an e-copy once it had been examined.

Attending a media workshop held by QUT's public-relations unit, I spoke with an organizer and pitched the idea of a media release on the Aussie movie industry. Expecting difficulties in arguing my case, I was surprised when the representative took down my contact details and a week or so later the head of public relations telephoned to tell me that they would produce a release. The workshop also gave me an excellent introduction to the media, which helped me understand why my story appealed to QUT PR and later the media. There are several key news values that determine a story's newsworthiness: timeliness, proximity, prominence, human interest, impact, conflict, or oddity. My own research appealed to both oddity and timeliness. For QUT PR, it was also a chance to promote a unique story with potential for popular appeal.

Over the next three weeks, and many telephone conversations and emails later, Amanda Vine (the PR officer assigned to my story) and I drafted a media release titled "Aussie horror rises from the grave." The release's angle focused on the Australian film industry's poor box-office performance in recent years, and argued that by contrast Aussie horror-movie production has been booming. The media release had a strong industry focus, picking up on the core drive of my research.

At first it was extremely difficult to be hands-off during this process. All I was doing was making the release more academic. I kept adding details that Amanda kept taking out; trying to qualify every point. In the end, I trusted Amanda's ability to draft a PR release while I concentrated on ensuring the factual accuracy of my statements, and adding flair for horror fans—expressions like "undead from beyond the grave." Once the release was finally drafted, the story was circulated on October 14, 2008, across national media wires; released strategically to coincide with Halloween and the release of the strongly publicised cannibal movie *Dying Breed* (2008). During this period, media organizations are often searching for stories on the dark side of popular culture, and in particular horror movies, as Halloween is a key release date for scary movies. My story was thus released at a time of year when audiences are hungry for spook stories, tales of the uncanny, and dark folklore.

The Australian Associated Press (AAP) newswire wrote a story titled "Horror brings film industry back from grave" (AAP, 2008), which was syndicated across a large number of metropolitan and regional newspapers. Numerous live and pre-recorded radio interviews followed. Stories ranged from general Halloween features, to stories on recent horror-movie releases (particularly *Dying Breed*), to why Australian horror movies have been so popular in recent years. A highlight of the media coverage was an interview I gave for the Halloween special of the current affairs programme "Hack" on the national radio station Triple J. In between *Psycho* sound effects and the *Jaws* theme song, I talked about the success of Aussie horror movies, while Leigh Whannell, the co-creator of the modern classic *Saw*, commented about why people watch horror movies.

Following the success of the first media release, QUT's PR unit decided to release another story once my research had been completed. While the study was officially finalized in early 2009, the second release was once again released before Halloween. On October 14, 2009, QUT issued the press release "Horror, Aussie style: Fear in the Outback." The media release's message was quite simply that the outback is a central feature of Australian horror movies, and such movies are popular with overseas audiences.

An AAP journalist had read a report from an Australian tourism conference observing that international tourists perceive Australia as a destination filled with "deadly snakes, spiders, stingers and sharks." Drawing upon both the media release and the report, he wrote an article titled "Horror movies bugging tourists" (Gray, 2009a), which asked whether Australian horror movies attract tourists, or scare them away. From this article, more than 60 stories circulated between October 14 and 19 in print, online, or broadcast media, with headlines such as "Horror films may be killing Aussie tourism industry" (Grey, 2009b), "Aussie horror scares tourists away" (N.A., 2009a), and "Are we scaring tourists away?" (N.A., 2009b).

From QUT PR's perspective, the volume of coverage was great, and although the headlines were controversial, the stories never actually claimed that my doctoral research found that horror movies were scaring away audiences. Frustrated and worried the coverage would damage my credibility as a researcher—as the story had nothing to do with my research—I wanted to issue a statement refuting the claims. I contacted Ian Eckersley, QUT's new PR manager who had been in the job for a few weeks. He assured me that any media coverage is good media coverage, and suggested I use the ongoing coverage to redirect readers towards key findings of my research. To do this, Ian's advice was to have a simple and clear message, stay on message, and redirect any questions off topic back to my central message. His advice was invaluable. In radio interviews that followed, my message was that horror movies do not scare away audiences, and what my research found is that the Australian landscape is central to local horror flicks. To an extent, I was able to shift the media's focus back towards the distinctiveness of chillers from down under.

On November 3rd, following the announcement of *The Reef* (2011)—a shark horror filmed off the Great Barrier Reef—another wave of media coverage broke, influenced by the first media story. Investigating claims by Townsville tourism operators that the movie would scare away tourists and ruin their businesses, I was interviewed by *Brisbane Times* journalist Scott Casey for the article "Killer shark movie to bait tourists" (Casey, 2009). In contrast to the original story, drawing upon my comments, the article argued that *The Reef* may in fact generate tourism, similar to the way in which *Wolf Creek* has placed Western Australia's Wolfe Creek Meteor Crater on the map as a tourism destination. It was a satisfying end to the saga.

Media Exposure and Outcomes

Overall, my research received strong national and international media exposure. In both 2008 and 2009, my research received more than 150 media stories in broadcast, print and online media—including the BBC's World Service, the UK's *Daily Mail*, Australia's Channel 7, *Daily India*, Sky News, ABC Radio, Triple J, and *The Australian*. My research received coverage in Australia, the United Kingdom, Canada, India, Pakistan, the Philippines, and New Zealand, among others.

After the horror movies and tourism media coverage, I received requests for interviews on a wide range of topics. In November 2009, I was a guest on the national commercial radio breakfast programmes *The Cage* on Triple M, and Jamie Dunn's *4BC Breakfast Show* to talk Edward Cullen, Bella Swan, and the popularity of the Hollywood smash-hit *Twilight* (2008). This was followed by guest appearances on Red Simon's (a popular national television celebrity) breakfast radio show in Sydney, and a Queensland-wide ABC radio program on Christmas Eve to recommend movies to watch over the festive season.

As an indirect result of the media coverage, I was a speaker for the Australian Cinémathèque's *Dead Country: Australian Horror Classics* and *Be Afraid: Fear in North American Cinema* movie festivals; I was a member of national radio panels including *Australia Talks* to discuss cinema and popular culture; and was commissioned by the national public broadcaster ABC to review the 2009 Oscars. I learned from this experience that popular and intellectual outcomes are not always mutually exclusive. My academic research provided rich detail and historical background for talks at movie festivals, while radio conversations with critics and opinion pieces written for newspapers later shaped my thinking in scholarly papers.

My media coverage resulted in valuable academic outcomes and career opportunities. I had a limited academic profile before this publicity. Following the media coverage, I was invited to guest edit the "Australasian Horror" (Ryan, 2010a) special issue of the journal *Studies in Australasian Cinema*, the first academic journal devoted solely to the academic discussion of Australian and New Zealand horror-movie traditions. I was also invited to edit the "Horror Movies" section for the *Directory of World Cinema: Australian and New Zealand Cinema* (Ryan, 2010b), among other outcomes. In July 2010, I was awarded the QUT Creative industries Dean's Award for Excellence in Research for the impact and utilization of my research by the media and industry.

Lessons from Working with the Media

The media are tools for promoting one's research, or an ongoing research project, to a broad general audience. Such media coverage can significantly raise an academic's profile and generate general interest in their research but rarely leads to increased citations counts or reviews in prestigious journals, which are often measures of quality and esteem for the academy. It can also consume a deceptive amount of time, depending on the scale of coverage, as you may need to prepare for telephone interviews and face-to-face interviews, and travel to radio studios for hour-long interviews, and so on.

At the core of popularizing research through the media is finding the right angle. In drafting the first media release, I wanted to talk about production, financing, and distribution models, and how the current boom in Aussie horror movies builds upon a tradition emerging in the 1970s. In the end, my three-year research project was boiled down to the simple catch-line "The Australian film industry is languishing, while Aussie horror flicks are booming." Most importantly, what a researcher values—as one who is intimately involved in the research—may not be what the media, and audiences, find interesting. To an extent, research needs to be simplified for journalistic stories and perceived readerships.

Advice I would give to a researcher is to be very careful with what you go public with. Working with a relatively simplistic media release, and sometimes a quick interview, details of what may be a complex research project can easily be misconstrued, particularly the further the media release travels. While *Wolf Creek* and *Daybreakers* have achieved box-office success, most local horror titles perform poorly at the Australian box office but perform well in video and cult markets, and low-budget titles can make returns from presales. Yet unable to capture this complexity in the initial release, some commentators were quick to say "Yeah, but *Rogue* (2007) and *Dying Breed* (2008) didn't make money at the box office, and most don't receive domestic cinema release so they can't make money." This is not the case; the low-budget *Black Water* going into profit from sales to international territories alone is an example.

Also, be prepared for the unexpected. No matter how well you prepare for an interview, journalists may ask you something completely unexpected—be it an angle you hadn't anticipated, or something so left of field that you're startled. One question I received was "what are the five crappiest horror movies of all time?" It seems logical now that a general audience may want to know this, but the question was difficult to answer in a live national radio interview when I had mentally prepared for countless other questions. A tip is, when you are live on radio, never freeze and think of an answer. A few seconds is a long time on radio. If you need to stall for time, repeat the question: "What are the five 'crappiest' horror movies of all time? Ok, well..." Practising off-the-cuff questions with colleagues helped manage similar situations.

A key benefit of media coverage is the immediacy of knowledge diffusion. Scholarship has long been plagued by the time lag between the completion of the research and its publication in scholarly journals, which can often take a year or more to go through peer-review processes, editing, and publication. Conference papers are published faster than journal articles or book chapters, but even this process may take several months. On the other hand, media coverage can circulate stories to national and international audiences within days.

Another positive outcome is that your research can reach a wide mainstream audience, broader than any subscription base for a prestigious academic journal. It was hugely satisfying knowing that after all the hours I'd invested into my research, people read about my project at the breakfast table, heard about it on radio, or were sent an online news story about it from a friend. This, however, is both a pro and a con. Because a research project must be condensed into a simple catch-line, complexity and details are often lost in a media story, and as a result general audience members may criticize your work in public forums or via blog posts. Once a story goes public, your work is open to attack from anyone, often without detailed understandings of the subject. So be prepared for negative comments or rants about your work.

Media coverage can lead to industry engagement and public outreach. As institutional research revolves increasingly around industry and interdisciplinary partnerships, one way of engaging with industry and the broader public can be facilitated through media coverage. Media coverage can often result in invitations to speak in public forums, be part of expert groups, among many other examples.

In conclusion, although I remain principally a researcher, I regularly do interviews for the media and I enjoy the public outreach activities that come with a public profile. On the other hand, I am now very cautious about undertaking major media campaigns and will only commit after serious consideration. Overall, popularizing my research has broadened my perspective on academic research and its audiences; it has influenced my writing style; and has brought an exciting new dimension to the research experience.

References

Australian Associated Press (AAP). (2008, October 13). Horror brings film industry back from the grave. *The Age*.

Casey, Scott. (2009, November 3). Killer shark movie to bait tourists: producer. *Brisbanetimes.com*. Available at http://www.brisbanetimes.com.au/travel/travel-news/killer-shark-movie-to-bait-tourists-producer-20091103-hujz.html.

Gray, Steve. (2009a, October 14). Horror movies bugging tourists. *Australian Associated Press* (AAP).

Gray, Steve. (2009b, October 16). Horror films may be killing Aussie tourism industry. *Courier Mail*, p. 21.

N.A. (2009a, October 18). Aussie horror scares tourists away. *Sunday Territorian*, p. 47.

N.A. (2009b, October 14). Are we scaring tourists away? *Special Broadcasting Service* (SBS) *Online*.

Ryan, M. D. (Ed.). (2010a). Australasian Horror. *Studies in Australasian Cinema*, 4(1).

Ryan, M. D. (2010b). Horror. In B. Goldsmith & G. Lealand (Eds.), *Directory of world cinema: Australia and New Zealand* (pp.188–207). Bristol: Intellect.

CHAPTER TWENTY-NINE

Publishing and Publicity

The Path to Popular Audiences

Mara Einstein

After almost 20 years in the marketing and television industries, I decided to leave corporate America and go into academia. On one hand, this was an incredibly easy decision. After five years working at the National Broadcasting Company (NBC) television network in New York, I felt my job had grown stale and redundant. I also couldn't help but think that getting people to watch more television—yes, *more television*—couldn't possibly be what I was put on this planet to do. On the other hand, it wasn't all an easy decision. It was going to be a little hard to extricate myself from a cushy office on the 48th floor of 30 Rock with a TV, a couch, a refrigerator, and a view of Central Park.

Even so, once the decision was made, it was with the understanding that I didn't walk away from the glamorous world of television—and its accompanying six-figure salary—only so that my work would gather dust and mold in the ivory towers of academia. I'd given up far too much for that to happen.

This chapter tells the story of my journey through the publishing learning curve and what I did—and continue to do—to ensure that my work reaches a wider audience. Like most writers, my path has had its ups and downs, but thankfully mostly up. Also, like many of us who write as a supplement to our teaching duties, the choice of books or articles to write are often dictated by issues of tenure as much as by tantalizing topic. However, these are only obstacles if you make them so. You are building a career and a point of view for the long term, and what you have to say is important, or you never would have put pen to paper—or, rather, fingers to keys.

Getting My First Book Published

The hardest thing for an unknown author to do is to get his or her first book into press. For many of us, particularly those coming out of an academic environment, our first significant full-length publication is likely to be a dissertation or some derivative thereof. That was true in my case.

I believed I had a good piece of work, but I had no idea how to go about getting it published. So I did what any newly minted PhD might do—more research. I looked on the websites of university presses to find out what they required in terms of submissions. I asked people with whom I worked what I should do about putting a proposal together. I even called some colleagues who had recently been published. They all said the same thing about framing the argument and reworking the manuscript and using what I call "doctoral words" like bifurcate and pedagogy and epistemology. Quite frankly, most of it went straight over my head. Even so, based on their advice, I tried to write an erudite, academic-y sounding proposal that would demonstrate my complete and utter transition out of the corporate world into the world of the scholar. Frankly, I don't remember how many proposals I sent out. What I do remember is that every last one was rejected.

At that point I realized I had to sit down, regroup, and start again. Then I had my "light bulb moment"; I realized that the book proposal is nothing more than a marketing sales tool. The publisher simply wants to know whether they will be able to sell this book—first internally to the editorial board and the marketing department, and ultimately to a wider audience. The objective, therefore, became how to position my book as a product with considerable sales potential. I didn't need to change my research, just the packaging around it. That's the advice I wish someone had given me, because that is what made the difference. I stopped trying to sound like an academic and started writing the proposal as the marketer I am. I had a contract shortly thereafter.

The book derived from my dissertation—*Media Diversity: Economics, Ownership and the FCC [Federal Communications Commission]*—is not the focus of this chapter. However, I want to include a quick lesson about publicity as it relates to this work. Research from *Media Diversity* was used by the FCC in revising the ownership rules in 2003. That occurred simply because I sent an email to the chairman of the FCC under the subject line "I have research I think you might be interested in." A few months later, I got a call from the Commission asking to see my research, which subsequently was included as one of 12 studies used in relationship to the new rulemakings. When the Commission released the studies, there was a flurry of publicity (not all good, I might add), but I was able to capitalize on that. The research still lives on the FCC website.

I include this story because it provides an example of how to publicize your work through nontraditional methods. Is there a large institution that might be interested in what you are researching? Can they be a source of publicity for you? I don't suggest here that you should compromise your values or change your findings to suit the institution for the sake of publicity. However, if a simple email can get your work to a wider audience, there's no harm in sending it. If you never ask, you'll never know.

Getting My Second Book Published

My second book—*Brands of Faith: Marketing Religion in a Commercial Age*—was the book I had been waiting to write since I left NBC. I originally wanted to write my dissertation on media and religion, but felt there was too much learning that had to occur for that to happen, and frankly I wasn't getting any younger. I needed my doctorate to begin teaching.

Once my first book was published, however, I could turn my attention more fully to continuing the work of *Brands of Faith*. This text broadly looks at how marketing and media have altered faith practice in the United States—a big topic with important social implications and certainly one worthy of popularization in light of the fact that 90 percent of Americans believe in some kind of higher power.

Before I get into the publishing and publicity aspects of this work, let me briefly explain the research and the theory within which the work is rooted. *Brands of Faith* is about why religious marketing is proliferating today. This entailed researching how more sophisticated techniques are being used by religious institutions, examining the impact of marketing on the super-sizing of religious institutions (so-called megachurches), and how promoting religion was affecting American culture and more specifically the American political climate.

The book examines why religious marketing has grown exponentially in the last 20 years. There are several factors at play here. First, religious marketing is tied to the growth in media—both cable television and the internet—and to the increasing influence of corporate marketers who have entered the fields of religious film production and book publishing. Social trends—notably the ability to choose one's faith rather than having to stay in the faith of one's birth—have contributed to a shopping mentality when it comes to belief systems. Finally, the concept of branding and its importance to the development of personal identity are explored. Building on this, I argue that religious institutions have had to brand themselves in today's market in order to remain culturally relevant. Two overarching theoretical ideas are woven throughout the book: marketing and evangelizing are similar processes; and there is a blurring of the sacred and the secular in American culture.

Throughout the book, I use a wealth of popular-culture examples to demonstrate these ideas. Rick Warren's *Purpose Driven Life*—the bestselling nonfiction book of all time after the Bible—and the growth of megachurches are examples of the explosion in marketing. To demonstrate the blending of the sacred and the secular as a means of promoting faith, I compared Joel Osteen with Oprah Winfrey (Osteen is the *New York Times* bestselling author and leading televangelist who sells books and tapes and tours via his program and website. Winfrey is the talk-show host who readily evokes God and spirituality in her very secular program). Finally, I presented information about the Kabbalah Centre and the then-ubiquitous red string, as well as the fluctuating fortunes of the New Age, an ideology considered to be the fore-runner of faith marketing, to examine this question.

In writing this book, my goal was to marry my two passions—religion and marketing—and make sense of how these two institutions interact with each other. Importantly, I wanted to do so in a way that was readily accessible to both an academic and "well-read" lay audience.

Promoting the Book

Brands of Faith was published by Routledge, a reputable academic publisher who had some inroads into trade bookstores. What I learned after the book was published, however, was that the trade division of the company was being pulled back considerably. What I also learned—far too late—was that because the book was being published as part of a series, there was no flexibility in affecting the price point. The paperback was being sold at $35, and there was nothing I could do to change that. Moreover, as an academic book, you have the obstacle of Amazon.com putting up the hardcover version of the book (sold to university libraries at $125) when prospective buyers look for your work.

This did not sway me, however, because I was determined that this work would be the book that would solidify my reputation as a scholar in the area of media and religion. I had learned from my first publishing experience that the only way the book would get any kind of publicity is if I promoted the work myself. So that's what I did.

First, I researched online for book publicists. This is an expensive route to take, but can be worthwhile if you select a really good one. I was lucky as I was able to work with someone who was honest and realistic about what could be achieved. She told me that because of the topic of the book, it was going to be difficult to get some national radio shows. This is because religious radio markets (the so-called flyover states in the middle of country) are hesitant to air a discussion about a book that isn't blatantly pro-religion. Their concerns cause programmers of national shows to steer clear of what may be perceived as controversial. That said, however, my publicist was able to get me local radio interviews in close to 30 markets, and they were programs for key audiences. These enabled me to generate additional appearances on my own, including *Marketplace* on National Public Radio (NPR) and a spot on the ABC radio affiliate in New York City. (Important caveat: Be level-headed when working with a publicist. Some will promise you the moon. But beware, you pay for their time whether they get you on *Oprah* or not.)

The other thing I knew I needed to do was to create a blog (www.brandsoffaith.com). This is not for the faint of heart. A blog takes a lot of work. Yet the more you write, the closer your site appears on the top of the Google search list. Importantly, if your topic is really specialized (and thankfully mine is), this task is not particularly onerous. However, being well positioned on Google is important because the blog comes to be a valuable means for national reporters to find your work. Search engine optimization (SEO) is not just about writing; it's about picking the right names. For example, not only did I buy the URL for *Brands of Faith*, I also bought the URLs for marketing religion—the search term I expected reporters would use when researching the topic. To this day, Brands of Faith is the first item that comes up when you Google "marketing religion." Depending on how much time you have and how aggressive you want to be, you can also contact others to include you as part of their blog roll or ask if they would like you to do a blog interview. If you have time, do it. However, I would caution against spending too much time writing content for others for free unless they have a significant following. It does little to promote your work and takes time away from more fruitful ventures.

In terms of print promotion, there are a number of ways to develop this. First, push your publisher as much as you dare to get them to promote your book. Most academic books don't tend to get reviewed in major publications, so don't expect too much in this regard. Second, in addition to a blog, an important tool is an expert list. Reporters search these regularly to find sources for their articles. A list may be organized through an academic organization (for my work, I am on the expert list with the American Academy of Religion) or a public-relations association. In this case, Profnet is broadly used and is part of the PR Newswire. A free, major competitor to the PR Newswire is Help a Reporter Out (links are provided on www.popularizingresearch.net). Simply go to the website and sign up for their twice-a-day email. These emails list the types of sources that reporters are looking for based on broad categories. One caveat: don't claim to be an expert in something you are not; they will kick you off the list.

The upshot of all of this is that I have commented on topics such as Jesus on wine bottles; churchgoers getting better rates on car insurance; and Godtube, a religion-based version of YouTube. These articles have appeared in the *New York Times, Los Angeles Times*, Religion News Service, Associated Press, *Chicago Sun-Times, Atlanta Journal-Constitution, Naples Daily News, The Daily Record* (Baltimore, MD), *The Record* (New Jersey), and the *United Methodist Reporter*.

What I Learned

No matter what the project, in today's overcrowded media environment everyone has to learn how to be their own publicist. Here are some helpful hints to promoting your writing:

1. Learn how to condense your topic down to three key elements—that's all anyone is going to want to listen to when you're giving a pitch. You can get into detail later once you book an appearance.

2. Know what your purpose for publicity is—do you want to promote yourself, your work, both? Are you trying to establish yourself in a very limited space or a broad one? Are you looking for tenure? These will affect how and when you promote yourself.

3. Don't be a snob. If someone asks you to speak, be there and be gracious.

4. Get a landline and make sure it doesn't have call waiting. Most radio is done by phone, and a cell phone won't cut it.

5. Be excited about your work. If the reporter becomes interested in what you have to say, they may write more about it.

6. Be polite and be friendly. Reporters come back to sources that are helpful. Tied to this notion is if you think the reporter can be helped by a colleague, give the reporter their name. Publicity is not a zero-sum game. Maybe you'll both get quoted and that person will recommend you to someone else next time.

7. If you create a blog, keep up with it. Write as often as you can and make sure to respond to those who post. Another important aspect of having a blog is that bloggers read each other.

I know there are academics who will eschew this type of promotion. That's fine. It's not for everyone. But there's nothing that says that someone who takes this route is any less of a scholar for having done so. *Brands of Faith*, I'm happy to note, was named a Choice Magazine Outstanding Academic Text for 2008—certainly recognition of the value of this research. That said, I would not recommend using these tactics on a first book or before someone has received tenure, as taking a popular approach is still frowned upon in many parts of the academy. However, take heart. Having your first book be decidedly academic is a small price to pay for being able to do the work you are passionate about for the remainder of your career.

The net takeaway: while my book did not become a bestseller, I did get tenure and I am recognized as a leading authority on marketing religion, which were ultimately the objectives I was looking to achieve. Moreover, because of the publicity I was able to generate, when reporters look for a source in this area, I am the one they call. (And when they do call, I ask where they found me. In most cases, it's either through an expert list or a Google search.)

Building on these experiences, my forthcoming work, *Compassion, Inc.: How Corporate America Blurs the Line between What We Buy, Who We Are and Those We Help*, will be published by an academic press—the University of California Press—but this time as a trade publication. They have promised that I don't need to hire my own publicist—but I still have her on my speed dial.

My advice to all who venture down this path is to listen to all the advice you get, but ultimately listen to your own counsel. You know what you have to say, and you will find out quickly enough if other people want to hear it.

CHAPTER THIRTY

Reaching Mainstream Audiences

Media Tips for Academics and the Challenge of Storytelling

Philip A. Saunders

My background is in journalism, where for 15 years I worked in print, radio, and television news—both on short- and long-form content production. For the past six years, however, I've worked as a media-relations expert for Royal Roads University. As a result, my later career has been characterized by an intuitive understanding of mass audiences and the language most effectively used to engage them through mainstream media. Conducting proactive and reactive media relations on behalf of an academic institution has meant facilitating access for researchers to mass audiences in support of building their own positive reputation, that of the institution, and the funding agencies that support their work.

In this chapter, I will argue that in order to make research publicly relevant, academics must seek out and capitalize on opportunities found in local, regional, and national news media, or seize opportunities to tell stories to audiences through popular online media channels. In this way, academics can insert themselves and their ideas into a wider public discourse, thereby influencing how mass audiences see the world or make decisions both collectively and individually as participants in civil society. I will argue that researchers can seize the opportunity of a public conversation about their research and thus fortify a tangible connection to the lives of the people who may be in a position to support its continued funding.

In my role at Royal Roads University, I often field calls from reporters seeking commentary on specific aspects of a news story. The paradigm of the news reporter is unique in that they are often looking for a specific point of view in an effort to provide balance to their story. Thus academic experts are often called upon to provide an external, third party—dare I say "neutral"—context to a story that has a conflict (real or created) embedded into it as a narrative device by the journalist. Academic experts, depending on their personal experience with the media, can see this environment as volatile or unsafe. As a result, I often coach academics on how to pitch their knowledge on a particular subject area in a way that is both satisfactory for them and for the general news audiences they are hoping to reach.

This chapter will explore opportunities found in this environment for popularizing research. It will also provide some structural advice to academics to make research more understandable and engaging to general audiences. I won't explore pedagogical concepts or how people understand complex ideas. I will focus on the tools of my trade and those that have been successful for academics with whom I have worked.

Finally, this chapter will attempt to show that new audiences can be reached through contemporary online communication channels, more frequently referred to as "social media" or "social networking." I will make the argument that a refined sense of how to wedge rigorous research in a more popularly understood context of storytelling frames it for larger audiences and increases its value in the public domain.

Know Your Media and Know Their Audiences

Depending on the medium being engaged, audiences can vary and their attention will most certainly be different depending on how they access the information.

The most common broadcasting channel I use in my work is the talk-radio format. Public and private broadcasting approaches differ slightly. A public broadcaster, because of its freedom from advertising interruptions, provides a more thoughtful, in-depth channel that in many ways is less volatile for the inexperienced or uncomfortable researchers. However, audiences in private talk radio are larger, though their attention spans are shorter and the pace tends to be much faster—making the opportunity for a more thoughtful approach fleeting, and in fact possibly absent, depending on the style of the host announcer. Talk radio is more popular during the day, when the attention audiences pay to programs is often split as listeners go about the business of their day, listening to the programs in short bursts, often with divided attention.

The second most available channel that I use for academic expertise is the local television newscast. TV audiences tend to be more engaged than the radio audiences, but if used properly, the structure of a typical news item—never longer than a few minutes—provides a relatively easy access point for researchers to reach mass audiences. However, the constraints of the medium require some skill at packaging information in digestible chunks for mass audiences.

Opportunities in print are a third way I encourage members of our teaching and research faculty to access large audiences. The constraints of the printed narrative and the limited space allocated by most print media can sometimes be very strong. Without proper preparation, the potential for being quoted out of context is high. On the other hand, opinion and editorial pages can be the best place to communicate research and insights in a controlled way. Moreover, an opinion piece in a newspaper can result in subsequent radio and television opportunities as reporters pick up on the story and try to tell it in a different way. Of course, this kind of coverage can also backfire because the instinct of a reporter is to identify a conflict and frame the story in an adversarial way, thereby making your point of view the focus of a critique by others. In this context, it is vitally important for researchers who choose this channel to be prepared for the media spotlight and understand the importance of focusing messages with key audiences in mind.

So what is a media audience? What can academics tell them? How receptive are they? What tools do we need to work in this kind of system? These are important starting points for academic experts seeking to popularize their work.

The Tyranny of Short Attention Span

As a rule of thumb, a standard length of an interview on a public-affairs program is around six minutes. As a result, researchers and academics have the opportunity to get two or three messages across. During a television news item, they have the opportunity to deliver one or two messages in short bursts ranging from 10 to 20 seconds each. So what messages can be gotten across, how they are planned, and most importantly, how they are delivered, is critical for success.

Simplicity is among the most important elements of a strong resonating message. The clearer the articulation of a message—for example using analogies and examples that connect with broad cross-sections of your audience—the higher the likelihood the relevance of your research will stick with the receiver of your message.

Simplicity is counterintuitive to most academics. A strong element in a successful academic career is complexity and rigor. The instinct of an academic is to unpack simplicity to reveal underlying complexities that most people take for granted. In fact, for some academics, that kind of ponderous exploration is what has drawn them to academe. So asking an academic to simplify research that he or she has spent years exploring could be a challenge. Also, what is simple to an academic may not be so simple to broad audiences, or even to the journalist with whom the academic is speaking. So understanding the constraints of the media and the scope that an audience can deal with is critical for engaging audiences. Analogies and examples thus become a valuable tool in this battle of balancing complexity with simplicity. When I train academics to speak to the media, I prompt them to identify key audiences and think of two or three messages and analogies for those audiences.

Because I have a background in broadcasting, I can work as a go-between with the producer/announcer and the academic. Not only does this save the academic time in preparation, but in some respects I am prompting both sides on the topic of discussion and making it easier for both of them to craft an engaging item for public consumption. Scoping a story or interview with the journalist is crucial for making the transition from the request to a live or taped interview more efficient. In some cases I can get the journalist to tell me exactly the sort of things they'll be asking the researcher and then explore the topic with them—suggesting angles, or elements they haven't thought of. I may even suggest some experts and offer which area they may be able to discuss. This strategic dance with the journalist unfolds more quickly when I have a rapport with them and can quickly run through some options. It goes without saying that it's very important for an academic to be well acquainted with the personnel of one's institution's media and public relations office.

Talk-radio programs, usually publicly funded or large market private stations, have researchers or associate producers who seek out expert voices for their programs.[1] These individuals may call around looking for an expert on a story of the day. In this case, a pre-interview may take place. This is ideal as it allows both the announcer and the academic to be prepared for the live interview, and in some cases it provides both with an opportunity to gather more information on the topic at hand. Sometimes the academic/expert will prepare an interview plan, in order to avoid going into areas he or she is ill prepared to discuss. Others will simply gather some useful analogies or facts to better explain the topic at hand.

A popular faculty expert I work with regularly at Royal Roads University is Michael Real, a communication professor who is an expert on sports spectacle. He has published a number of writings on the Super Bowl; has researched and explored the Olympic movement with some depth; and has a broad understanding of media and film history, popular culture, and communication theory. During the recent Vancouver Olympic Winter Games, Real was frequently called upon for comment. Recently he has also been speaking to the media about international sporting events such as the World Cup and the Commonwealth Games. Real is very comfortable in the live media environment. He is a veteran communication professor and understands how to effectively use the sound bite and message within the context of a media opportunity. He has a clear voice and confident poise. His popularity largely has been due to his comfort in a mass-communication environment and because he is superb at presenting information in bite-sized chunks that are understandable and palatable to broad audiences. He has also mastered the art of driving interviews, thus controlling the tone of the discussion and the topics he's willing to discuss.

An example of where expertise has laddered from the more traditional written opinion or editorial commentary to larger audiences in broadcasting is the media work of the editor of this collection, Phillip Vannini. In his case, Vannini wrote a series of opinion pieces (op-eds) and media releases in which he illustrated his research in the local ferry transportation system. He then approached me to pursue placement in local community newspapers. The incentive for Vannini was higher than most of his peers, since the very nature of socio-anthropological research he conducts benefits greatly from public engagement, so his articles were written in a way that would capture the imagination of his audience. He always mentioned the nature of his research in the biographical detail provided in the column, providing his contact information as a way of connecting with more volunteer informants.

Typically Vannini would craft a piece, addressing either an issue currently in the news that related to his research, or identifying an issue that may capture the public interest, usually connected to his research. His topic, ferry travel in Canada's west coast, was easily engaging for the people in the communities he was accessing. I'd work with Vannini on the final edit, bringing my editorial skills to bear on the piece, stripping out jargon and tightening the language for mass audiences. Thus we would provide a properly crafted and concise article that resource-starved local and regional media could easily accept and publish, while also presenting the researcher with an engaged pool of data subjects. With my help, Vannini would time these articles to appear in the week he would be in the community conducting his research. While there, he'd likely get picked up by local private and public radio stations, thereby increasing his opportunity to gather data while in the area. It was a win-win-win situation: media organizations would have interesting free content, audiences would read or hear about a topic as common as the day's weather, and he would increase his sample of interviewees following his appearances.

These days, upon publication of his work, when any policy decision affecting the service or any big news about ferry fare increases breaks locally on the ferry system, my phone regularly rings or my email box flashes with journalists looking to speak to Vannini about it. Thus his expert opinion regularly informs political debate and policy formation.

But both these examples also present a fundamental weakness in the system of content gathering: that resources are fewer and fewer in traditional media channels. Drawing on the critique of Robert McChesney, the business of media production is under siege by economic considerations. Thus the opportunities to access the media, particularly in small markets, is significant for those who are imbued with the reputation of an academic institution. Certainly, the position of an expert is a loose one, especially as I've described it above, but the opportunities for accessing mass audiences are considerable.

The Opportunities Found in Social Media

The expansion of new technology for delivering information over the World Wide Web has been a watershed in modern communication. Not since the creation of the printing press and the first broadcast signals were sent out over the air has there been such a transformation in the way that humans communicate and share information.

Fifteen years ago we could not have imagined being able to create and broadcast our messages without the use of highly expensive delivery systems. Tools for storytelling are now broadly available, to the point that the internet has become not just an avenue for the transformation of information flow, but in a way that has put the primal social skill of storytelling back in the hands of common people who would otherwise wallow in obscurity.

As academics, a skill that was once the dominion of lecture halls is now available online to anyone, anywhere, anytime. Although audiences are splintering, in a traditional sense, content is now available on demand, through social channels and attentive networks of friends, thinkers, and storytellers.

The skill of storytelling, earlier found primarily in traditional face-to-face human interaction, can now be explored and developed with specific audiences in mind, while social networks provide the easy, unfettered access to those audiences. Facebook, for example, has an approximate user base of over 800 million people. Each of these users may have hundreds of friends, followers, and colleagues, and most importantly, each of them has the power to broadcast your message. These networks can show video, broadcast audio, photographs, provide text and documents, all at a relatively low cost.

The challenge we face today is one of engagement. There are so many opportunities for audience distraction, so much more information. How will storytelling be affected by this change? Will text survive, or will audiences be seduced to other, oral forms of communication? The key is for us to be able to access those audiences in the media they choose to find us. So it is incumbent upon academics to seek out opportunities for engagement and to nurture an accessible body of research that engages the public. The opportunity is to use those tactics honed in traditional media in new media and further spread the knowledge we explore as academics and researchers.

The skills of a modern researcher would thus be well served by some training in storytelling. The ability of a researcher to capture her work with the modern technical tools of a contemporary storyteller could be the difference between continued funding and obscurity. Younger generations imbued in the abilities of a Web 2.0 have a distinct advantage over those less apt in oral storytelling techniques. Even traditional media are starting to organize themselves for this eventuality as magazines start to look more like web pages than picture books.

As mass publics are driven to more oral forms, academics must seize the opportunities found in modern internet technologies to expand relevance and knowledge around their research. It is a matter of survival for many and a matter of being understood for others. The challenges are daunting, but the opportunities are great and the impact potentially long lasting.

I wish to conclude with a simple and concise list of tips to academics on how to better relate to the world of news media and popular media:

1. Properly scope out an interview request. Be sure about the angle of the interview or story and prepare for it. Ask what it is the reporter or producer is looking for from you. If you can't scope it yourself, make sure you have someone you trust do

it for you. Understand that you are jumping into an ongoing narrative and speak to it.

2. Be concise and to the point. Don't be afraid of silence, especially during a live interview. It's not your job to fill the air. That's the job of the announcer.

3. Be conversational. This is especially important in broadcast media. Most people don't understand jargon, acronyms, or in-depth context, and people are not engaged by long lists of numbers and trend data. Pretend you are at a cocktail party and people are enrapt by your story. Keep them engaged.

4. Use analogies that appeal to large sectors of the population. Make comparisons that occur in everyday life. Use images that are commonplace.

5. Make stark contrasts instead of nuanced differences, unless you can tell a good story to illustrate the nuance you are trying to make. Ask yourself if you can do it in 30 seconds. If not, rethink the point you are trying to make.

6. Tell a story as though you are telling it to a 12-year-old.

7. Speak slowly.

8. Answer questions directly and if you don't know, say so, especially in print as you can always ask the reporter if you can get back to them before the deadline.

9. Respect the reporter's deadlines and their professionalism. Don't ask to review the story before publication. They aren't likely to share it anyway. Offer to go over anything with them over the phone. Be available if they call back.

10. Respect questions the reporter is asking, no matter how stupid they sound.

11. Maintain a positive tone and be positive in your responses. Be appreciative when responding to the questions being asked of you.

12. There is no such thing as off the record, especially if there is a microphone nearby. This is true even if you think the camera isn't on. If you don't want it to appear in the story or be broadcast on the air, don't say it.

13. Don't try to be funny. You are an expert, not a comedian. Sarcasm never translates in print or over the air. Don't be sarcastic.

14. Breathe.

Note

1. This is becoming a luxury as economic pressures and audience shares diminish in mainstream private radio; producers are sometimes called to do two or three hours of programming on their own these days. In these instances, very little preparation is done and reliance on scoping increases.

CHAPTER THIRTY-ONE

Interacting with News Media Journalists

Reflections of a Sociologist

Christopher J. Schneider

While the public presentation and dissemination of academic research is important, I must confess that I never actually had any intention of participating in media interviews. As a matter of fact, when filling out my employment paperwork, I distinctly remember checking the box to indicate that I did not wish to be contacted by media. In spite of this, in just the last three years I have appeared in over 200 print, radio, and television interviews—a handful of these featured across North America. I also appear as a frequent guest commentator on three different large-market radio stations, one of which is consistently ranked among the highest-rated radio stations in Vancouver, British Columbia. In recognition of my contributions, I received the 2009–2010 *Provost's Public Education Through Media Award*, one of three major university-wide awards presented at my institution. This award acknowledges faculty members who "actively and creatively" share their research expertise through media. In this essay, I reflect upon some of my experiences and offer comment on some of the lessons that I have learned while interacting with media journalists.

Interacting With News Media Journalists

Upon completion of my PhD in the United States in 2008, I accepted a tenure-track position in a country that was foreign to me. My immigrant status accorded me a certain cultural ignorance to Canadian-specific media. After only a few months of living and working in Canada, I received an unsolicited email interview request from a national magazine. I later learned that this was Canada's only weekly national current-affairs magazine. At the time I had no idea. I asked my then fiancée (now spouse and Canadian citizen and herself an academic) about the interview request, including her knowledge about the magazine. She was shocked. "They want to interview *you* about *your* research?" I remember her asking, her face agape. The journalist was interested in writing a story about cell phone ringtones and wanted to interview me about my published research. I had initially wished to avoid media interviews because I was afraid that they would be a distraction from my academic work (I address this later). While initially reluctant, I sheepishly agreed.

In preparation for my interview, I spent quite a bit of time reviewing my extensive data and notes that were part of my dissertation research on ringtones. I spent approximately an hour speaking to the journalist over the phone. I remember the experience was a friendly one, and the discussion fun; however, my fond memory soured once the article was published. I was surprised that I was quoted rather minimally considering the time that I invested in the conversation. The quotations were also not quotations that I would have selected, especially considering that they were taken largely out of context. I was also very upset to see that much of my research was woven throughout the article but not attributed to our conversation. I guess I was not really sure what to expect. Lesson learned.

Lesson #1: You are not in control of how journalists will use your research or your ideas. To minimize this risk of what you may find to be improper use of your materials, you should ask questions about how your research and interview will be used. This is especially important when dealing with print-media journalists, as you cannot control what will appear in print. After this experience, I have since asked journalists if I may review their articles before they go to print. My requests are always denied. I first suggest "interviewing" the journalist before you respond to any questions. Find out how much homework the journalist has done. Ask how they heard about your research and why they are interested in speaking with you. Do not spend large amounts of time preparing and presenting your materials. Do not give your work away. Remember, in most if not all cases, the journalist needs you—be mindful of this very simple fact when you are contacted for an interview.

Among the various functions of campus media-relations and public-affairs departments is to locate and promote faculty appearances in media. Due to the national exposure of the above-mentioned magazine, it was not long before other journalists started calling. I was soon thereafter invited to discuss my ringtone research on a popular morning show on a local radio program. I thought that this would be a fun opportunity to be able to rid myself of my uneventful interview experience (noted above) because I would be able to say things that would be directly attributed to my research. Besides, this was a live radio broadcast and I was already freshly prepared to discuss my research at length. Too prepared, as it turned out. I remember the host cutting me off in midsentence to end the segment. Depending on the station, radio interviews can be quite short, usually in the range of three to five minutes, and if you are very lucky in the exceptional case, ten to twelve minutes (including a commercial break). Stay on task. Be clear, concise, and avoid being verbose. Get in, make your points, and get out. This brings us to the next lesson.

Lesson #2: Time constraints and rhythm. Find out about the interview segment and find out exactly how long you will have to speak. Some radio producers (and sometimes hosts) will tell you this upfront, but others will not. Like everyday conversations, radio interviews always have a rhythm. However, unlike everyday life, radio interviews most always have a very distinct rhythm. The format, flow, and direction are usually the same, without fail. It is a good idea to learn this in advance. Keep in mind that radio stations and their hosts are mostly interested in keeping the show on a tight schedule. Believe it or not, they are usually less concerned with what you have to say. Make sure you get the points you wish to make across early. You should consider beginning an interview with the basic point that you wish to make.

Speaking to media can be a useful way to promote your research to diverse and broad publics. How you present your materials is very important, particularly to print journalists. As academics, we often borrow from and play with other people's ideas for a living. Journalists often do the same but with a different sort of ethos. Journalists, in my experience, are a whole lot less concerned with citing specific sources to individual authors. It is usually good enough if it can be affirmed that an identifiable person (you) made a particular statement (said something). Journalists are always looking for that perfect sound bite. The sound bite is to news media as the abstract is to an article. Like an animal stalking its prey, journalists (unlike journal editors!), will usually hang on your every word waiting for you to make what I call the "golden utterance": the perfect sound bite. Problems arise, however, when that golden utterance happens to draw from the work of another. This brings us to Lesson #3.

Lesson #3: Watch what you say and how you say it. Be very mindful when drawing from a body of academic research, and be careful when speaking identifiable statements that are not entirely your own. Journalists will sometimes latch on to these statements, and you may see them in print attributed to you even if you verbally identify the statement as not your own and provide a source. When we pass off another's statements or ideas as our own, this is plagiarism, the most serious academic offense. When journalists publish statements, it often only matters that someone else said them. The specific citation is of less importance. This is sometimes called good journalism. Be mindful of this when speaking to journalists.

In my experience, news media personnel, including radio and televisions hosts as well as journalists, most always have a pretty good idea if not an exact idea of how their story will look, read, or sound when it is completed. Keep in mind that your remarks are only a very small piece of the puzzle. The finished product usually fits into an existent debate or narrative about a particular issue deemed worthy of coverage, and/or it provides a validation of existent statements and/or it supports the beliefs or opinions of the journalist. These things are always beyond your control. Let me provide an example.

As a sociologist with a specialty in criminology, I was once invited by two local media outlets (one of these a television station) to offer comment on California's Proposition 19 to legalize marijuana and the possible implications of this proposition including the impact (if any) on the British Columbia black market. The questions asked were reflective of those already discussed in news media. Would crime increase or decrease? Would more people smoke marijuana? Rather than rehash these drab debates, I tried instead to shift the focus of the interview to the comparatively less-discussed racial discrepancies of California's correctional system. I provided what I felt was a relatively sound argument with some supporting evidence to suggest that if marijuana were in fact legalized (it was not), this would be one way to directly address the vast racial discrepancies present in the criminal "justice" institution. To my disappointment (but not to my surprise), these comments were deleted from the final broadcast and edited to better fit with the ongoing debates concerning crime and speculation about increases in marijuana use.

Journalists are sometimes looking to support the statements of others or to interject their own opinions and beliefs in the news media, but I have found they need someone with credentials (you) to do that for them. While the opinions of the everyday member are also important, in most circumstances they are not perceived as equally important as those of a university professor. In my experience, it sometimes seems like stories are already written and are missing a person with the appropriate credentials to allow the story to go to press. During one interview (which was picked up by the national press), the journalist asked a question to which I responded that I would rather not offer comment as my research expertise did not cover the scope of the question. Instead, I offered an alternative response to this question. The journalist was persistent and again asked the question, only this time as a hypothetical. I reiterated my lack of knowledge, but affirmed the hypothetical while careful not to repeat the statement. Even so, the statement, while not technically made by me, was nevertheless attributed to me in print. This brings us to our next lesson.

Lesson #4: If you can, find out the "angle" of the story. To do this, I recommend engaging in small talk prior to your interview (during *your* interview of the journalist, see lesson #1), and if you can, inquire about the journalist's personal position on the matter at hand, keeping in mind how your comments may or may not be used. Ask if the journalist has spoken with others and how their comments will be used with respect to your remarks. In the above example, for instance, my remarks (i.e., hypothetical affirmation) were used to support a preexisting statement of a high-ranking police officer.

The more media interviews that you do, the more requests you will likely receive. That is, of course, assuming you give a good interview: that you are available, speak clearly, and address questions effectively. Much of these interview requests will be sent and filtered through your university institution where the understanding of your research expertise can quite often be limited to just a few words such as "social control" or "cell phones," and, depending on these keywords, it may be easy to set you up with interviews that might not pertain exactly to your research expertise. Once I was called upon to give an in-studio radio interview about these very issues (social control and cell phones), presenting materials from my research on these matters. I learned seconds prior to the interview that I was to speak as an authority on cell-phone etiquette, an area that I am not trained in, nor particularly comfortable speaking about. Fortunately, I was able to shift the focus of the interview in the direction of my research interests so that it was not a total disaster. This happened to me only once, and, while a very rare circumstance that worked out in the end, the situation taught me an important lesson.

Lesson #5: Make sure to get all the information before the interview. You should also select your research expertise words with care. The vaguer, the more likely you will fall into situations like the above (such as preparing for the wrong interview).

Journalists are in the business of publishing good, accurate, and reliable stories; a basic part of this includes locating confirmed credible sources. In several private conversations with reporters, radio hosts, and TV journalists, many whom I've come to know personally, I've learned that having reliable go-to sources is an important, indeed basic, part of the profession. These individuals can be called upon to offer comment on timely issues, and importantly, can be contacted in circumstances of necessity, such as when an interviewee cancels or is a no-show (this is especially the case for live radio). I have been contacted on several such occasions (sometimes with as little as 15 minutes of prep time). If you are available and you can manage these situations, you'll get on the go-to list of reliable contacts. This may mean more phone calls and emails. However, in my experience, I have found that the requests tend to expand a little beyond (while not entirely removed) from the scope of your particular research expertise. This may require extra preparation time and can be good or bad depending on how you approach the issue. I have used these requests and preparation time to further develop my interest in pursuing other research. Preparation for the average seven-minute radio interview can take as much as four hours, resulting in two or three single-spaced pages of notes. These notes can be placed in a future or developing projects folder for further development.

Lesson #6: Time management. While perhaps a little less to do with interacting with journalists, time management is important nonetheless. For those media requests in your area but outside your specific expertise, I suggest you accept only those that can fold into developing research ideas, projects, or even classroom materials (having myself developed several into course lectures).

The media world, like the academic world, is a small one. Journalists know one another and sometimes share information, including contacts. The more materials and topics that you can address, the more requests you will likely receive to address these and other topics. This can mean additional phone calls and emails. For instance, I was once called upon to offer comment on distracted driving, specifically drivers who use cell phones behind the wheel after the passing of a new law in British Columbia. While this is linked in some ways to my research on communication and information formats as features of social control, it was not an area that I have directly researched. I used the opportunity to connect distracted driving to some of my existent research. This opportunity served to broaden my research agenda and contributed to my developing ongoing research interests related to policing and social control. I teach a policing course at my institution, and the opportunity also allowed for the creation of lecture materials as well as the development of a paper that I later presented at an academic conference.

While I view the aforementioned as positively related to the development of my academic persona, one must be careful how journalists will use such materials. This connects with various lessons presented above, and in my view, remains the most consistent and important lesson of interacting with journalists.

Lesson #7: Resist the sound bite if you can. I received a few other requests for comments not very long after I gave the radio interview about distracted driving. One of these was a prerecorded segment for a different local radio station. I was aware that our conversation was going to be prerecorded, but it was not made clear to me that my comments were going to be reduced to ten-second sound bites and used as local public-service announcement to curb distracted driving. The reduction of your research into snippets of information can distort or change the context of your message in unforeseen ways. The most important lesson that I have learned when speaking to journalists is to resist providing the sound bite as much as possible. This may require that you only commit to giving live radio or television interviews (rather than print or prerecorded segments).

Conclusion

The public presentation of your research can be fun, rewarding, and, most importantly, a good way to stimulate debate on matters of public importance. News media journalists can be interested in your perspectives for many different reasons. These reasons are mostly instrumental. Most of the time, you are simply unable to control how a journalist will represent you or your comments (and research materials). This is the case with most interviews, including print, radio, and television. When possible, you should always stick to live interviews, most of which will emerge in the realm of radio. When possible, ask for in-studio interviews (remember, they need you). Such opportunities allow you the freedom to either not answer questions or redirect such questions to those that more adequately reflect your research expertise, or to stay within your comfort zone.

While you cannot necessarily control how your research will be used, you can—drawing from some of the lessons noted above—somewhat control factors that will reduce the risk of journalists misusing your comments. In any event, you take a chance when interacting with journalists and you should do so at your own risk!